Arab Worlds beyond the Middle East and North Africa

Arab Worlds beyond the Middle East and North Africa

Edited by
Mariam F. Alkazemi and
Claudia E. Youakim

LEXINGTON BOOKS
Lanham • Boulder • New York • London

Published by Lexington Books
An imprint of The Rowman & Littlefield Publishing Group, Inc.
4501 Forbes Boulevard, Suite 200, Lanham, Maryland 20706
www.rowman.com

6 Tinworth Street, London SE11 5AL, United Kingdom

Copyright © 2021 The Rowman & Littlefield Publishing Group, Inc.

All rights reserved. No part of this book may be reproduced in any form or by any electronic or mechanical means, including information storage and retrieval systems, without written permission from the publisher, except by a reviewer who may quote passages in a review.

British Library Cataloguing in Publication Information Available

Library of Congress Cataloging-in-Publication Data

Names: Alkazemi, Mariam, editor. | Youakim, Claudia E., 1979- editor.
Title: Arab worlds beyond the Middle East and North Africa / edited by Mariam F. Alkazemi and Claudia E. Youakim.
Description: Lanham, Maryland : Lexington Books, 2021. | Includes bibliographical references and index. | Summary: "By providing migration experiences of Arabs to various nation-states, this volume examines socio-historical factors that allowed Arab communities to settle in several places, including Latin America, Asia, the United States, Europe and Africa. It bridges several fields to provide context that is useful in today's globalized world"— Provided by publisher.
Identifiers: LCCN 2021014922 (print) | LCCN 2021014923 (ebook) | ISBN 9781793617668 (cloth) | ISBN 9781793617675 (ebook)
Subjects: LCSH: Arabs—Foreign countries. | Middle East—Emigration and immigration.
Classification: LCC DS36.95 .A73 2021 (print) | LCC DS36.95 (ebook) | DDC 909/.04927—dc23
LC record available at https://lccn.loc.gov/2021014922
LC ebook record available at https://lccn.loc.gov/2021014923

∞™ The paper used in this publication meets the minimum requirements of American National Standard for Information Sciences—Permanence of Paper for Printed Library Materials, ANSI/NISO Z39.48-1992.

To anyone who has struggled to find a community and anyone that accepts the complexity of a truly cosmopolitan identity. May these chapters help you feel understood and inspire you to connect with other people and yourself.

Contents

List of Figures and Tables		ix
Acknowledgments		xi
Introduction *Mariam F. Alkazemi and Claudia E. Youakim*		1
1	*Turcos* and *Chilestinos:* Latin American Palestinian Diaspora Nationalism in a Comparative Context *Michael Ahn Paarlberg*	11
2	Politics, Media, and Society: Argentina's Response to the Syrian Conflict *Jodor Jalit*	29
3	Can We Be Governed by Someone Who Eats Kibbeh? Lebanese Migrants and Brazilian Politics *Diogo Bercito*	49
4	The Arab Community of Cuba: Past and Present *Rigoberto Menéndez Paredes*	67
5	Exploring the Roots and Identity Politics of the Hadhrami Diaspora in Singapore *Aisha Sahar Waheed Alkharusi*	83
6	Whither "Integration"? Children's Television, Immigration, and Arab Diasporas in Germany *Christine Singer, Jeanette Steemers, and Naomi Sakr*	99

7	Maghrebis in France: From "Arab Immigrants" to "Muslims" *Imène Ajala*	115
8	Arab Youths' Sense of Belonging to Canada: Integrated and Hyphenated Identities *Bessma Momani and Nawroos Shibli*	129
9	Mahjari Musicians: The Recorded Sounds of Arab Americans in the Early Twentieth Century, 1912–1936 *Richard M. Breaux*	151
10	"Welcome, But Be Ready to Work": Negotiating Gender Norms as Refugees in America *Manal al-Natour and Rita Stephan*	171
11	The Influence of Nativity (or Lack Thereof) on Arab-American Muslim Attitudes and Behaviors *Youssef Chouhoud*	187

Appendix 1: Question Wording	201
Index	205
About the Contributors	213

List of Figures and Tables

FIGURES

Figure 2.1	Keyword Count Mentions in Selected Argentine Press	38
Figure 10.1	Adeebah's Paintings	177
Figure 11.1	Multivariate Analyses: Predicted Probability of Being U.S. Born (90% CI)	194

TABLES

Table 1.1	Profile of the Palestinian Diaspora in the Top Three Countries by Population in Latin America	14
Table 2.1	Syrian Program Visa Requests, Approval, and Use (by year, 2014–2019)	42
Table 3.1	Members of the Grupo Parlamentar Brasil-Líbano	62
Table 3.2	Administrative Regions Represented by Members of the Caucus	63
Table 3.3	Party Affiliation and Political Orientation of the Caucus' Members	63
Table 4.1	Arab Immigrants Arriving in Cuba (1920–1931)	72
Table 4.2	Main Settlements of Arab Immigrants (1900–1955)	74
Table 8.1	Self-Identity, Sense of Belonging, and Level of Happiness in Canada	139
Table 11.1	Demographic Differences	192

Acknowledgments

There are a number of people whose hard work made the publication of this book possible.

When we received our first contract, several people helped us evaluate it. Some of these people came from our personal networks and others came from our professional ones. We would like to thank Dr. Joshua M. Langberg, the associate dean for research at the College of Humanities and Sciences at Virginia Commonwealth University (VCU) and Dr. Brooke Newman the director of the Humanities Research Center at VCU. We would also like to thank Dr. W. Wayne Surles and Dr. Andrew James Naughton for providing practical insights on the terms of contract. Finally, we would like to thank Hillary Miller from VCU Libraries for providing a number of resources, including the distribution pattern of books by different publishers, to help us decide a course of action; we would also like to thank Devin Bowers for the introduction to her.

There are several scholars we would like to thank for their reviews as well. We would also like to thank Dr. Rita Stephan for reviewing the introduction to our book and providing us with feedback. Furthermore, we would like to thank Dr. Iain Walker and Dr. Mara Leichtman, two reviewers who helped connect us to scholars and provided input on a chapter that focused on Africa. They were both extremely helpful in providing insight that the Arab communities in the East and West coasts of Africa are very complex and deserve more depth than we were able to produce in a timely fashion. Ultimately, this led to the decision that we would have to exclude the chapter because we could not do the communities justice at the current time. Their work provides many examples of the Arab influences in either coast of Africa, and we want to emphasize that this work deserves its own volume and more focused inquiries in the future.

We also would like to thank the Director of Communication for the VCU Robertson School of Media and Culture, Professor Joshua J. Smith. His design consultation was helpful in the technical parts of the book cover. A special thank you to Manal Deeb, who debuts the cover of the book with her beautiful artwork. Thank you for listening to our vision and for sketching and suggesting designs that would be a good fit for this book theme. Your contribution truly illustrates the interdisciplinary perspective that we value as you are able to communicate to audiences that go beyond words.

We would like to thank two students who helped with indexing and formatting of the book. Marilynn Oetjens and Judi Aldalati were both very helpful, showing dedication and consistency that is exceptional. Their work allowed us to finish our book by the deadline in a timely manner.

Finally, we would like to thank the pedagogy workshops for graduate students organized by Dr. Martin Simpson at the University of Florida. For it was at these workshops that Dr. Alkazemi and Dr. Youakim first met. Dr. Alkazemi and Dr. Youakim began the conversations that would end up resulting in the conception of this book over coffee and frozen yogurt. When this volume began, we did not realize Dr. Youakim would be living in Lebanon during the Beirut port explosion or that Dr. Alkazemi's brother would die unexpectedly. Neither of us thought we would live through a global pandemic, but our work together solidified a bond whereby we can listen and learn from each other, especially during these unprecedented times.

We would also like to acknowledge every contributor of this book, who has dedicated the time and effort during an unprecedented time of the COVID-19 pandemic. We want to genuinely thank you for your commitment and valuable work that made this volume possible. Similarly, we are grateful to Joseph Parry and Alison Keefner Lexington Books and also the production and marketing teams that have worked with us to make this book available on the market under such trying circumstances.

To thank some of the scholars that have impacted our development and encouraged our growth both in our disciplines and across disciplines, we separately want to thank a few people for their support and encouragement of our professional development and confidence that allowed us to create this book.

Dr. Mariam Alkazemi: I want to thank Dr. Wayne Wanta, Dr. Spiro Kiousis, Dr. Cory Armstrong, and Dr. Patricia Wood from my doctoral committee. I also want to thank other mentors, including Dr. Mark Tessler, Dr. Amaney Jamal, Dr. Michael Robbins, Dr. Charles Kurzman, Dr. Toby Dodge, Dr. Courtney Freer, and Dr. Fahed Al-Sumait for fostering my interest in Middle East Studies. I want to thank Dr. Deb Aikat for his support in working with me as a Carnegie Fellow at a Center for the study of the Middle East and Muslim Civilizations. I would like to thank Dr. Marcus Messner for his support of this interdisciplinary project and his trust in my ability to contribute to a number of fields. I would also like to thank Dr. Claudia Youakim for being the type of friend who turns dreams into collaborative realities.

Last but not least, I'd like to thank Dr. Faisal Alkazemi, the first PhD who instilled the love of innovation, the joy of creativity and an insatiable curiosity about culture in me. My father raised me in vastly different world regions, taught me to question my environment and laid the foundation that fostered my intellectual contributions.

Dr. Claudia E. Youakim: To my academic advisors, Dr. Tamir Sorek and Dr. Milagros "Milly" Peña, thank you for your support and inspiring my work through your own. A few women, in particular, have paved the way for me in ways that are noteworthy: Dr. Constance L. Shehan, Dr. Rita Stephan, and Dr. Charlotte Karam, thank you for providing me with opportunities that have helped shape my interdisciplinary academic career and life journey. To my co-editor, Mariam, thank you for collaborating with me and for your friendship throughout this creative process.

I want to acknowledge with gratitude the love of my immigrant Palestinian family, who have shaped my identity and academic interests. I often reflected on my parents' journey in this work. Both my parents are part of the Palestinian diasporic community. My father lived in Santiago, Chile, before settling in Chicago and my mother journeyed to Chicago from Bethlehem after marriage. Their experiences have sparked my interest in migration studies, ethnic identity, and national belonging, which have shaped my scholarly career. Lastly, a sincere thanks to my life partner, Andres, thank you for your encouragement and unwavering support.

Introduction

Mariam F. Alkazemi and Claudia E. Youakim

The roots of globalizations have a rich history, some of which are embedded in migration patterns that impact people and various facets of our society. In this book, we work assiduously and purposefully, alongside authors from various disciplines, to compile stories that span different fields and time periods to examine how Arab communities have settled in nations outside of the Middle East and North Africa (MENA) and across the globe. What we see are stories of Arab people grappling with quite personal and ancestral ties in these new spaces, facing prejudice and discrimination, and others where they are seated in political positions of power as members of that society. Each chapter illustrates the wide array of migration patterns that have impacted the social, economic, and political spheres for Arab persons who have emigrated from their ancestral homeland and settled in a new nation, voluntarily or involuntarily.

Migration patterns and collective identities of Arabs include a number of factors that result with Arab diasporic communities in nations outside of one's ancestral homeland. Generally speaking, people have been pushed out of their home country and/or pulled in another for economic, social, political, and environmental reasons, to name a few (IOM 2019). We see some of these migration patterns within the MENA region itself (IOM 2004); however, this compilation focuses on unpacking the Arab diaspora who have emigrated outside of the region.

THE ARAB IDENTITY

In this section, we will provide some clarification that will help explain our selection criteria of the Arab ancestral homeland, identity, and diaspora.

This is a universal problem across the Middle East/North Africa, demonstrating that even non-Arab nations like Israel, Turkey, and Iran have similar issues. Kumaraswamy (2006) attributes this dynamic to six factors described in this paragraph. First, the legacy of colonialism is important to recognize as the MENA was organized into nation-states after the fall of the Ottoman Empire. Individuals grouped together into nation-states sometimes included different ethnicities, such as the Kurdish population in various parts of the region. Many countries in the region had no historical roots to the state boundaries. Second, these nations buttress their identities through the use of religion, and the role of religion in public and private life, particularly Islam, is obvious in the majority of the region. This complicates the question of national identity of the minorities that exist throughout the region. Third, approximately a third of these states often have a dynastic identity which does not relate to the populations governed. Fourth, several wars among Middle Eastern states demonstrate that these nations prefer to expand rather than define a national identity. These efforts have not been successful and often exasperate existing problems in the region. A transnational identity was seen as a hopeful solution to overcome the national identity crisis associated with the individual identities based on their territory. Kumaraswamy (2006) explains how even this identity was problematic, pointing to how Syria and Iraq used the Baathist ideology differently. As individual nation-states faced differences, the Arab League ostracized different Arab nations. Finally, there is a stateless identity, from the Kurds to the Palestinians that sought refugee status in various parts of the region and world. The autonomy of stateless people threatens the national identities of the individual states in the Middle East.

Against this backdrop, two trends are worthy of examination: the growth of Arab communities outside the Arab world and the development of Arab transnational media networks across the globe. First, Alrasheed (1994) explained the phenomenon of the myth of return that is common among the Iraqi population in London. Alrasheed (1994) notes that members of the Assyrian ethnic group that left, in the 1950s, and did not return to Iraq afterward for many reasons, including not belonging to the Arab ethnic group that is prominent in Iraq. This myth is common in studying refugees, and the last few decades have led to the displacement of many individuals from several Arab nations. Tabar (2010) explains that the waves of Lebanese immigration trace back to 1840–1860, between 1860 and 1900, between 1945 and 1960s, during the Lebanese Civil War of 1975–1990, and after the 1990s. More recently, the Syrian humanitarian crisis has led a large number of refugees to enter Europe from the Arab world (Dekker et al, 2018). As groups of Arabs move outside the MENA, there are some ways that the Arab identity becomes important despite the many national origins from which these individuals may originate.

Second, the advancement of communication technologies and the recognition of the importance of the media in the aftermath of the Iraqi invasion of Kuwait in 1990 led to the development of some transnational Arab media outlets. Aljazeera began in the mid-1990s in Qatar, followed by the development of the Saudi-funded Alarabiya and the American-funded Alhurra (Fahmy, Wanta & Nisbet, 2012). Noha Mellor (2008) explains that transnational Arab media outlets have revived the pan-Arab identity, allowing journalists to serve a particular function. According to Mellor (2008), journalists serve as "cultural intermediaries" (p. 471) in which they form communities of "shared narratives and discourse" (p. 473). By setting their own rules, Arab journalists work together to gain more power in the field of journalism. Since journalism is a field in which representation is particularly concerned, journalists gain political, cultural, and economic capital as they reach near-celebrity status. One of the unifying factors that distinguishes multilingual, Arab journalists is their knowledge, pride, and use of Modern Standard Arabic, which has become symbolic of the pan-Arab national identity (Mellor, 2008). In doing so, transnational Arab identities develop organizational cultures that allow individuals to set aside their national identities and work together in organizations that increase the market share in a competitive media landscape. Many of these news organizations increasingly had offices outside the Arab world, which then highlights the role of being a cultural intermediary in the diaspora (Mellor, 2008).

In addition to the historical, political, and commercial reasons an Arab identity is relevant, understanding the origins of the Arab League is relevant. For this book, we have limited the discussion of the diaspora to the Arab ethnic identity or national identities that are related to the Arab League. The internal conflict in the aftermath of the Ottoman Empire and the conflict with Western powers impacted the development of the Arabist ideology (Dawn 1988). In 1945, the Arab League's member-states were established to strengthen economic and political programs and mediate disputes among member-states, officially adopting the pan-Arab identity (Encyclopædia Britannica, n.d.). The Arab League, an association of twenty-two independent member-states to-date, identify an Arab as persons in the MENA who have cultural, ethnic, and racial similarities. For the purpose of this book, if communities in the diaspora originate in a member-state of the Arab Leagues' and refer to themselves as Arabs, they have been included in our definition as "Arab diaspora."

UNPACKING ETHNIC IDENTITY

To unpack ethnic identity, it is important to reflect on its collective (macro) and individual (micro) components. The macro constitutes the socio-historical dynamics in the receiving countries, which have, to some extent, united and divided the Arab population. The micro, on the other hand, is one's understanding of their ethnicity that results in their self-determination as, for instance, "Arab" or a pan-ethnic identity, such as "Chilestino" (Palestinian-Chilean) or "Arab American". This ethnic formation process involves negotiation and contestation that are influenced by cultural and contextual components, thus it is referred to as *situational* (Fenton, 2010). Scholars argue this process includes various socio-political, religious, and/or personal elements (Jenkins, 1997) that are dynamic and intersect over time (Dekovic & Buist, 2005). Although a receiving country may have a rather fixed criterion to describe an ethnic group, such as a "white" racial category for persons from the Middle Eastern North Africa in the United States, for example, the group may contest the formal classification despite its reinforcement by government officials (U.S. Census, 2005).

DIASPORA AS A THEORETICAL FRAMEWORK

There is a growing number of self-defined diasporas, for many reasons, including a crisis of the nation-state and related global economic challenges and war (Butler, 2001). In examining Arab communities around the world, it is easy to see they fit into the definition of a diaspora that Butler (2001) lays out:

1. "the dispersal to a minimum of two locations,"
2. "the relationship to an actual or imagined homeland,"
3. "the self-awareness of the group's identity," and
4. "the existence of the community for more than one generation."

These factors are featured in personal essays of the Lebanese in Canada such as Abboud's (2009) personal and ethnographic account of being the daughter of a Lebanese Canadian. It also exists in less personal accounts of Assyrian and Arab Iraqis living in England that Alrasheed (1994) recounts.

Before we demonstrate how our chapters contribute to the study of the Arab diaspora, we would like to qualify our work in several ways. First, a natural question is why nationality is not used to describe one's origin in today's world. Historically, the dispersion of Arabs around the world happened before the existence of the nation-states that today make up the Arab League. Our chapters should shed more light on this issue, particularly the Arab diaspora in Latin America.

Second, the scope of this book is limited to Arab communities that exist outside the boundaries of the Middle East/North Africa due to definitional criterion of a diaspora. In Cohen's (2015) criteria for distinguishing a diaspora and other migrants, his first factor is the existence of cultural characteristics that include strong emotional ties to a language, religion, history, and culture of their original homeland. He argues that these cultural characteristics must remain strong despite public proclamations of assimilation, and they must serve as a basis for connection with other diasporic groups across the world. By this definition, Arab migrant communities based in Arab nations are beyond the scope of this book.

While religion can be a factor that sets a diaspora apart, it alone does not designate a diasporic community (Butler, 2001). Butler (2001) explains that this is true of the Jewish diaspora, for example. Having said that, the Arab diaspora is not strictly Muslim or Christian, showing Butler's (2001) insistence that no diaspora is monolithic, which applies to the Arab diaspora.

Finally, it is important to distance ourselves from fallacies that have been debunked. While approximately a quarter of the conflicts in the last 200 years took place in the region, it is important to note that the Middle East/North Africa is not more violent than other world regions (Mundy, 2019). Regardless of the reason for immigrating, Abboud (2009) reminds us that there is a feeling of immigrancy that combines "the senses, the challenges, and the spirit" of an individual immigrant (p. 372).

Diaspora discourse becomes a method to connect an individiual with their home country or nation-state, resisting erasure as they maintain, revive or reinvent themselves against the hegemonic culture (Clifford, 1994). By bringing in examples from various countries and disciplines, we weave together in one manuscript many narratives that have seldom appeared together. This book is neither exhaustive nor cumulative, and each chapter can be read separately. Combined, the chapters shed light on communities that have thrived (i.e., Argentina) and others that can no longer be witnessed (i.e., Cuba). The purpose of this book is to learn about the history of Arab migration, the development of Arab communities, and the representation of Arabs in cultural products, such as television shows in Germany or music in the United States. By including successes and failures, our book both acknowledges the weaknesses and celebrates the accomplishments of the Arab diaspora.

It is important to also note the limitations of this text. Although we are shedding light on the diversity of Arabs as an ethnic group, the label "Arab" is not only contested but it also conflates a heterogeneous group into one term though they do not possess a monolithic ethnic identity. Arab countries and people in the Middle East and North African region are heterogeneous in terms of linguistic, ethnic, and religious groups, to say the least. Our intention in this volume is to share some of this diversity, but we acknowledge that aside from the selection criteria we use, our book is just the beginning of a plethora of literature on the topic of Arab migration and communities that exist around the world. We also limit the story of immigration/emigration, a group's arrival to a nation, which involves the experiences of a community and their dynamics and development in the nations where they settle. The literature cited here about the Arab identity and the literature relating to studies of diaspora are by no means exhaustive. Still, they help justify why we chose an ethnic identity rather than a certain nationality to study for this book.

The goal of the book is to highlight the diversity that exists in and outside of the Arab MENA in terms of identity patterns and experiences. Emigration patterns of Arabs from the MENA to nations outside the region have not been captured in one text and as persons with ancestral ties to the region we wanted to ensure that a book existed that shed light on these patterns.

REFLEXIVE NOTE FROM THE EDITORS

The question may arise as to why a communication scholar and a sociologist are co-editing a book on the Arab diaspora around the globe; and to this point, we would like to be explicit and reflexive. We are both academics who believe that the complexity of a topic, particularly on ethnic identity and representation, necessitates a number of perspectives to grasp a level of appreciation. Like us, the authors in the volume also come from various disciplines and professional experiences, including scholars in the social sciences and humanities, to directors and diplomats who work in governmental institutions. This interdisciplinary intention produces the work you see before you today that unpacks the topic on emigration from the Middle East and North African region.

What our disciplines have in common, as do our contributors, are that we are focusing on human interaction. The way we come to articulate these dynamics rely heavily on our positionality, which includes a number of socially significant dimensions (race, ethnicity, nationality, class, gender, etc.) that go beyond our academic or professional training (see Muhammad, Michael et al. 2014 on positionality). These set of distinctions are of value in our examination, as they produce perspectives of the Arab diaspora in various nations that would not be captured if we were working in silos or echo chambers, particularly in a digital age. By curating a number of chapters that bring in a host of disciplines, we hope our volume allows us to learn from the Arab communities that have existed, and continue to exist, in various political, social, cultural, and temporal contexts.

The liberal arts are all about informed inquiry, and our contribution provides ideas that we hope will inspire our own communities' development—whether academic or otherwise. Our attempt is in no way comprehensive, but we hope that ours is the beginning of a line of examinations of the Arab communities around the world. We hope this inspires individuals in Arab communities to find ways to honor their heritage and fit into their society in a way that supports the sense of belonging that their individual members feel.

OVERVIEW OF THE CHAPTERS

Rigoberto Menéndez Paredes writes about how Cuba served as an initial destination from which Arabs arriving from the Ottoman Empire would move on to other countries in Latin America. Drawing on historical records, he explains the demographics and professions of those who arrived as well as the factors that led to the decline of the Arab diasporic community in Cuba. Unlike the rest of the chapters, the community in Cuba left during the revolution in 1959. This chapter describes the remnants of the Arab diasporic community in Cuba. The Cuban Arab community can be starkly compared to other Arab diasporic communities that are outlined in Latin America in other chapters.

Jodor Jalit writes a case study about the Arab diaspora in Argentina and its role in the Argentinian response to the Syrian refugee crisis. In doing so, he traces the history of migration from the Ottoman Empire to Argentina, and how the diasporic community influenced the news media. In the process, Jalit argues that the Arab diaspora was unsuccessful in advocating for policy that would have been favorable to the Syrian refugees. This contribution demonstrates that the Arab diaspora and the Argentinian media are both actors that influence Argentina's response to the dire humanitarian crisis in Syria and around the globe. This chapter pertains to the role of the diaspora in contemporary international affairs, particularly with regard to refugees.

Diogo Bercito describes the strong participation among Brazil's politicians of Lebanese descent. To unpack this pattern of political representation, the chapter opens with a historic foundation that includes the ability of Lebanese persons to transfer their homeland political engagement to Brazil and the role of social mobility in political life. While supportive socio-political conditions in Brazil induce the process for minority participation, Lebanese immigrants' geographic spread in the country assisted in gaining support of constituents. Lebanese political presence shaped Brazil's national and foreign policy decisions as a result, despite the fact that they were and continue to be a minority group.

Bessema Momani and Nawroos Shibili present a case study of Arab youth in Canada to understand their acculturation process as Arab, ethnically and culturally, and as Canadians by means of their community. Using a mixed methods approach to collect data, the authors examine the identity, and the socio-cultural integration and belonging of Arab youth to Canada and their homeland. A number of variables contribute to the complexity of the process, including demographic and socialization factors. This chapter illustrates how the self-identification process as a hyphenated, or hybrid identity, is a result of the acculturation and transnational connections that youth possess.

Imène Ajala describes the ethnic and diasporic diversity of Maghrebin in France, which ranks as the second country in Europe to house the largest Muslim population. The author describes Maghrebin as an Arab population whose ethno-political mobilization and acculturation process in France has been impacted by the Islam and its religious understandings of its host society. With religion as an identity marker, the perception and evolution of Arab immigrants in France

Richard M. Breaux's chapter celebrates the creative contributions and entrepreneurial spirit of Arab Americans in the United States. He shows that Arab American contributed to the American music scene before the Great Depression of the 1930s. Unlike some of the chapters that focus on some of the challenges facing Arab diasporic communities, this chapter feels very celebratory of the Arab heritage that has seldom been remembered in the United States. He provides the names of streets and neighborhoods in New York City where Arab communities thrived and records of Arabic language music were sold prior to World War II.

Manal al-Natour and Rita Stephan apply an ethnographic framework to uncover how Syrian refugees, those who have fled from persecution, are adapting to life in Connecticut. Paying particular attention to the role of Syrian refugee women in the family, the authors take into consideration how their gender identity, performances, and norms are applied in navigating economic challenges faced in the United States through various levels of agency: active, ambivalent, or passive. This chapter highlights the conditions and content that shape acculturation patterns. Since the majority of Syrian refugees in the United States are women and children, this chapter is an important contribution because it addresses their sense of empowerment.

As a career diplomat, Aisha Sahar Waheed Alkharusi traces back the migration of an Arab population from Hadhramout, Yemen to Singapore. In her chapter, she points out the long-lasting impact of their settlement in Singapore such as the Arab district that continues to exist today. She also shows how this group eventually integrated into the Malay Singaporean population. Hers is an example of successful integration of an Arab community into an Asian culture. This is the only chapter from the Asian continent, and its inclusion serves as a reminder of the diverse communities that have absorbed Arabs for over a century.

Michael A. Paarlberg focuses on the Palestinian diaspora in Latin America, with the largest concentration in Chile, followed by Honduras and El Salvador. Despite the presence of Palestinians in Latin America, literature on Palestinians has been scarce in comparison to other Arab ethnic migration from the Middle East. Through a comparative analysis, Paarlberg sheds light on this pattern, which began in the mid-to-late 1800s while Palestine was under the rule of Ottoman Empire to date. The chapter captures the historic and socio-political journey with its challenges and successes for Palestinians as they navigate life in Latin America and build a nationalist movement and through socio-political participation in their new communities.

In stark contrast to the rest of the chapters, Christine Singer, Jeanette Steemers, and Naomi Sakr focus on children's media in the diaspora. Their analysis of two television shows that focus on the arrival of Arab children in Germany relies on theory relating to integration. It shows that the diaspora is heterogeneous and reminds us that Syrian refugees are not the first from the Arab world to seek asylum in Germany. This chapter focuses on media representations of children, a vulnerable population, within a vulnerable population, refugees. These media representations are varied, showing different experiences that young refugees may experience and highlighting the range of joyful and difficult emotions that come with them.

REFERENCES

Abboud, V. M. (2009). (Trans) Planting Cedars Seeking Identity, Nationality, and Culture in the Lebanese Diaspora. In *Arab Voices in Diaspora* (pp. 371–393). Brill Rodopi.

Al-Rasheed, M. (1994). The Myth of Return: Iraqi Arab and Assyrian Refugees in London. *Journal of Refugee Studies, 7*(2–3), 199–219.

Bureau, U.C. (2005). Retrieved August 11, 2020 from https://www.census.gov/prod/2005pubs/censr-21.pdf.

Butler, K.D., 2001. Defining Diaspora, Refining a Discourse. *Diaspora: A Journal of Transnational Studies, 10*(2), 189–219. Elsevier. Retrieved June 25, 2020 from https://vcu-alma-primo.hosted.exlibrisgroup.com/permalink/f/1shm02o/TN_crossref10.1353/dsp.2011.0014.

Clifford, J. (1994). Diasporas. *Cultural Anthropology, 9*(3), 302–338.

Cohen, R. (2015). Diaspora. In *International Encyclopedia of the Social & Behavioral Sciences* (Second ed., pp. 353–356). Elsevier. Retrieved June 28, 2020 from https://vcu-alma-primo.hosted.exlibrisgroup.com/permalink/f/1shm02o/TN_elsevier_sdoi_10_1016_B978_0_08_097086_8_12054_9.

Dekker, R., Engbersen, G., Klaver, J., & Vonk, H. (2018). Smart Refugees: How Syrian Asylum Migrants Use Social Media Information in Migration Decision-Making. *Social Media+ Society, 4*(1), 2056305118764439.

Deković, M., & Buist, K. L. (2005). Multiple Perspectives Within the Family Relationship Patterns. *Journal of Family Issues, 26*(4), 467–490.

Encyclopædia Britannica. (n.d.) "Arab League." In *The Editors of Encyclopaedia Britannica. Encyclopædia Britannica, inc.* Retrieved Aug. 10, 2020 from *https://www.britannica.com/topic/Arab-League.*

Fahmy, S., Wanta, W., & Nisbet, E. C. (2012). Mediated Public Diplomacy: Satellite TV News in the ARAB WORLD and Perception Effects. *International Communication Gazette, 74*(8), 728–749.

Fenton, N. (2010). *New Media, Old News: Journalism and Democracy in the Digital Age.* Sage Publications.

International Organization for Migration. 2005. *Arab Migration in a Globalized World* (pp. 1–257). Retrieved August 10, 2020 from https://publications.iom.int/system/files/pdf/arab_migration_globalized_world.pdf.

Jenkins, R. (1997). *Rethinking Ethnicity: Arguments and Explorations.* Sage.

Kumaraswamy, P. R. (2006). Who Am I? The Identity Crisis in the Middle East. *Middle East Review of International Affairs, 10*(1), 63–73.

McAuliffe, M., & Khadria, B. (2020). "World Migration Report 2020." United Nations International Organization for Migration (pp. 5–498). https://www.un.org/sites/un2.un.org/files/wmr_2020.pdf.

Mellor, N. (2008). Arab Journalists as Cultural Intermediaries. *The International Journal of Press/Politics, 13*(4), 465–483.

Muhammad, Michael et al. 2014. Reflections on Researcher Identity and Power: The Impact of Positionality on Community Based Participatory Research. *Critical Sociology, 41*(7–8), 1045–1063.

Mundy, J. (2019). The Middle East is Violence: On The Limits of Comparative Approaches to the Study of Armed Conflict. *Civil Wars, 21*(4), 539–568.

Rubinstein, H. (2020). Constructing a Transnational Identity: the Three Phases of Palestinian Immigration to Chile, 1900–1950. In *Migrants, Refugees, and Asylum Seekers in Latin America* (pp. 85–107). Brill.

Shils, E. (1957). Primordial, Personal, Sacred and Civil Ties: Some Particular Observations on the Relationships of Sociological Research and Theory. *The British Journal of Sociology, 8*(2), 130–145.

Tabar, P. (2010). *Lebanon: A country of Emigration and Immigration* (p. 7). Institute for Migration Studies.

The Arab League: Algeria, Bahrain, Comoros, Djibouti, Egypt, Iraq, Jordan, Kuwait, Lebanon, Libya, Mauritania, Morocco, Oman, Palestine, Qatar, Saudi Arabia, Somalia, Sudan, Tunisia, United Arab Emirates, Yemen.

Chapter 1

Turcos and *Chilestinos*

Latin American Palestinian Diaspora Nationalism in a Comparative Context

Michael Ahn Paarlberg

In 2019, El Salvador elected as president Nayib Bukele, a 38-year-old former mayor and business owner of Palestinian heritage. Bukele became El Salvador's first ever millennial president, but not its first Palestinian president; that milestone went to Tony Saca, president from 2004 to 2009. The 2004 election which brought Saca to office, in fact, was notable, in that both of the major party candidates, Saca and his leftist opponent Schafik Handal, were Palestinian.

Bukele's landslide victory in 2019—he won with a first round majority in a three-way race— put to rest doubts about his electability as an outsider. This identity, which he conspicuously cultivated with his relentless social media presence, had three parts. First, as a political outsider: as mayor of first Nuevo Cuscatlán and later San Salvador, he ran with the left-wing FMLN, but later broke with the party's leadership, was expelled, and ran with a smaller right-wing party. His victory was the first for a third-party candidate in the country's postwar period marked by a deeply institutionalized two-party system. Second, an economic outsider: Bukele was a successful business owner, running a Yamaha dealership in the exclusive San Salvador neighborhood of Escalon, among other properties. However, he did not come from *las catorce*, El Salvador's famous fourteen families which made up the historical business oligarchy, to whom business owners such as Bukele were viewed with suspicion as new money upstarts. Third, a cultural outsider: despite the history of Palestinian Salvadoran participation in the country's politics at the highest level, rumors abounded of Bukele's religious identity. Although Bukele is a self-professed Catholic (reflecting the vast majority of Palestinian Salvadorans—indeed Latin Americans of Arab descent generally—who are Christian, largely Orthodox or Catholic), his father was the imam of the Salvadoran Islamic Center and a leader of the city's small Muslim community. Bukele had been photographed praying in a mosque in Mexico City, leading to "secret Muslim" rumors about the candidate. Such rumors might have been politically disqualifying in a country as overwhelmingly Christian as El Salvador. A smear campaign by his rival to the right, purporting to expose Bukele's secret faith, took on comical proportions, including a doctored photograph depicting the candidate wearing "Muslim clothing." The photograph turned out to be of Bukele at a costume party, dressed as a Jedi Knight from Star Wars, complete with a plastic lightsaber (*Última Hora*, 2018).

Yet while both Saca and Bukele have publicly acknowledged their Palestinian heritage, their expressions of Palestinian nationalism have been muted. Among Latin American countries, El Salvador has had unusually close ties to Israel cemented in the years prior to the country's 1980–1992 civil war, when 83 percent of the Salvadoran government's arms imports came from Israel (SIPRI 1980). El Salvador maintained an embassy in Jerusalem before the United States moved its embassy to the city, and was the last country to move it to Tel Aviv, during the Saca presidency. Saca's family name also adorns a plaque at Plaza Palestina in San Salvador, the inauguration of which provoked criticism from El Salvador's small Jewish community for featuring a map of the pre-1948 British Mandate of Palestine. The dedication of a second plaza by Palestinian community leaders provoked harsh criticism from the Israeli embassy due to its designation as Yasser Arafat Park, with the installation of a bust of the PLO leader nearby. Nevertheless, Saca was the preferred candidate for Israel supporters in the 2004 election given the support of his opponent, Handal, and his leftist party, by the PLO (Jewish Telegraph Agency, 2004).

Bukele, for his part, has spent his political career distancing himself from any politically problematic aspects of his Palestinian identity. He has downplayed his father's Muslim faith— noting that his father converted to Islam as an adult and describing himself alternately as Catholic and not religious. And he has emphasized his support for Israel, including prior to his presidency. As mayor of San Salvador (and all-but-declared presidential candidate), Bukele visited Jerusalem as an invitee to the International Mayor's Conference. During the visit—co-organized by the American Jewish Congress and viewed by the Palestinian press as an effort to delegitimize the Boycott, Divestment, and Sanctions Movement (Fallas 2019)—he prayed at the Western Wall, visited the Yad Vashem Holocaust museum, and emphasized the Sephardic Jewish roots of his wife at a meeting with his Jerusalem counterpart (Ahren 2019). Previously, in San Salvador, Bukele had met the mayor of Bethlehem to less fanfare, at a private gathering of twenty people. The meeting was friendly and lasted forty minutes (Valencia 2018). Among Latin American leaders, Bukele enjoys unusually warm personal relations with Donald Trump. For all Salvadoran leaders, maintaining friendly relations with Israel is instrumental for two more important political considerations: first, winning the support of the country's growing Evangelical Christian population (approaching the size of the Catholic majority) and especially the politically influential Tabernáculo Bíblico Bautista Amigos de Israel mega-church; and second, securing favorable policies from the United States.

The ambivalence of El Salvador's two Palestinian presidents toward questions of Palestinian nationalism is reflective of that of the Palestinian Salvadoran community as a whole, and that of neighboring Honduras, a country with an even larger Palestinian community. Of Latin America's estimated half million people of Palestinian ancestry, the vast majority reside in three countries: El Salvador, Honduras, and Chile—the country with the largest Palestinian-descended population, and the only one which can be described as having an active and politically salient Palestinian nationalist movement. How political attitudes and expressions can vary within the same broader diaspora—indeed, sharing not only the same religious profile (largely Christian), the same period of migration (1880s to 1920s), and even the same geographic origin (principally Bethlehem)—is worth examining. A comparative historical analysis suggests that in Chile, the greater degree of pluralism, with a more diverse political and occupational profile of the Palestinian community, has allowed for greater success in constructing a Palestinian nationalist movement than in Central America.

WEST FROM BETHLEHEM

Among Arab diaspora communities in Latin America, Palestinians in Latin America are a relatively understudied community in comparison to the more numerous Lebanese and Syrian descended populations which make up the majority of Arab Latin Americans in larger countries like Argentina, Brazil, Colombia, and Mexico. Other Levantine Latin Americans are well-known throughout the region and have reached the highest positions of power. They include presidents like Argentina's Carlos Menem, Brazil's Michel Temer, Colombia's Julio César Turbay, Dominican Republic's Jacobo Majluta Azar, Ecuador's Julio Teodoro Salem, Abdalá Bucaram, and Jamil Mahuad, and Paraguay's Mario Abdo Benítez, as well as businesspeople such as Mexico's Carlos Slim and celebrities like Colombia's Shakira and Mexico's Salma Hayek.

Likewise, scholarship on the broader Arab diaspora of Latin America is extensive and cross-disciplinary, including history (Klich and Lesser 1998, Civantos 2006, Alfaro-Velcamp 2007, Karam 2007, Hyland 2011), cultural studies (Hu-DeHart 2009, Alsultany and Shohat 2013), and international

Table 1.1 Profile of the Palestinian Diaspora in the Top Three Countries by Population in Latin America

	Chile	El Salvador	Honduras
Population	350,000	65,000–100,000	280,000
Origin	Bethlehem, Beit Jala, and Beit Sahour	Bethlehem, Beit Jala, and Beit Sahour	Bethlehem, Beit Jala, and Beit Sahour
Period of immigration	1880–1930	1880–1922	1876–1930
Areas of concentration	Patronato, Santiago	San Salvador and Sonsonate	San Pedro Sula and Atlantic coast
Industries	Architecture and design, banking, higher education, law, media, medicine, real estate, retail, textiles	Banking, construction equipment, food products, furniture, media, retail, textiles, tobacco products	Banking, biofuel, coffee, food products, media, retail, textiles
Notable families	Abdala, Abumohor, Chahín, Chahuán, Hasbún, Hirmas, Jacir, Jadue, Kassis, Littin, Massis, Meruane, Said, Saieh, Salah, Sumar, Tarud, Yarad, Yarur, Zalaquett	Bahaia, Barake, Bukele, Daboub, Handal, Hasbún, Hirezi, Jacir, Kattán, Nasser, Saca, Safie, Salume, Samour, Sedán, Simán, Zablah	Abud, Abufele, Asfura, Atala, Bendeck, Canahuati, Facussé, Gabrié, Handal, Jaar, Kattán, Kawas, Larach, Mitri, Musa, Nadal, Nasralla, Saybe, Siryi, Siway, Yuja, Zablah
Political leaning	Mixed	Right*	Right*
Nationalist sentiment	High	Medium-to-low	Low

*With certain high profile exceptions such as El Salvador's late Schafik Handal, FMLN military and political leader and Hato Hasbún, former FPL guerrilla and later minister of education under Mauricio Funes (2009–2014), and Honduras' Salvador Nasralla, presidential candidate of the Anti-Corruption Party.

relations (Amorim 2011, Amar 2014), while that of the Palestinian diaspora specifically is more limited. Notable exceptions include González's *Dollar, Dove, and Eagle* (1993), Amaya Banegas' *Los árabes y palestinos en Honduras 1900-1950* (1997), Raheb's *Latin Americans with Palestinian Roots* (2012), and Baeza's "Palestinians in Latin America" (2014), although earlier scholarship has considered the community, albeit instrumentally, with regard to the Arab-Israeli peace process (Glick 1959, Sharif 1977, Abugattas 1982, Bahbah 1986, Karam 2013).

The relative obscurity of Latin America's Palestinians is in part a matter of numbers and geography, which are linked. As the much larger Lebanese-Syrian population settled into major cities and in Latin America's larger countries (Buenos Aires, Argentina; Rio de Janeiro and São Paulo, Brazil; Barranquilla, Colombia; Mexico City and Veracruz, Mexico; Caracas, Venezuela), newly arrived Palestinian migrants moved further from these established Arab communities to avoid competition with more established Lebanese and Syrian merchants. As a result, Palestinians came to be a majority among Arab migrants only in countries with relatively small Arab populations: Chile, Peru, Honduras, and El Salvador.

This relative isolation from the broader Arab community built strong endogenous bonds in business, social, and family relations (intra-community marriage was the norm), creating Palestinian identities lasting multiple generations after arrival, even after descendants no longer spoke Arabic and largely assimilated into receiving country society.

Reinforcing such tight social networks were several shared characteristics including period of migration, religious faith, and geographic point of origin. In comparison to Palestinian diaspora populations elsewhere created by multiple migration waves, Palestinian Latin Americans have a largely uniform background: overwhelmingly Christians from Bethlehem and surrounding villages of Beit Jala and Beit Sahour who migrated in the late nineteenth and early twentieth century, and made their livings as merchants—first as itinerant vendors, later as store and factory owners. This diaspora can thus be described more specifically as a Bethlehem diaspora in Latin America—one which by now greatly outnumbers the population of its home community (today roughly 25,000).

Palestinian migration to Latin America began in the 1870s and 1880s, under the Ottoman Empire, earning the new migrants the inaccurate and pejorative moniker *turcos*, or Turks. That many were fleeing Ottoman—and by extension Turkish—oppression of their homeland was an irony not lost on the new arrivals. The peak of the migration wave, in 1910, succeeded a new military conscription law of 1909 which motivated many Christian families to send their military-age children abroad to avoid forced service to the new Young Turk regime (Caro 2010). World War I followed, sparking more waves of migrants facilitated by their newly settled relatives in the Americas.

In both South and Central America, the new arrivals gained a reputation—not always positive—for business acumen. This created resentment, in some cases violence (the "War of the Comb," an anti-Arab pogrom in Curitiba, Brazil), and discriminatory laws. In 1921, El Salvador declared Arabs and Chinese as "pernicious" races, and in 1933, the dictator Maximiliano Hernández Martínez barred all immigration of Africans and Asians, naming specifically "new immigrants from Arabia, Lebanon, Syria, Palestine, or

Turkey, generally known by the name *turcos*" (Valencia 2018). Such laws barring entry on the basis of nationality mirrored similar laws in the United States (the Chinese Exclusion Act of 1882), Colombia (an 1887 law banned Chinese migration, later expanded to include Syrians and then all "Orientals" by 1913), and other countries (Dolan 2020).

Compounding legal restrictions on immigration to Latin America were those on return migration to Palestine. In the post-Ottoman Empire, the establishment of a new Palestinian nationality by British Mandate authorities in 1925 placed new visa restrictions on emigrants, for whom circular migration between the Americas and Palestine had been easy and frequent under Ottoman nationality. Many Palestinian migrants were unable to obtain documentation required to establish legal residency or Palestinian nationality; many became stateless. Those who left under the Mandate were unlikely to be able to return. The formation of the State of Israel in 1948 not only ended legal Palestinian nationality but gave finality to the one-way nature of Palestinian emigration. While previous generations of migrants to Latin America had planned to work and save money to return to Palestine in retirement, and many did, this was no longer an option.

Thus, despite discrimination and social marginalization, Palestinian migrants to Latin America had little choice but to settle in their new homes. Marriages outside the community increased. Children became monolingual Spanish speakers. Families Hispanicized their names: Al-Farid became Alfredo, Yamil became Emilio (Zahdeh 2012). And although shunned by the entrenched business elites, Palestinian merchants became more established, and came to corner the then-underdeveloped markets of retail business, while national business owners concentrated their wealth in land and commerce in cattle and agricultural export goods. As the expansion of Palestinian-owned businesses spurred diversification of investment into manufacturing and banking, the *turcos*—for whom the still-pejorative term had evolved from signifying poor peddlers, carrying products by mule, to *nouveaux riches* (Baeza 2014)—reinvested their financial capital into social and political capital, electing community members to local office by the 1930s and national office by the 1950s.

Bukele embodies this trajectory: the grandson of Christian Palestinians from Bethlehem and Jerusalem who migrated as Ottoman nationals in the early twentieth century, he pursued a political career after his success in business, owning El Salvador's Yamaha franchise and directing an advertising company. The political persona he successfully built is that of a wealthy outsider, at war with the hegemonic two-party system. If he believes his trajectory was at all hampered by his background, he does not express it, telling *El Faro* "It doesn't bother me if they call me *turco*, although I know some continue to use that word in a pejorative manner" (Ibid).

Despite a broadly shared identity, however, South and Central America's Palestinians exhibit divergence in their political makeup, with consequences for diaspora nationalist movements. As the following sections will elaborate, the relative political pluralism of Chile's Palestinian population—by far the largest in Latin America—contrasts with the more uniformly conservative and business profile of Central America's, despite notable exceptions. As a consequence, Chile exhibits a far more pronounced and organized nationalist movement within Latin America's Palestinian population.

The *Chilestinos*

It is nearly accidental that Chile became the top destination for Palestinian migrants to Latin America, due to both push and pull factors. By the late 1800s, largely Christian Palestinians escaping unemployment and Ottoman discrimination of religious and national minorities, such as the *jizya* tax on non-Muslims,[1] end of the millet system, and rising Turkish nationalism, and lured by then-booming economies in the Americas, left for other destinations in both North and South America. Though the United States remained the top destination of choice, the migration wave coincided with a period of selective encouraged migration policy in Chile. Seeking to both develop its mining and agriculture sectors and "improve the race," Chile encouraged the immigration of Europeans—principally British and Germans—to industrial cities like Osorno and Valdivia. Although Palestinian migrants were not given the same level of support, those unable to reach the United States, or who sought less competition with other Arab merchants in larger Atlantic coast cities in South America, were able to enter Chile, making the arduous journey over the Andes by horse.

The new migrants concentrated in a specific neighborhood in Santiago: Patronato, in the capital's North Mapocho sector, with subsequent generations moving to the more elite neighborhood Las Condes. From 1860 to 1925, some 40,000 Palestinians migrated to Chile. Before 1930, 81 percent of the country's Palestinian population had arrived, at which point Chile began restricting its relatively open-door migration policy (Agar and Saffie 2005).

The first migrants were overwhelmingly single men who worked as ambulatory street vendors, gradually establishing stores and concentrating in the clothing business, including retail, tailoring, and later textile manufacture. Patronato came to be both the commercial and cultural center of Palestinian life, where the community established its first Orthodox Church in 1917. To non-Palestinian Chileans, Patronato came to be a shopping destination for the "four Bs": products that were good, nice, cheap, and abundant (*"Bueno, Bonito, Barato, y aBundante"*), as well as Arabic food, drink, and music (Caro 2010). Migrants founded pan-Arab mutual aid community organizations starting in 1904 with the Ottoman Benevolence Society, and later the Arab Union Club and Arab Benevolence Union, business organizations (Syrian-Palestinian Commercial Association) and even firefighter squads (The Eduardo Farley Chilean Arab Firefighters in Valparaíso). These coincided with the founding of other Arab descended hometown associations (Sociedad Juventud Homsiense Siria, in 1913, Club Sirio Unido, in 1935, and Círculo Libanés in 1943).

Despite facing often blunt racism and misrepresentations of their faith (the newspaper of record, *El Mercurio*, described Palestinian migrants as "Mohammedans" who "are dirtier than the dogs of Constantinople"), Palestinians' Christian background hastened their early assimilation into broader Chilean society. And though their businesses were dismissed as small and cheap, some merchants took advantage of the ascendant economic nationalist model of Import-Substitution Industrialization in the post-Depression era to avail themselves of close relations with the government. This in turn opened doors to state support, while splitting the community during the subsequent period of intense political polarization.

The business and political history of the Palestinian-owned textile industry, and especially of the Yarur family, detailed in Winn's *Weavers of Revolution* (1986), is illustrative. First generation migrants from Palestine in 1902, the Yarur brothers first opened a retail store, then a textile plant in neighboring Bolivia. Under the industrialization policies of Chile's Alessandri administration, the Yarurs were coaxed into opening a much larger textile plant in Santiago with the patronage of the Chilean government, which included a loan from the state bank and subsidized investments in machinery, eventually employing 3,000 workers. Other Palestinians opened textile plants, and the industry came to be dominated by Palestinian owners like the Hirmas, Kassis, Said, and Sumar families. Eventually, the Yarurs opened their own bank, BCI, to finance their investments. Growing worker radicalism in the 1960s and 1970s led to increasing labor-management conflict and demands for worker ownership. In 1971, following the election of democratic socialist president Salvador Allende, workers took over the Yarur plant and ran it collectively, with other Palestinian-owned factories nationalized by the government in short order. The subsequent military regime of Augusto Pinochet, who overthrew Allende in a 1973 coup, violently suppressed these worker movements and returned the factories to their owners. However, these owners were wiped out in the financial crash brought on by the dictatorship's 1975 economic shock therapy, facilitated, ironically, by a fellow Palestinian Chilean, Pinochet's economic minister, Jorge Cauas Lama. The Yarurs' textile factory failed, however their bank, BCI, remains one of the largest in Chile.

Throughout this tumultuous Cold War period, Palestinian Chileans took up prominent positions on both sides of the political divide. Some were unapologetic supporters of the dictatorship; Alberto Kassis founded the Pinochet Foundation. Others held positions in left-leaning administrations, including Rafael "El Turco" Tarud, economic minister under the government of socialist-supported Carlos Ibañez del Campo, and Mahfud Massis, ambassador under the socialist Allende government. Another prominent Allende supporter was movie director Miguel Littin. All three were forced into exile by the military regime.

Palestinian Chileans' political pluralism at the elite level also allowed for a broader base for Palestinian nationalist political activism. By the 1930s, Palestinian Chileans had founded a Spanish language reformist newspaper, *Al Islah*, which reported on news from Palestine and which has a counterpart today in Revista Al-Damir (Alsutany and Shohat 2013). The community raised money for family members of those who had died in the 1936–39 Arab Revolt against the British, and in 1947, lobbied the Chilean government not to support the UN resolution on Partition. In 1963, a commemoration of the Nakba was read in Chile's Congress (Baeza 2014).

Explicitly nationalist institutions emerged in Chile in the 1960s: poet and future ambassador Massis founded FRELIPA (Palestine Liberation Front) in 1964, along with its affiliated newspaper, *Palestina Patria Martir* and radio station Voz de Palestina, which organized support for the Palestinian Liberation Organization. PLO delegates visited Chile in 1966, and later opened a Palestine Information Office in 1978, operating uneasily under the military regime. Intent on renewing nationalist sentiment among the Latin American diaspora through the Sanaud movement, the PLO (and later Palestinian Authority) was sensitive to both the Christian background of Chile's Palestinians and the allergy of business owners to any form of radicalism, sending as their first delegate a Catholic priest from Bethlehem. Pro-Palestinian activism and the BDS movement have been especially pronounced on college campuses, organized by the Chile branch of the General Union of Palestinian Students. Though associated with the left during the Cold War period, it has been increasingly common for politicians across the political spectrum to pay lip service to Palestinian causes. In 2011, right-wing president Sebastián Piñera visited Palestine and declared support for Palestinian statehood. In 2014, left-wing president Michelle Bachelet recalled Chile's ambassador to Israel in protest of Operation Protective Edge in Gaza (Legrand 2014). In Chile's Congress, a Palestinian Chilean Inter-Parliamentarian group today includes members from parties across the political spectrum.

Nationalist sentiment extends beyond electoral politics and into community, religious, and educational organizations. Fundación Palestina Belén 2000 (Palestine Foundation Bethlehem 2000) formed in response to Pope John Paul II's jubilee call that year, with the mission to "form a strong and participatory community made up as much of Chileans as of Palestinians and their future State" and to "support actions to achieve peace in Palestine" (Caro 2010).[2] The University of Chile houses a Center for Arab Studies and publishes the *Revista de Estudios Árabes*. The *Juventud Palestina* (Palestinian Youth) organization has chapters is most major cities in Chile, and today includes membership that is not of Palestinian descent. Diaspora feminist organizations have existed since the 1970s, beginning with the Chilean Arab Feminist Association, continuing through the present day with the *Yo Soy Palestino* (I Am Palestinian) movement founded by Leyla el-Massou, Leyla Haibeh, and Nadia Garib (Palma Troncoso 2017).

The most visible symbol of the Palestinian community's social capital is Club Deportivo Palestino, a professional soccer team in Chile founded in 1920 by Palestinian migrants. Though today its players and management are not necessarily of Palestinian ancestry, the team has always been a vehicle for nationalist sentiment, with its colors—black, white, green, and red—an explicit reference to the Palestinian flag. Fans at Palestino games often wear keffiyehs and fly Palestinian flags, and the team's social media broadcast nationalist statements: "For us, free Palestine will always be historical Palestine, nothing less" (BBC 2014). The club faced controversy in 2014 when it unveiled new jerseys in which the number "1" was replaced by an outline of Mandate-era Palestine. Jewish Chilean groups protested the design as implicitly denying the legitimacy of modern-day Israel, and Chile's soccer federation banned the jerseys and imposed a fine. Following the controversy, the number 11 jerseys became bestsellers in Chile. Palestino has won the national championship; its legacy as a highly visible vehicle for Palestinian identity that is no longer exclusively Palestinian in its makeup symbolizes the degree to which Palestinian nationalist sentiment has become mainstream, not just in the diaspora community but within broader Chilean society.

Central America's *Turcos*

The other major destination for Palestinian migrants to Latin America became the Northern Triangle of Central America, principally Honduras and El Salvador, where together the Palestinian-descended population is roughly equal to that in Chile. In comparison to the *chilestinos*, Central America's Palestinians can be characterized by their more uniform conservative political orientation and concentration in business, and less developed nationalist sentiment and institutions.

The late nineteenth-century Ottoman migration waves coincided with a period of openness in Central America, particularly in Honduras with a new permissive immigration law in 1866 and the Liberal Reforms of 1876.

Although aimed at encouraging migration from Europe, especially France and Germany, and the United States, the reforms established Honduras as a destination for Palestinians slightly before Chile. While European migrants settled in the country's south, Palestinians settled along the country's Atlantic coast, concentrating in the city of San Pedro Sula. In El Salvador, the period of migration was cut short relative to other destination countries, largely ending by 1922 with a reform to that country's immigration law which blocked entry to Chinese and Arabs. Future laws targeted established immigrants, prohibiting the opening of new stores, factories, and farms by any persons of Arab descent. In part due to such official discrimination, and in part the greater concentration of Palestinians in Honduras, many Palestinians migrated from El Salvador to Honduras and established homes and businesses in San Pedro Sula and other towns in the north.

As in Chile, Palestinian business owners got their start in the textile industry. In the 1930s, coinciding with the opening of the Yarur factory, Jacobo Kattan established Central America's first clothing company in Honduras. Central America's business oligarchy, characterized by El Salvador's *las catorce* (the fourteen), concentrated in agricultural export goods, primarily in coffee, agave, bananas and sugar, financed by investments from the United States and United Kingdom. This left a vacuum in the neglected retail, manufacturing, and finance sectors which Palestinians came to fill. Such businesses were family owned and operated and closely linked within the Palestinian communities, with business relationships fortified by intermarriage. By the 1980s, the Honduran government, seeking to further develop the clothing manufacturing sector, established duty-free export zones on the Atlantic coast, where the Palestinian population and businesses concentrate. Palestinian business owners came to dominate the new maquila sector.

Nationalist activity was not always low. Like their Chilean counterparts, Palestinians in Honduras raised funds for those displaced in the 1936 Arab Revolt and successfully lobbied the Honduran government to abstain from the 1947 UN Resolution on Israel. Following the foundation of the State of Israel, however, Palestinian activism in Central America went into steep decline. Palestinian community newspapers disappeared. Efforts by the PLO in the 1960s to revive Palestinian identity met little enthusiasm, though delegates from Honduras visited Chile in 1966 to elect Latin American delegates to the organization's Palestinian National Congress. The PLO found greater support in countries with little to no Palestinian population, notably Cuba and Nicaragua, and opened offices there.

This association of late 1970s Palestinian nationalism with nearby left-wing regimes had a chilling effect on Palestinian activism in Central America, then dominated by right-wing regimes supported by the United States as anti-communist bulwarks in the Cold War. Palestinian Central Americans, concentrated in the business sector, feared a communist takeover by rebels inspired by the 1975 Sandinista Revolution in Nicaragua. The subsequent Sandinista government maintained close ties with the PLO and included one prominent Sandinista of Palestinian descent, Moises Hassan. A 1982 hostage crisis in which Sandinista-inspired Honduran rebels took 100 hostages in the San Pedro Sula Chamber of Commerce, including several Palestinian business owners, brought to sharp relief these fears.

Palestinian-descended business owners provided strong support to the Honduran government's counterinsurgency program in the 1980s. The business and political career of Miguel Facussé, the wealthiest person in Honduras, illustrates the close ties between the government and Palestinian business community. Having received support from the state National Investment Corporation during Honduras' adoption of Import-Substitution Industrialization policies, Facussé developed businesses in diverse industries including textiles, food products, biofuels, soaps, commercial airplanes, and pharmaceuticals. He later advised president Roberto Suazo Córdova and became a leader of the Association for Progress of Honduras, an organization founded to forge close relations between business owners and military officers. As an owner of the Dinant palm oil company, Facussé is alleged by the U.S. State Department to command an extensive private militia targeting landless peasant activists with violence, and to be involved in cocaine trafficking from his vast landholdings in the Aguán Valley (Wikileaks 2004). Facussé and fellow Palestinian Honduran business owners Camilo Atala, Juan Canahuati, and Fredy Nasser, made up four of the ten principal financiers the 2009 coup against left-wing President Miguel Zelaya, whose reforms of the energy sector diminished the profits of Dinant and other biofuel companies (Salomon 2009, Thale 2009, Chayes 2017). These business owners have maintained close ties with subsequent post-coup governments.

There have been some notable exceptions to the political one-sidedness of Palestinians in Central America. In neighboring El Salvador, Palestinians played a role on both sides of the 1980–1992 civil war. The guerrilla forces under the umbrella group FMLN were led by Schafik Handal, member of one of that country's most prominent Palestinian families. Handal's roots made him something of a class traitor. The guerrilla movement attracted other Palestinian Salvadorans, including Hato Hasbún, who joined the rebels and later became a politician in the postwar era, rising to education minister under Mauricio Funes, the first democratically elected left-wing president. Héctor Samour, a former vice minister of education, also of Palestinian descent, was a collaborator with Archbishop Oscar Romero, a martyr of the Salvadoran left whose assassination in 1980 formally started the war. In Honduras, the candidate declared to have lost in the disputed 2017 presidential election was

Salvador Nasralla, a business owner and television personality of Palestinian ancestry, who founded the Anti-Corruption Party, and has been stridently critical of several Honduran government, including those largely supported by the Palestinian Honduran business establishment.

Exceptions aside, El Salvador and Honduras' Palestinian community is more right-leaning than Chile's. This reflects its continued uniform concentration in the business sector. In Chile, Palestinian merchants leveraged their commercial success into educational attainment and careers in law, medicine, media, universities, and politics. In Honduras and El Salvador, where the higher education system is more limited, the preferred career path of Palestinian families has been to maintain the family business, usually passed down from father to son. In all three countries, the threat of expropriation during periods of worker radicalism provoked a right-wing backlash among business owners, Palestinians included. However in Chile, this political and occupational diversification had occurred prior to this period of Cold War upheaval, as well as prior to the inroads of Palestinian nationalist organizations, principally the PLO. Thus by the time of the 1973 coup, there had already been notable Palestinian Chileans associated with the left, and Palestinian nationalism had found purchase among the otherwise conservative business sector. In El Salvador and Honduras, the Cold War turned hot a decade later, in the 1980s, when counterinsurgency efforts received much more sustained support from the United States. Yet by this time, a Palestinian left had not emerged, nor indeed had any Palestinian social sector outside of that of wealthy business owners. Politically, this had a reinforcing effect, with Palestinian identity taking on elite, right-wing, and anti-democratic associations among the broader Honduran public, particularly in the aftermath of the 2009 coup.

The Question of Nationalism

The relative neglect of the Palestinian Latin American community, particularly within the Palestinian diaspora as a whole, is reflective not only of its minority status within the broader Arab Latin American population but also the visibility of the issue which has largely defined Palestinians in the eyes of the world: the national question. Palestinian nationalism is a less salient issue among those of Palestinian descent in Latin America than those in the Middle East, for whom migration was more recent and associated with a shared narrative of forced displacement and dispossession (the *Nakba*), the desired temporary nature of their settlement (refugee status), and a denied aspiration to come home (right of return). As Baeza 2014 notes, the term "diaspora" is itself fraught with controversy when it comes to Palestine, as it may be understood to suggest a permanent settlement in a new home, which does not reflect the aspirations of the post-1948 migrants for whom the term "refugee" is more appropriate. Nevertheless, "diaspora" can also have nationalist connotations as well, as exemplified by the nineteenth–twentieth-century Zionist movement, and thus is not fundamentally incompatible with aspirations for an as-yet-unrealized homeland.

Nationalist sentiment can often develop in contest with competing nationalisms. Within the Middle East, there is considerable research on the development of Palestinian nationalism in relation to Zionism, not simply in opposition but also adopting certain aspects of Zionist rhetoric as a strategy of validation: terms such as exodus and diaspora evoking a forced dispersion from a historic homeland, brought on by a catastrophe. Because migration to Latin America occurred prior to 1948, however, under less violent circumstances, the early development of Palestinian nationalism in Latin America was not in response to a new Israeli identity but newly constructed out of an older imperial Ottoman identity, and later in response to a new ethnonationalist Turkish identity. For both competing identities, the uniqueness of Palestinian identity at the time was seminal, aspirational, and as yet unclear. Palestinian migrants to Latin America accompanied those from what became Syria and Lebanon, and these other Arab migrants shared with Palestinians many customs, traditions, as well as a history of dominance by Turkish Ottomans. They also largely shared a religious identity which set them apart as minorities within the majority Muslim empire. Among early migrants, distinct identities between Syrian, Lebanese, and Palestinian migrants were more amorphous and less politically relevant than those of post-Nakba refugees. What distinguished Palestinian migrants was the largely shared hometown ties of Bethlehem in particular.

For Arab Christian migrants, including Palestinians, the appeal of nationalism depended in large part to its association with secularism. Prior to the PLO's Latin America outreach, it was Nasser's pan-Arabism which attracted the most support within the Latin American diaspora, which by design deemphasized unique national identities. Later, the PLO was careful to cultivate a Christian-friendly image and underscore its secular ideology. Nevertheless, the global association of Palestinian nationalism in the 1970s with radicalism and terrorism did much to undermine the movement among conservatives and business elites within the Latin American diaspora, a trend that was only counterbalanced in Chile by the development, decades earlier, of social networks outside of the business world and the political right. In the latter twentieth century, the association of Palestinian nationalism first with revolutionary leftist regimes in Cuba and Nicaragua, and, in the twenty-first century, with Hamas and other Islamist organizations, further alienated conservative Latin American Palestinians who were by then multiple generations removed from their ancestral homeland.

Yet the decline of Palestinian nationalism in Latin America is neither linear nor inevitable. Nationalist sentiment has risen and fallen in waves, long after the initial period of migration. There have been revivals of nationalist sentiment in the Americas in response to events in Palestine: the 1936 Arab Revolt, the *Nakba*, the 1967 war, the Sabra and Shatila massacre, the Intifadas, and the Gaza wars. External forces, most notably outreach by the PLO in the 1970s, had some measured success, while U.S. influence has had opposite effects, by constraining official expressions of nationalism, particularly in Central America due to its dependence on the United States. This trend has been compounded especially in Central America by the rapid growth of a Christian Zionist evangelical community.

However, comparing diverging nationalist sentiments and activity in Chile, El Salvador, and Honduras—three countries which experienced both significant U.S. intervention and PLO outreach during the Cold War era—suggests that the most notable factor in determining the purchase of nationalism is not foreign but domestic: the relative political and occupational diversity of the Palestinian community. In Chile, we can see the cultivation of a strong Palestinian identity despite generations of successful assimilation, through media, student groups, civic organizations, and sports teams. The emergence of high profile Palestinian figures beyond the business sector, on both the political left and right, has given Palestinian nationalism a bipartisan veneer and disassociated the movement from radicalism. In Central America, where high profile Palestinians are firmly and nearly uniformly entrenched in the business sector and on the political right, and where Palestinian nationalism came to be associated with Marxist threats to business interests, there has been little appetite for the movement. Like in Chile, community associations, Palestinian clubs, and official monuments exist. But expressions of Palestinian identity have been largely depoliticized and limited to a cultural sphere.

The Palestinian Latin American experience illustrates the challenges of building a nationalist movement within a dispersed and diverse diaspora. Notably, it is not impossible. Despite more than a century of removal from the homeland, loss of language, decline of endogenous marriage, and religious minority status in relation to the broader nation, Palestinian nationalism has found purchase among the *chilestinos* and, to a lesser extent, other Palestinian-descended Latin Americans at different moments in history. The Chilean case shows it is possible for national identity to survive and revive through generations of assimilation into the host community, for organized nationalist movements to have an impact on policy and diplomacy and to achieve a degree of mainstream and cross-party support. It is also possible for nationalist movements to become radioactive in the context of contentious and polarized politics, within diaspora communities defined by their political and economic insularity, as the Central American cases demonstrate. Social ascension by itself is not determinative. Rather, it is pluralism that allows diasporas to leverage social capital into political capital, to redefine homeland issues as host country issues, and to de-radicalize and legitimize national causes. Contrasting with the pitfalls of the Palestinian case, the experience of other nationalist movements—including, in the case of Zionism, oppositional ones—can illustrate the potential successes of this dynamic.

NOTES

1. *Jizya* was a tax levied by the Ottoman Empire on its non-Muslim, principally Christian and Jewish, subjects intended to substitute for both military service, for which non-Muslims were exempt, and the *zakat* which Muslim subjects were obliged to pay. In 1856, after the empire allowed for military service (and conscription) of non-Muslims, the jizya replaced by a new tax, *baddal askari*, with which a non-Muslim subject could pay in lieu of military service.

2. Though the Palestinian population is overwhelmingly Christian, organizations for the Muslim minority of Palestinian and other nationalities include the Muslim Society of Chile, the Islamic Center of Chile, and the As-Salam, Bilal, and Coquimbo mosques. Such organizations have largely avoided politics, owing to Islamophobia in the early 21st Century, and sectarian divides, including accusations of Wahabbi radicalism by the Shia-oriented Center for Islamic Culture against the Sunni Defenders of Islam.

REFERENCES

Abugattas, Juan. 1982. "The perception of the Palestinian question in Latin America." *Journal of Palestine Studies* 11(3): 117–128.

Agar, Lorenzo and Nicole Saffie. 2005. "Chilenos de origen árabe: La fuerza de los raíces." *Revista Miscelánea de Estudios Árabes y Hebraicos* 54: 3–27.

Ahren, Raphael. "His dad was an imam, his wife has Jewish roots: Meet El Salvador's new leader." *Times of Israel* February 7, 2019. https://www.timesofisrael.com/his-dad-was-an-imam-his-wife-has-jewish-roots-meet-el-salvadors-new-leader/.

Alfaro-Velcamp, Theresa. 2007. *So Far from Allah, So Close to Mexico*. Austin: University of Texas Press.

Alsultany, Evelyn and Ella Shohat. 2013. *Between the Middle East and the Americas: The Cultural Politics of Diaspora*. Ann Arbor: University of Michigan Press.

Amar, Paul (ed.). 2014. *The Middle East and Brazil: Perspectives on the New Global South*. Bloomington: Indiana University Press.

Amaya Banegas, Jorge Alberto. 1997. *Los árabes y palestinos en Honduras, 1900–1950*. Tegucigalpa: Editorial Guaymuras.

Amorim, Celso. 2011. "Brazil and the Middle East: Reflections on Lula's south-south cooperation." *Cairo Review of Global Affairs* 1(2): 48–63.

Baeza, Cecilia. 2014. "Palestinians in Latin America: Between assimilation and long-distance nationalism." *Journal of Palestine Studies* 43(2): 59–71.

Bahbah, Bishara. 1986. *Israel and Latin America: The Military Connection*. New York: St. Martin's Press.

BBC. "Chile bans Palestino football club 'anti-Israel' shirt." *BBC News* January 21, 2014. https://www.bbc.com/news/world-latin-america-25821058.

Caro, Isaac. 2012. *Islam y Judaísmo Contemporáneo en América Latina*. Santiago: RiL Editores.

Chayes, Sarah. "Getting to Such a State." Carnegie Endowment for Peace May 20, 2017. https://carnegieendowment.org/2017/05/30/getting-to-such-state-pub-70001

Civantos, Christina. 2006. *Between Argentines and Arabs: Argentine Orientalism, Arab Immigrants, and the Writing of Identity*. Albany: State University of New York Press.

Dolan, Thomas Simsarian. 2020. *Unusual Figures: The Global Middle East, Citizenship and Racial Injury*. Unpublished dissertation. George Washington University.

Fallas, Amy. "El Salvador's Bukele at crossroads in relations with ancestral land." *Palestine Square* June 28, 2019. https://palestinesquare.com/2019/06/28/el-salvadors-bukele-at-crossroads-in-relations-with-ancestral-land/.

Funk, Kevin. 2016. "How Latin America met the Arab world: Toward a political economy of Arab-American relations. In Tawil Kuri, M. (ed). *Latin American Foreign Policies toward the Middle East: Middle East Today*. New York: Palmgrave.

Glick, Edward. 1959. "Latin America and the Palestine partition resolution." *Journal of Inter-American Studies* 1(2): 211–222.

González, Nancie L. 1993. *Dollar, Dove and Eagle: One Hundred Years of Palestinian Migration to Honduras*. Ann Arbor: University of Michigan Press.

Hu-DeHart, Evelyn. 2009. "Multiculturalism in Latin American studies: Locating the 'Asian' immigrant or, where are the *chinos* and *turcos*?" *Latin American Research Review* 44 (2): 235–242.

Hyland, Steven Jr. 2011. "Arisen from deep slumber: Transnational politics and competing nationalisms among Syrian immigrants in Argentina, 1900–1922." *Journal of Latin American Studies* 43(3): 547–574.

Jewish Telegraph Agency. "El Salvador candidate who vowed to move embassy to Tel Aviv loses." *Jewish Telegraphic Agency* March 24, 2004. https://www.jta.org/2004/03/24/archive/el-salvador-candidate-who-vowed-to-move-embassy-to-tel-aviv-loses.

Karam, John Tofik. 2007. *Another Arabesque: Syrian-Lebanese Ethnicity in Neoliberal Brazil*. Philadelphia: Temple University Press.

Karam, John Tofik. 2013. "On the trail and trial of a Palestinian diaspora: Mapping South America in the Arab-Israeli conflict, 1967–1972." *Journal of Latin American Studies* 45(4): 751–777.

Klich, Ignacio and Jeffrey Lesser (eds.). 1998. *Arab and Jewish Immigrants in Latin America: Images and Realities*. Portland: Frank Cass.

Legrand, Christine. "Chile's Gaza sympathisers rally behind Palestinian football colours." *The Guardian* December 4, 2014. https://www.theguardian.com/world/2014/dec/01/chile-palestine-palestino-football-santiago.

Palma Troncoso, Jorge. 2017. *Programa "Yo Soy Palestino": Resistencia y Resignificación Cultural de la Comunidad Palestina en Chile.* Bachelor's thesis. University of Chile Department of Historical Sciences.

Raheb, Viola (ed.). 2012. *Latin Americans with Palestinian Roots.* Bethlehem: Diyar.

Salomon, Leticia. "Conozca las diez familias que financieron el golpe de estado en Honduras." *El Libertador* August 8, 2009.

Sharif, Regina. 1977. "Latin America and the Arab-Israeli conflict." *Journal of Palestine Studies* 7(1): 98–122.

Stockholm International Peace Research Institute (SIPRI). 1980. *World Armaments and Disarmament: SIPRI Yearbook 1980.* London: Taylor and Francis.

Thale, Geoff. "Behind the Honduran Coup." *Foreign Policy in Focus* 1 July 2009.

Última Hora. "ARENA intensifica campaña sucia contra Bukele al grado de lo ridículo." *Última Hora* November 4, 2018. http://ultimahora.sv/arena-intensifica-campana-sucia-contra-bukele-al-grado-de-lo-ridiculo/.

Valencia, Roberto. "Los turcos y el olor de la berenjena. *El Faro* 25 April 25, 2018. https://elfaro.net/es/201804/el_salvador/21762/Los-turcos-y-el-olor-de-la-berenjena.htm.

Wikileaks cable Re: Honduras, March 19, 2004. http://www.hondurasnews.com/wikileaks-cable-re-honduras-031904/.

Winn, Peter. 1986. *Weavers of Revolution: The Yarur Workers and Chile's Road to Socialism.* Oxford: Oxford University Press.

Zahdeh, Abdelmalik. 2012. *La Comunidad Palestina en Santiago de Chile: Un Estudio de la Cultura, la Identidad, y la Religión de los Palestinos Chilenos.* Masters thesis, Bergen, Norway: University of Bergen.

Chapter 2

Politics, Media, and Society

Argentina's Response to the Syrian Conflict

Jodor Jalit

INTRODUCTION

"They will be provided with a permanent residency, work permit and education,"[1] said Argentina's President Mauricio Macri at the high-level meeting on Large Movement of Refugees and Migrants hosted by the United Nations (UN) General Assembly (GA) in September 2016 ("Asamblea de la ONU Macri en la ONU," Clarín, September 20, 2016). President Macri was referring to the 3,000 refugees Argentina promised to receive as part of the global effort to ease the latest Syrian humanitarian crisis. All that, in line with the government's will to "become part of the world again" ("Macri: 'Queremos volver a ser parte del mundo,'" Casa Rosada, September 19, 2016). Nevertheless, Argentina started to receive Syrian refugees, as early as 2012, and implemented a policy to facilitate family reunification in September 2014. Hence, the new compromise did not imply the implementation of a novel policy as much as reform of the one already in place. The successive modifications introduced led to a change in the policy's objective and exclusion of its original driving force: the Argentine-Arab community. All that against a background marked by the election of a government with different international preferences than its predecessor. For all these reasons, this chapter analyzes the factors that contributed to shaping Argentina's humanitarian response to the Syrian refugee crisis.

Drawing on professional experiences as a member of the National Syrian Committee and journalist covering the Syrian conflict, this chapter presents an analysis of the Special Humanitarian Visa Program for Foreigners Affected by the Conflict in the Syrian Arab Republic, commonly referred to as the Syrian Program, and implemented in Argentina since September 2014. This analysis includes interviews with Argentinean government officials,

NGO representatives, and Syrian immigrants to Argentina. More, the analysis sheds light upon the interaction between society, the press and the state that helped shape the Syrian Program.

Since its beginning in 2011, the Syrian conflict caused a renewed interest in the *motherland*. This has sparked a debate in the Argentine-Arab community on the best way to address the ensuing humanitarian crisis. The most important questions were whether Syrians, refugees or not, should be relocated to Argentina? If so, which Syrians? Should women and children inside Syria be given priority or should the priority be given to Syrians already residing in refugee camps? Also, who is responsible for the economic burden of relocation? These are the most immediate questions faced by the Argentine-Arab diaspora, and its Syrian component in particular, as the humanitarian crisis has worsened since 2014.

Argentina's effort to address the Syrian refugee crisis was facilitated by the adoption of pro-immigration policies by neighboring countries. Brazil, Uruguay, and Argentina reacted to the Syrian refugee crisis almost simultaneously, in great part due to a demand from the Arab diaspora to the state for a humanitarian response.[2] By the time the Syrian conflict began, the leftist governments were dominant in South America, including those of the Southern Cone. Moreover, their political ideology supported human rights and facilitated the incorporation of the Syrian refugee crisis into the public agenda. Hence, the drafting and implementation of humanitarian policies in Brazil, Uruguay, and Argentina to address the Syrian refugee crisis was facilitated by a coincidence between a demand from below and a like-minded regional ideology. More, the acknowledgment of the Arab diaspora's demand must be understood as a reaffirmation of an ideological inclination that is linked to a past of humanitarian abuses which dates back to the authoritarian regimes of the 1970s. That is, a time when the infringement of human rights took the form of a regional security policy labeled Condor Plan.[3] For the same reason, the regional character of the South American response to the Syrian refugee crisis in front of other initiatives led by northern countries should come as a no surprise. However, the implementation of policies by each country differed slightly, and the Argentine case will be examined here.

This chapter argues that Argentina's humanitarian program—regardless of the financial challenges and constraints—is the result of the interaction of society, the press, and the state. In summary, the Syrian Program was spearheaded by the Argentine–Arab community, mediated by the press and modified by partisan interests. To explain the role assigned by the policy to each actor, this chapter is divided into three parts. First, it analyzes Arab immigration to Argentina. Second, it examines the representation of the Syrian conflict by Argentina's media. And third, it outlines the Syrian Program by explaining its origins, implementation, and reforms. To conclude, observations will be made to show the relationship between the Arab diaspora, media outlets, and government officials that helped shape the Syrian Program implemented during the 2014–2019 period.

METHODOLOGY

For this analysis, the preferred methodology is qualitative and draws from the historical analytical narrative within the institutionalist approach for a case study (Hernández Cortez 2019). This approach allows for the identification of organizational arrangements and isolation of particular scenarios to direct attention toward critical junctures and path dependence during the implementation of the Syrian Program (Person and Skocpol 2008). All that to, first, identify a shift in policy objectives, and second, describe the relationship between relevant actors. Before the analysis of the policy itself, two actors will be introduced: the Argentine-Arab community and the Argentine media.

IMMIGRATION TO ARGENTINA AND THE BIRTH OF THE ARAB DIASPORA

Argentina's social cloth is embroidered with many national threads, and the Argentine elite made a concerted effort to populate a land and develop an economy in the nineteenth century. Moreover, a net immigration of 3,300,000 between 1857 and 1914 increased Argentina's total population from 3,955,110 to 7,885,237.[4] According to the National Census of 1895, one in four people were born abroad. That proportion had risen in the 1914 census to one in three (Sarramone 1999, 15). Moreover, the Italian and Spanish contribution to Argentina's population growth accounted for 2,283,882 and 1,472,579, or about 82 percent of total immigration. The remainder consisted of individuals of French (214,198), Russian (160,672), Ottoman (136,079), and various other origins. Lebanese, Palestinian, and Syrian immigrants would be included in that last category, because their respective republics would not be established until the early 1920s, after the fall of the Ottoman Empire, and by 1914 its count amounted "approximately 65,000, or 1.6 percent of the population" (Klich 1993, 179). The First Great War limited world immigration in general. Upon the conclusion of the war in 1918, fewer Arab immigrants were settling in Argentina (Akmir 2011, 39–49). These raw data attempts to shine a light on the Arab diaspora in Argentina and serves as the starting point for a deeper look into its origins, characterizations, and social participation.

The arrival of immigrants to Argentina throughout the second half of the nineteenth century was no accident. North American and Northern European immigration was promoted by Argentina's political elite as a basis for its social, economic, and cultural development. It was a policy adopted and pushed by the so-called 37's Generation and implemented by the 80's Generation (Halperín Donghi 1976, 443–60). Moreover, the policy was summarized by the member of the 37's Generation, revered lawyer and author of the 1853 Argentine Constitution, Alberdi, who wrote: "To rule is to populate" (Alberdi 2017, 18). In short, the author promoted immigration as a means for effective governance over the territory. Arab settlers were not targeted for migration. For example, Faustino Sarmiento, another member of the 37's Generation and Argentinian president (1868–1874), in the classical piece of Argentinian literature, *Facundo o Civilización y Barbarie*, asks: "Are we to intentionally close the door to the European immigration that is repeatedly asking to populate our desert, and make ourselves, under the shadow of our flag, a nation countless as the grains of sand in the sea?" (Sarmiento 2018, 40). A few years later, Alberdi states in *Bases y Puntos*, a work that defined Argentina's constitution: "Do we wish to plant and grow British freedom, French culture, the industriousness of European and the United States in America? Let us bring living parts of them in the customs of their inhabitants and settle them here" (Alberdi 2017, 22). Such endeavors, paraphrasing Halperín Donghi, could lower high salaries by appealing to new forms of labor (Sarramone 1999, 18–19). In short, Argentina's elite wanted to civilize the *gaucho* and reduce the cost of labor through an aggressive migration policy that sidelines Arab settlers.[5]

The push for a pro-immigration policy for Argentina during the nineteenth century targeted specific populations and was not driven by a humanitarian concern. Expectations, however, were not fulfilled (Halperín Donghi 1976, 443). Northern European and American settlers chose not to emigrate to Argentina in large numbers, but predictably Southern European population of Spaniard and Italian origin emigrated through Buenos Aires (see National Commission 1914, Vol. II, 114–25). In part, such incongruence was the consequence of Northern Europe and America's better response in front of its Southern European peers when faced with the Demographic Revolution that accompanied the Industrial and Urban revolutions by the end of the 1800s (Sarramone 1999, 67–80). In other words, Southern Europe's late arrival to the revolutions meant that surplus population had no difficulty finding employment in farms or factories, and many decided to relocate outside of Europe. Those conditions help explain why Italian and Spaniard farmers filled most of the ships sailing for Argentina's coasts during the second half of the nineteenth century. Among them, were many Arabs escaping the Ottoman Empire in search of a country free of political violence and religious persecution and with ample economic opportunity for immigrants and refugees (Akmir 2011, 21–7). Arab immigration to Argentina grew stronger during the 1870s to reach a zenith half way through the 1910s, with a yearly rate of 6,000 immigrants (Sarramone 1999, 311–70; Akmir 2011, 39–49). Unlike the routes taken by Arab migrants today, Europe was for the nineteenth century Arab immigrant a necessary layover for cargo ships filled with silk arriving from the East Mediterranean. Once in Argentina, Arab immigrants were not easily assimilated nor integrated, and discrimination is well-documented in the records of the Migration National Directorate (MND) (Akmir 2011, 33), and legislation was enacted to limit the flow of Arab immigrants and growth of petty traders (Klich 1993, 178). Moreover, Arab migrants were officially labeled "unhelpful" by then Migration General Director, Juan Alsina, and Ottoman Consul General for Argentina, Emin Arslan Bey, because of their preference for commerce over agriculture (Akmir 2011, 32-6; Klich 197–8). The First Great War interrupted maritime immigration, but the basis of the Arab diaspora in Argentina had already been settled.

The geographical origin of the Arab diaspora in Argentina is difficult to identify, because immigration authorities used many different labels in its records. Turk, Ottoman, Arab, Lebanese, Palestinian, and Syrian are the most common among those registered by immigration authorities and the national censuses. Nonetheless, the first two were the most widely used until the fall of the Ottoman Empire (Akmir 2011, 39–42). Such preference by immigration authorities is a direct consequence of, first, immigrants usage of Ottoman issued travel documents, and second, the inauguration of official relations between Buenos Aires and Istanbul, and designation of the first Ottoman consul to Argentina, Emin Arslan, in August of 1910 (Akmir 2011, 41–42; Klich 1993, 181–82). After the fall of the Ottoman Empire, and more specifically since the establishment of the French Mandate for Syria and Lebanon, and British Mandate for Palestine, both in 1922, government records began to discriminate between national identities (Akmir 2011, 43). Thus, Turks and Ottomans turned into Palestinian, Lebanese, and Syrian. In turn, these early immigrants established social, financial, and confessional institutions which were closely related to a regional, national, and/or religious identity, for example, Arab Union Society of San Juan (1899), Maronite Mission (1901), Arab Cultural Center of Tandil (1907), Syrian-Lebanese Society of Mutual Aid of Catamarca (1910), Israeli Sephardic Community Association Agudat Dodim (1913), Al Nahdat-Ul-Adabiat Society (1914), Israelite Association of Corrientes (1914), Naim Al Baiez Society of Villa Maipú (1917), Orthodox Center of Córdoba (1918), Syrian Lebanese Union of Salta (1920), Sephardic Congregation of Education, Religion, and Aid Yesod Hadath (1920), Syrian Lebanese Bank (1921), Islamic Society (1922), Homs Youth (1925), Syrian Lebanese Chamber of Commerce (1929), Alawite Islamic Union (1929), Yabrudi Association (1932), Syrian Lebanese Club "Honor and Motherland" (1932), Cultural Syrian Association (1932), and Homs Club (1938, later Syrian Club of Buenos Aires and today Syrian-Lebanese Club) (Akmir 2011, 125–44; Veneroni and Abú Arab 2004, 68–169; Veneroni and Taub 2004, 277–303). Consequently, through these organizations' founding documents can traced the origins of the early Syrian diaspora in Argentina to the districts of Alepo, Al Tall, Al Qutayfah, Al Nabk, Homs, and Damascus. Also, some organizations secular in name were intimately associated with particular confessional communities. For example, the Homs Club is closely tied to the Christian Orthodox community, while the Yabroudi Beneficiary Association to the Muslim Shia community, and the Syrian Cultural Association to those identified with secularism. In short, the Syrian diaspora in Argentina replicated the social and communal differences found in Syria.

In general, the first Arab immigrants of the nineteenth century settled in the city of Buenos Aires, and specifically in the neighborhood of Retiro (Akmir 2011, 105–9). They were mostly involved in commercial activities, and many of them, as street vendors (Akmir 2011, 32–6; Klich 197–8). The location and profession were, however, a stepping stone for other more familiar destinations and affluent ways of living. Argentina's national expansion of railroad transportation during the first quarter of the twentieth century made it easier for Arabs to move beyond the city of Buenos Aires and into regions that resembled their origin. Hence, the regions of Cuyo and the Northwest became very popular among the Arab diaspora in Argentina, although many cut their trips short and settled predominantly in the Pampas and Litoral regions (Asfoura 2004, 413–22; Jozami 1987; Akmir 2011, 109–11). Those who reached the furthest regions became an influential force in the textile business, while their peers continued within trade and commerce and some ventured into agriculture (Akmir 2011, 51). Today, Arabs are found throughout Argentina, including in remote localities, among a majority of Italians and Spaniards of Christian Catholic confession. Moreover, there is no social, economic, or political activity in which the Arab diaspora do not participate (Akmir 2011, Anexo).

To recapitulate, the Arab diaspora in Argentina found its origins in the second half of the nineteenth century and reached its immigration peak just before the First Great War. Arab immigrants were not among the targeted population for Argentina's socioeconomic development. Still, Arabs arrived from territories that are today part of Lebanon, Palestine, and Syria to settle in Buenos Aires and engage in petty trade. Eventually, they moved beyond the capital city to all corners of the country. Once established, Arabs founded social, economic, and religious institutions that replicated social divisions of their origins. These are the fundamental characteristics of the Arab and Syrian diaspora in Argentina, and as it will be shown later, the original driving force behind the Syrian Program.

ARGENTINA'S PRESS AND THE SYRIAN CONFLICT

After reaching its zenith during the late 1920s, Arab immigration steadily declined (Akmir 2011, 39–49), as Argentina continued to prioritize its European and North American commercial partners throughout the twentieth century (Jozami 2013, 27–34). That preference for northern settlers, combined with geographical distance and the systemic peripheral condition of both Argentina and the Arab countries, helps explain the low feature of Middle Eastern news in Argentina's international news sections (see Pizarro 2012, 217–220). For the same reason, it is worth examining the features of the current Syrian conflict in Argentine newspapers and the information available to Argentinian society. Specifically, this section will examine Argentina's press coverage of the Syrian conflict in two parts. The first, introduces some concepts about media bias, and the second, applies them to a resounding case.

The involvement of core countries and the level of registered violence, as well as the active presence of the Argentine-Syrian community in the media, allowed the Syrian conflict to overcome the news gatekeepers (see Bennett 1–31; Pizarro 2012, 225–247). In other words, the Syrian conflict drew the attention of the Argentine media, in part, thanks to a mix of the conflict's own characteristics and an interest in it by the Arab diaspora in Argentina. More, it debuted by the end of March of 2011 in a column published by *La Nación* and headlined: "Violent Repression in Syria: 15 Dead" ("Violenta Represión en Siria: 15 Muertos," March 24, 2011). Three weeks later, the television show *TV Pública Internacional* dedicated its weekly emission to a special report titled: "Crisis in Syria" (Visión Siete Internacional 2011). The coverage provided by two popular and ideologically opposite media outlets meant the Argentinian society was made aware of the ongoing Syrian conflict. Regardless of media politics and social awareness, the Argentinian press suffered from the same bias experienced by other Western media. That is, framing, personalization, dramatization, fragmentation, and the authority-disorder bias (see Bennett 2007, 38–45). Hence, this section analyzes the way in which media biases affected Argentina's press coverage of the Syrian conflict. The analysis will address the narratives and raw data from two news outlets: one opposite to the Syrian government, *La Nación*, and the other favorable, *Diario Sirio Libanés*. All that, to answer to the following questions: what is the way in which the news is presented that affects the Syrian Program?

According to Lance Bennett, the news that crosses the gatekeepers is characterized by five news bias: framing, personalization, dramatization, fragmentation, and authority-disorder bias. The first element, framing, refers to the theme organizing a story's elements. The second, personalization, concerns the inclination to downplay the big picture. The third, dramatization, indicates a preference for simple and dramatic stories. The fourth, fragmentation, has to do with the lack of connection between stories and the larger context. Lastly, authority-disorder bias refers to a preoccupation for stories about public (dis)order and (in)security. Consequently, audiences lack quality information required to draw informed conclusions (Bennett 2007, 38–45). In the following paragraphs, these concepts will be applied to the reporting of the Syrian conflict by the Argentine media to better understand the information upon which Argentinians acted upon to promote, implement, and engage with an active immigration policy for Syrian refugees.

The five news bias mentioned above affected Argentine reports on the Syrian conflict. Therefore, although the Argentinian society was aware of the Syrian conflict, it was unaware of the effort required to confront the ensuing refugee crisis. According to the daily news published, starting September 2015, Syrian refugees travelled to Europe to find shelter and food. More, Argentinians only learned about the Syrian refugee crisis through the picture of dead 3-year-old Syrian immigrant, Ilan Kurdi. Kurdi's body washed up on a Turkish beach after the boat carrying his family and about 200 refugees capsized in the Mediterranean Sea. Also prominent in the news was journalist Petra László's aggression to immigrants, including a young girl and a father carrying his daughter, near the Serbian-Hungarian border. Mariano Winograd, President of Argentine Humanitarian Refuge, said "I saw the image of that boy. . . . and decided I had to do something" (Pura Vida 2016). All that, in spite of the fact that Argentine media published stories about Syrian refugees since March 2012 ("Exodo de Siria por la ofensiva de Al-Assad," *La Nación*, March 5, 2012) and the Argentine government deployed a policy to address the Syrian refugee crisis in September 2014 (Regulation 3915/2014). Hence, it can be concluded that Argentinian citizens were poorly informed, and consequently ill prepared to respond in a timely and effective fashion to the refugee crisis. Many were ignorant about the security and socioeconomic drivers pushing Syrians to Europe, and the reasons to search for alternative host countries, like Argentina. Thus, framing, personalization, dramatization, and authority-disorder bias affected coverage of the Syrian conflict. Consequently, Argentinians lacked quality information to understand and respond to the Syrian refugee crisis.

The widely publicized arrival of Syrian refugee Haneen Nasser offers an opportunity to further examine Argentina's media coverage of the Syrian conflict and refugee crisis. After Nasser's arrival, *La Nación* published an article which opened with the following sentence: "Haneen Nasser is 24 years old and left her native country, the convoluted Syria, to forge a future in

Argentina thanks to the help of a friend with a similar last name that she met online" (Loreley Gaffoglio. "En busca de paz: huyó de la guerra en Siria para vivir en un pueblo de La Pampa," *La Nación*, July 17, 2016). Meanwhile, *Diario Sirio Libanés* began its article with a differing tone: "On Friday night, the Syrian Haneen Nasser, 24, stepped on Argentinean ground after seven months of endless procedures and more than 20 hours of travel to turn a new page of her life story" (Redacción Diario Sirio Libanés. "Haneen Nasser: La Siria que Conmocionó a Todos al Llegar al País," *Diario Sirio Libanés*, July 18, 2016). In both articles, the news is framed by the ongoing Syrian conflict. Also, it is personalized by Nasser's journey to Argentina, dramatized by focusing on her suffering and sacrifice, fragmented by ignoring other similar stories and the refugee crisis, and biased toward public order and security by emphasizing over current violence in Syria. Moreover, while *La Nación* explicitly mentions the Syrian conflict, *Diario Sirio Libanés* centers on time-consuming bureaucracy. In the end, both articles appeal to emotion through a recount of Nasser's contact through Facebook with her host, Belén Nasser. Moreover, no detailed information is provided about the ongoing Syrian conflict, Argentina's immigration policies addressing the refugee crisis, and the challenges faced by refugees and hosts once settled. Hence, it can be concluded that media coverage of Nasser's arrival contains the bias elements introduced above. That is, framing, personalization, dramatization, fragmentation, and authority-disorder bias. All of which reflects an emotional–editorial line preoccupied with a political position within the Syrian conflict. Consequently, the reader was deprived of the meaningful information required to draw informed conclusions. What follows is an analysis of the language used by two Argentine newspapers to report on the Syrian conflict and refugee crisis. That, to shed light over the emotional–editorial lines and the information available to the Argentine society.

La Nación and *Diario Sirio Libanés* address different audiences and promote opposite perspectives on the Syrian conflict. While the first focuses the whole Argentinian nation and denounces the Syrian regime, the second appeals to the Arab diaspora exclusively and supports the Syrian government. Thus, each outlet approached the Syrian conflict from unique angles. For example, while *La Nación* referred to the Syrian government as the *Syrian regime* on 2,349 occasions, *Diario Sirio Libanés* did so only sixteen times (see figure 2.1).[6] More, the comparatively higher mention of the Syrian capital city, Damascus, by *Diario Sirio Libanés* is consequent with its use as an alternative to Syrian government. Also, while Damascus was the most mentioned Syrian city in both newspapers, *Diario Sirio Libanés* doubled its mentions of Aleppo against *La Nación*. In other words, the recovery of the city of Aleppo by the Syrian government was a great victory for the official narrative. Thus, *Diario Sirio Libanés* continued to report on Aleppo after

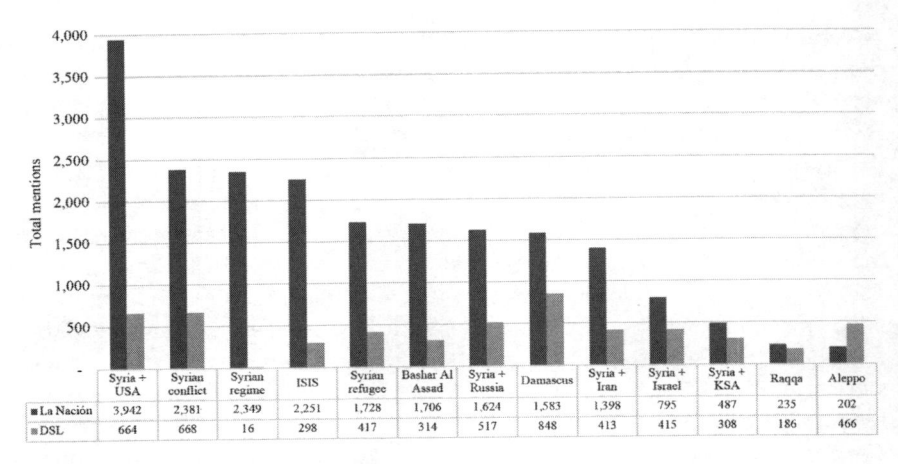

	Syria + USA	Syrian conflict	Syrian regime	ISIS	Syrian refugee	Bashar Al Assad	Syria + Russia	Damascus	Syria + Iran	Syria + Israel	Syria + KSA	Raqqa	Aleppo
La Nación	3,942	2,381	2,349	2,251	1,728	1,706	1,624	1,583	1,398	795	487	235	202
DSL	664	668	16	298	417	314	517	848	413	415	308	186	466

Figure 2.1 Keyword Count Mentions in Selected Argentine Press.

government forces took over the city while *La Nación* stopped. A similar attitude could be observed for the press coverage of Palmyra.

The conflicting narratives also included the representation of regional and international powers. Initially, *Diario Sirio Libanés* appears to downplay Saudi Arabia's role in the conflict against that of Iran and Israel, whereas *La Nación* emphasizes Iran's participation over that of Saudi Arabia and Israel. Here, there are two machinations at play. First, *La Nación* regularly cited international news organizations associated with Western political powers, for example, Reuters (UK), Associated Press (USA), *Agence France Presse* (France), and EFE (Spain). These agencies represented Iran as a challenger of the regional order, often negatively. Second, *La Nacion*'s reader is already familiarized with Iran through the accusation for the responsibility of two terrorist attacks in Argentina: the Israeli Embassy in 1992 and the Israelite Argentine Mutual Association in 1994. Iran was villainized in *La Nación* even before the Syrian conflict. All the while, *Diario Sirio Libanés* questions the narrative that points toward Iran because it too involves some Syrian responsibility for the terrorist attacks, and so it turned to politically opposite news organizations like RT (Russia) and SANA (Syria) or other alternative outlets like SouthFront. At an international level, the United States received the largest share of the narrative advanced by both news outlets. For *La Nación*, the United States was a partner for peace, and for *Diario Sirio Libanés* an instigator. For its part, Russia was characterized in the same tone, but always opposite to the United States. So, Russia for *Diario Sirio Libanés* was a partner for peace, and an instigator for *La Nación*. Thus, the reader's perception of warring parties and level of engagement depends on the news outlet chosen as a source of information. More, the proportionally higher count for DAESH in *La Nación* is a clear example of authority-disorder bias deployment revealed by a focus on the group's savagery. In short, *La Nación* adopted a narrative in support of the Syrian opposition while it denounced the Syrian government, and *Diario Sirio Libanés* attacked the opposition forces as a foreign element and turned itself into an official Syrian mouthpiece. In the end, the coverage did not offer the Argentinian society essential data to draw informed conclusions about the Syrian conflict and give a better response to the ensuing humanitarian crisis. That situation became evident when the Security Secretary Eugenio Burzaco warned about the presence of Argentine citizens trained by DAESH in the province of Corrientes ("Hemos Detectado Argentinos que se han Formado en Isis," *Primera Edición*, September 11, 2011), and President Macri announced Argentina would receive 3,000 refugees ("Macri en la ONU: Argentina Recibirá a 3000 Refugiados Sirios", *Clarín*, September 20, 2016), or the press reported that Syrian refugees returned to Syria due to inflation ("Los Sirios que se Vuelven a Alepo Porque acá los Mata la Inflación," *Perfil*, May 9, 2017). Such was the social confusion that an online campaign for a binding referendum opposing the arrival of Syrian refugees was launched at the online platform Change.org.[7]

In September 2015, the picture of Ilan Kurdi and images of Petra László caught the public's attention. That provided the news corporation with an opportunity to offer audiences quality information about the Syrian conflict and humanitarian crisis. The analysis of media coverage, however, revealed that *La Nación* and *Diario Sirio Libanés* included bias practices in the shape of framing, personalization, dramatization, fragmentation, and authority-disorder. All that, to make the news fit into a politically charged narrative. Such discourses did very little to provide the Argentine society with the required facts to draw informed conclusions. At this point it is worth asking, how did Argentina react to the Syrian humanitarian crisis? The following section will address this question.

THE SYRIAN PROGRAM

In September 2014, the Migration National Directorate (MND) approved Regulation 3915/2014. The legislative act called for the implementation of the Special Humanitarian Visa Program for Foreigners Affected by the Conflict in the Syrian Arab Republic (Regulation 3915/2014). Commonly referred to as the Syrian Program, the policy addressed a demand by the Argentine-Arab community for family reunification (Martín Arias Duval, pers. comm., December 16, 2019). In it, Argentina adopted a unique and original approach and sidelined the refugee status enacted by the Convention Relating to the Status of Refugees. Moreover, the following years saw the policy evolve from family reunification to large-scale refugee relocation. Among the most important reforms introduced were new security screenings, establishment of a host's registry, creation of a coordination office, and circumscription of humanitarian visas to Syrian refugees registered with United Nations High Commissioner for Refugees (UNHCR) in Lebanon (Regulation 4683/2016; Regulation 1025/2019). Thus, the analysis that follows will, first, introduce the Syrian Program in its original form, then, describe the successive reforms, and last, contrast results with objectives to evaluate Argentina's response to the Syrian refugee crisis, and its evolution.

The Syrian Program originates from a demand by the Argentinian-Syrian community, and the lobbying of late Galeb Moussa Hamad, President of the Federation of Argentine Arab Entities, Buenos Aires Chapter, to the then Migration National Director, Martin Arias Duval, for assistance to family members escaping the Syrian conflict (Martín Arias Duval, pers. comm., December 16, 2019). Hence, the Syrian Program's original stated purpose was to facilitate and guarantee family reunification (Regulation 3915/2014). The response meant that Argentina would issue a permit of entry in the form of a two-year humanitarian visa. That is, the beneficiary would not enter Argentina as a refugee and be granted all the rights and obligations associated with that figure (Law 26.165). To be very specific, any Syrian entering Argentina with a humanitarian visa would not receive, for example, a government-issued identity document, state subsidies, and other benefits granted to refugees by Argentinean law. Moreover, the MND was the only agency authorized to issue humanitarian visas which had to be retrieved by the beneficiary at the Argentinian embassy in Damascus. Additionally, the regulation required the beneficiary to hold a valid passport, certified criminal record, proven family bond, and have an interview with an Argentine diplomat. Previously, the host must have submitted a certified invitation letter, demonstrated the family bond, possessed a valid identity document, and credited a real address.

The MND established the Syrian Committee which held regular meetings with the participation of government agencies (Ministry of Interior, Ministry of Foreign Relations and Worship, Ministry of Federal Planning, Public Investment and Services, Ministry of Justice and Human Rights, Ministry of Security, and Federal Intelligence Agency), international organizations (ACNUR, International Organization for Migrations (IOM) and British Council), Argentine-Arab institutions (Argentine Confederation of Arab Institutions, Syrian-Lebanese Club, Yabrudi Club, Syrian Cultural Association, Islamic Center of the Argentine Republic, Arab Argentine Islamic Association, and Catholic Apostolic Orthodox of Antioch), and non-governmental organizations (Argentine Catholic Migration Commission Foundation, Youth With a Mission, Slaves of the Sacred Heart of Jesus,

Adventist Development and Relief Agency, Argentine Humanitarian Refuge).[8] The Syrian Committee met regularly to share the challenges faced and suggested modifications to the program. Some of the most recurrent topics discussed at the meetings were: extent humanitarian visas to all Syrians regardless of family bond, difficulties to visit the Argentinian embassy in Damascus to retrieve the permit, and certification of Syrian academic titles. Some of these issues were addressed by Regulation 4499/2015. For example, it eliminated the family bond requisite, and incorporated all Argentine embassies. Thus, form this point forward all Syrian citizens could apply for a humanitarian visa and retrieve the document from any of the 123 Argentine foreign representations. The Syrian Committee met for the last time on October 25, 2016, despite of the several requests by its members to government authorities to meet again.

The most important reforms to the Syrian Program were introduced after the New York Declaration for Refugees and Migrants, and then agreed upon at the high-level meeting on Large Movement of Refugees and Migrants, and ultimately hosted by the United Nations General Assembly on September 19, 2016 (Cyment et al. 2019, 13–17). Since Argentina signed the declaration, the Syrian Program became the subject of a global effort within the Emerging Resettlement Countries Joint Support Mechanism (ERCM), led by the UNHCR and the IOM. Also, the Syrian Program became involved with the Global Refugee Sponsorship Initiative (GRSI) sponsored by the Canadian government, the European Resettlement Network + Other Legal Pathways (ERN+), and the EU's Partnership on Inclusion of Migrants and Refugees (PI). As explained in the Syrian Program Institutional Memory document, the policy turned into an original international policy scheme which allowed the interaction of traditional humanitarian actors such as NGOs and the UN, as well as the private sector, civil society, including academia and religious groups. Moreover, it aimed not to replace individual state efforts to protect refugees, but to act as a complement in the promotion of a long-term sustainable model (*Ibid.*, 16). What spurred this action—the integration of the Syrian Program to an international plan for refugee relocation—was the government's urgency to secure the funding required by the relocation of 3,000 refugees. Funds which were conditional on the policy's reform.

Some of those modifications introduced were to take away from society the right to select beneficiaries, and limit beneficiaries UNHCR's registered refugee population in Lebanon, a complete health examination at Lebanese hospitals, a security screening assisted by foreign intelligence agencies, and cover of travel costs for migrants. The government, however, pushed other reforms on its own initiative and replaced the Syrian Committee by regional ones (Córdoba, Mendoza, La Rioja, San Juan, Salta y Tucumán) with the exclusive participation from government agencies and international organizations, and coordinated by a new Syrian Program National Cabinet (Decree 1034/2016). According to then Syria Program Coordinator Esteban Tomé Fuentes, the Argentine-Arab institutions were sidelined because the government did not receive from them the expected support (pers. comm., January 22, 2020). The revision of the Syrian Program took the right to choose the benefited refugee away from the host and transferred some financial responsibility to the state and international organizations supporting the policy (e.g., health check and travel costs). Thus, the modifications to the Syrian Program after the New York Declaration allowed for international partners to buy in, and in that sense the policy became a tool for the reorientation of Argentina's foreign policy away from South America and toward the North America and Europe. All that, in line with the Macri administration's desire to be part of the world again ("Macri: 'Queremos volver a ser parte del mundo'," *Casa Rosada*, September 19, 2016), it allowed the UNHCR to direct efforts away from relocation and toward integration (Cyment et al. 2019, 58–69). One thing that remained untouched since the beginning is the fact that, just like in the Turkish case, Syrians affected by conflict were deprived of the protection granted by the Convention Relating to the Status of Refugees through the creation of a new category.[9] What is left to analyze in the following section are the results of the Syrian Program and examine if the modifications introduced had any impact at all.

For the period 2014–2019, the MND reports the Syrian Program received a total of 961 special visas requests, 597 (62 percent) were accepted and 445 (46 percent) beneficiaries entered Argentina (see table 2.1). Moreover, 2016 records the highest number of requests submitted to the NDM. Ever since then, the decline in the submission and acceptance of applications for special visas, and entries to the country, exceeds 50 percent per year. However, not all Syrians entering Argentina did so through the Syrian Program, and many travelled first as tourists to Brazil only to later cross into Argentina and claim protection under the Convention Relating to the Status of Refugees. This alternative was recommended by institutions of the Argentine–Arab

Table 2.1 Syrian Program Visa Requests, Approval, and Use (by year, 2014–2019)

	Visa Applications Submitted	Visas Applications Resolved Positively	Visas Issued and Used by Syrians
2014	28	14	1
2015	209	180	81
2016	348	117	99
2017	261	226	166
2018	97	50	64
2019	18	10	34
Total	961	597	445

Note: Data provided by International Organization for Migrations. Table created by author.

community such as the Syrian Cultural Center and Druze Charity Association (Daniel Attar, pers. comm., February 24, 2020). According to the National Commission for Refugees, records between 2014 and 2019 a total of 397 Syrians were granted refugee status (see table 2.1); 2015 recorded the highest number of refugee states requests with 159 by Syrians, and it has declined ever since to reach a low of 8 for 2019. The fall is most interesting because immigration from Venezuela (3234), Haiti (1358), and Cuba (998) increased on the period 2015–2019, and total Syrian immigration (with and without the Syrian Program) during the same time totaled 842. Lastly, it should be pointed that only a third of the 3,000 refugees promised to be received have arrived to Argentina.

At the same time, there were a small number of Syrians who migrated to Argentina through alternatives to the Syrian Program and the refugee status altogether. Data, however, were not at the disposal for this analysis and should be considered for future research. Also, the possibility of accessing records of disaggregated data on Syrian refugees (e.g., sex, location of origin and destiny, education, and profession) should be included in following investigations. Most worrying for this analysis is the lack of data concerned with return rates, because the numbers can assist in the overall evaluation of the program, providing insights about the needs and challenges faced by the relocated populations. This last point becomes a reality when considering the committee meetings and the interviews by UNHCR and IOM that resulted in the publishing of two reports about the integration and profile of Syrians in Argentina (Kleidermacher 2019; Pérez Caraballo 2019). However, more importantly, both documents were published years after the Syrian Program deployment and did very little to change and revert the policy's declining results.

In summary, the Syrian Program started as a family reunification policy and ended as one gear in a global refugee relocation effort. This was done through policy reforms, and facilitated by both, a change of the government's external alignment toward Europe and North America, and the rise of regional right-wing parties inclined toward more traditional centers of power. All of this is reflected in the signing of the New York Declaration, the incorporation of international organizations to the Syrian Program, and the exit of Argentine–Arab institutions from the decision-making process through the elimination of the Syrian Committee. Although there is a temporal coincidence between the modifications introduced and the negative trend in the arrival of Syrian refugees, it remains challenging to prove any causality. However, that may be remedied with more disaggregated data on Syrians immigration. The lower number of requests may respond to conflict dynamics, the decline in the number of refugees, and the return to Syria of refugees in Lebanon, said Agustina Galantini, Project Assistant,

International Organization for Migrations (pers. comm., February 17, 2020). Although this may be true, it must be contrasted with the alternative to the Syrian Program promoted by Argentine-Arab institutions to secure the refugee status for Syrians arriving in Argentina. Also, it is necessary to inquire about the motives for the return of Syrian immigrants. Nonetheless, it can be affirmed with full certainty that the Syrian Program can be divided in two stages: family reunification and refugee relocation.

CONCLUSION: BETWEEN EXPECTATIONS AND REALITY

The analysis of the Syrian Program offers a clear picture of the challenges associated with geographical and cultural distance within the context of programs dedicated to relocating population. Even when the policy was promoted by the Arab diaspora, and met initial objectives, its progressive decline led interested actors to consider alternative plans. That, in detriment of a concerted effort by Argentine society which needed to engage as hosts and individual financiers. Moreover, media coverage provided insufficient information as it suffered from different types of media bias. For its part, the ex-Migration National Director, Arias Duval, administration addressed a demand from below although blocking access to the status of refugees, and the modifications introduced during President Macri's government transformed the Syrian Program into a foreign policy tool without offering wider protection to immigrants. Beyond the differences between the results reported by both administrations and the lack of disaggregate data, the policy's decline in terms of benefited Syrians is unquestionable. Thus, Argentina met the initial demand raised by the Arab diaspora, but failed to meet its self-assumed compromise with the international community.

The interviews with ex-Migration National Directorate Martin Arias Duval (2007–2015), Syria Program General Coordinator Esteban Tomé Fuentes (2016–2019), and IOM Project Assistant Agustina Galantini (2017–present) shed light on the failure by pointing out the challenges faced throughout the policy's implementation. While all of them were active participants at different times, and in representation of opposing political forces, their compromise with human rights through an active promotion of the Syrian Program was blurred by an over optimistic posture in regards to the effort required by such a policy. That is, criticism was scarce and blame was put on its political counterpart or Arab interlocutor. In that sense, Arias Duval blamed shortcomings on security apparatus' concerns about the infiltration of terrorists. In a differing tone, Tomé Fuentes pointed toward the Arab diaspora for its criticism of the policy's new objective. For its part, Galantini emphasized the refugees' expectations about the program's material provisions. Blame aside, neither has mentioned that a number of beneficiaries have never been granted a citizenship after the two-year period and are forced to periodically renew a provisional residency permit.

To end this chapter, the Syrian Program deserves to be praised for its novelty within Argentinian immigration policy and a contribution to ease an international problem. Thus, taking into account the growing number and places of origin of refugees, the development of new and innovative relocation programs are more than welcome. Consequently, improvements in social engagement through quality information could improve the results of those novel solutions offered to refugees while at the same time reinforce global efforts to eradicate conflict.

NOTES

1. All unofficial translations into English throughout this chapter were done by the author.

2. For the Brazilian policy regulating the arrival of Syrian refugees see, Normative Resolution 17/2013, National Commission for the Refugees, https://www.justica.gov.br/seus-direitos/refugio/legislacao. For the Uruguayan see, Resolution N° 707/014 of December 8, 2014 (https://www.impo.com.uy/bases/resoluciones/707-2014/3), respectively.

3. The Condor Plan was a regional initiative installed by autocratic regimes to disappear political rivals, activists and dissidents assisted and funded by North American and European governments. For an extended discussion on the authoritarian regimes in South America and implementation of the plan throughout the 1970's, see Guillermo O'Donnell. 1988. *Bureaucratic Authoritarianism: Argentina 1966–1973 in Comparative Perspective*. Translated by James McGuire and Rae Flory. Berkeley: University of California Press; Joan Patrice McSherry. 2019. "Operation Condor as an International System of State Violence and Terror: A Historical-Structural Analysis." In *The Politics of Violence in Latin America*, edited by Pablo Policzer, 269–72. Calgary: University of Calgary Press; Marie-Monique Robin. 2003. "Escadrons de la Mort: L'École Française." Directed by Marie-Monique Robin. Paris: Idéale Audience. https://www.youtube.com/watch?v=8_wXv2u3bxk.

4. The numbers shared here were taken from the National Census of 1914. To access an online copy for the document, please see National Commission, *Tercer Censo Nacional*.

5. According to the Random House Unabridged Dictionary of American English, *gaucho* is a cowboy of the South American pampas, usually one of mixed Spanish and Indian descent. More, throughout the eighteenth Century the Argentine ruling elite saw the *gaucho* as a social element that needed to be civilized and was characterized as procrastinate, unruly and costly. Such representation can be found in the Argentine classical literary works of, for example, Sarmiento, *Facundo*, and

Echeverria, *El Matadero/La Cautiva*. For a more nuanced description about the *gaucho*, see Hernández, *Martín Fierro*.

6. The figures reported were the result of simple online searches at each of the newspapers website using the keywords detailed in Figure 1. The searches were limited to the period January 1, 2011–October 17, 2019.

7. The campaign is currently closed, but it remains available online. To see the campaign and a brief statement of purpose, please visit: https://www.change.org/p/mauricio-macri-no-al-plan-para-recibir-a-3000-refugiados-sirios-en-la-argentina.

8. The mentioned government agencies, international organizations, Argentine-Arab institutions and non-governmental organizations participated in one or more of the meetings held by the Syrian Committee at the office building of the Migration National Directorate on Antártida Argentina Av., 1355, in the Autonomous City of Buenos Aires, between September 2014 and October 2016. More, the representatives present at the meetings were not always the institutional highest ranking authority, and lobbying was particularly effective amid particular institutional interests, as reflected by the modifications introduced to the program by Disposition 4499/2015.

9. For a discussion on the Turkish approach to the status of refugees and Syrian citizens seeking shelter in Turkey, see Verónica Sabrina Souto Olmedo. 2018. "La Humanidad en el Limbo. El Sistema de Protección Internacional de Turquía Ante la Crisis Humanitaria del Conflicto en Siria". *Foro Internacional* 58 (4): 719–54. https://forointernacional.colmex.mx/index.php/fi/article/view/2550.

REFERENCES

Abdeluahed, Akmir. 2011. *Los Árabes en Argentina*. Translated by Silvia Montenegro. Rosario: UNR Editora.

Alberdi, Juan Bautista. 2017. *Bases y Puntos de Partida para la Organización Política Argentina*. Buenos Aires: Editorial. Biblioteca del Congreso de la Nación. https://bcn.gob.ar/uploads/BasesAlberdi.pdf.

ARK Group DMCC. 2018. *Grey Noise: Migration and strategic communications*. https://static1.squarespace.com/static/5e9665731a6ca03856d5eb1c/t/5f2894b4bb61114b00930e46/1596495083587/ARK-Grey_Noise-Migration_and_StratComms.pdf.

Bennett, Lance. 2007. *News: The politics of illusion*, 7th ed. New York: Pearson Longman.

Cyment, Paola, Esteban Tomé Fuentes, Osmar Alza, Lorena Haupt and Mauricio Fallas. 2019. *Memoria Institucional Programa Siria 2014–2019*. Buenos Aires: Organización Internacional para las Migraciones. http://argentina.iom.int/co/sites/default/files/publicaciones/PDF%20Memoria%20programa%20siria_interior%20con%20tapas.pdf.

Decree 1034/2016, National Executive Power. http://servicios.infoleg.gob.ar/infolegInternet/verNorma.do?id=265715.

Doucet, Lyse. 2018. "Syria & the CNN Effect: What Role Does the Media Play in Policy-Making?" *Dædalus, the Journal of the American Academy of Arts &*

Sciences 147 (1): 141–57. https://www.mitpressjournals.org/doi/full/10.1162/DAED_a_00480.

Echeverria, Esteban. 1961. *El Matadero/La Cautiva*. Buenos Aires: Pellegrini Impresores.

Equipo OIM Argentina. 2019. *Informe de Actividades 2018*. Buenos Aires: Organización Internacional para las Migraciones.

Halperín Donghi, Tulio. 1976. "¿Para qué la Inmigración? Ideología y Política Inmigratoria y Aceleración del Proceso Modernizador: El caso argentino (1810–1914)." *Anuario de Historia de América Latina* 13 (1): 437–89. https://doi.org/10.7788/jbla-1976-0129.

Hernández, José. 2004. *Martín Fierro*. Madrid: Edimat Libros.

Hernández Cortez, Noé. 2019. "El Enfoque Sistémico en el Institucionalismo Histórico". *Reflexión Política* 21 (4): 134–45. https://doi.org/10.29375/01240781.3233.

Jozami, Gladys. 1987. "Aspectos Demográficos y Comportamiento Espacial de los Migrantes Árabes en el NOA." *Revista de Estudios Migratorios Latinoamericanos* 2 (5): 57–90.

Jozami, Julio. 2013. *Argentina y el Mundo Árabe: Un Nuevo Enfoque de su Vinculación*. Buenos Aires: Cámara de Diputados de la Nación.

Kleidermacher, Gisele. 2019. *Perfil Sociocultural de la Población Siria en Origen*. Buenos Aires: Organización Internacional para las Migraciones. http://argentina.iom.int/co/perfil-sociocultural-de-la-poblaci%C3%B3n-siria-en-origen.

Klich, Ignacio. 1993. "Argentine-Ottoman Relations and Their Impact on Immigrants from the Middle East: A History of Unfulfilled Expectations, 1910–1915." *The Americas* 50 (2): 177–205. https://doi.org/10.2307/1007138.

———. 2015. "Argentina y la Dimensión Humanitaria de la Guerra en Siria". In *Irak, Siria y el Califato: ¿Un nuevo Medio Oriente?*, edited by Ignacio Klich and Luis Mendiola, 185–207. Buenos Aires: Consejo Argentino para las Relaciones Internacionales.

Law 26.165/2006, General Law for Refugee Recognition and Protection. Honorable Congress of the Argentine Nation. http://servicios.infoleg.gob.ar/infolegInternet/verNorma.do?id=122609.

Mitchell, Amy, Katie Simmons, Katerina Matsa and Laura Silver. 2018. "Publics Around the World Follow National and Local News More Closely than International." In *Publics Globally Want Unbiased News Coverage, but Are Divided on Whether Their News Media Deliver*, 22–28. Pew Research Center. https://www.pewresearch.org/global/2018/01/11/publics-globally-want-unbiased-news-coverage-but-are-divided-on-whether-their-news-media-deliver/.

National Commission. 1914. *Tercer Censo Nacional, Vol. I and II*. Buenos Aires: Talleres Gráficos de L.J. Rosso y Cía. http://www.estadistica.ec.gba.gov.ar/dpe/Estadistica/censos/C1914-T1.pdf, http://www.estadistica.ec.gba.gov.ar/dpe/Estadistica/censos/C1914-T2.pdf.

Pérez Caraballo, Gimena. 2019. *Guía Informativa de Fortalecimiento de la Comunicación Intercultural para la Integración de la Población Beneficiaria del Programa Siria en Argentina*. Buenos Aires: Organización Internacional para las Migraciones. http://argentina.iom.int/co/gu%C3%ADa-informativa-y-de-forta lecimiento-de-la-comunicaci%C3%B3n-intercultural-para-la-integraci%C3%B3n -de-la.

Pew Research Center. https://www.pewresearch.org/global/2018/01/11/publics-a round-the-world-follow-national-and-local-news-more-closely-than-international/.

Pierson, Paul and Theda Skocpol. 2008. "El Institucionalismo Histórico en la Ciencia Política Contemporánea." *Revista Uruguaya de la Ciencia Política* 17 (1): 7–38.

Pizarro, Ana Marcela. 2012. *El "Mundo" de la Prensa Argentina: ¿Qué es noticia internacional para La Nación y Clarín?*. Saarbrücken: Editorial Académica Española. https://www.researchgate.net/publication/45220396_Dinamica_y_cont enidos_de_la_seccion_internacional_de_la_prensa_argentina_La_Nacion_y_Clari n_1980-1998.

Pura Vida. 2016. "Refugio Humanitario Argentino en Pura Vida, cada día." Filmed December 16 in Buenos Aires. TV Pública Argentina video 17:46. https://youtu.be/LYHo_F1Vlro.

Regulation 3915/2014. Migration National Directorate. http://servicios.infoleg.gob.ar/infolegInternet/verNorma.do?id=236705.

Regulation 1025/2019. Migration National Directorate. http://servicios.infoleg.gob.ar/infolegInternet/verNorma.do?id=320495.

Regulation 4683/2016. Migration National Directorate. http://servicios.infoleg.gob.ar/infolegInternet/verNorma.do?id=265236.

Sarmiento, Domingo Faustino. 2018. *Facundo o Civilización y Barbarie*. Buenos Aires: Biblioteca del Congreso de la Nación. https://bcn.gob.ar/uploads/Facundo_Sarmiento.pdf.

Sarramone, Alberto. 1999. *Los Abuelos Inmigrantes: Historia y sociología de la inmigración argentina*. Azul: Editorial Biblos Azul.

Veneroni, Rita. 2004. "La Situación de los Inmigrantes." In *Sirios, Libaneses y Argentinos: Fragmentos para una Historia de la Diversidad Cultural Argentina*, Yosef Abboud et al. Buenos Aires: Editorial Cálamo, 318–33.

Veneroni, Rita and Omar Abú Arab. 2004. "Cronología Institucional." In *Sirios, Libaneses y Argentinos: Fragmentos para una Historia de la Diversidad Cultural Argentina*, Yosef Abboud et al. Buenos Aires: Editorial Cálamo, 92–171.

Veneroni, Rita and Emmanuel Taub. 2004. "Los Judíos". In *Sirios, Libaneses y Argentinos: Fragmentos para una Historia de la Diversidad Cultural Argentina*, Yosef Abboud et al. Buenos Aires: Editorial Cálamo, 277–97.

Visión Siete Internacional. 2011. "Crisis en Siria." Filmed April 16 in Buenos Aires. TV Pública Argentina video, 12:35. https://www.youtube.com/watch?v=iuSZTyxc-rk.

Chapter 3

Can We Be Governed by Someone Who Eats Kibbeh? Lebanese Migrants and Brazilian Politics

Diogo Bercito

Looking at the ballots cast in Brazil since the second half of the twentieth century, one would be excused for thinking that these were Lebanese elections rather than Brazilian. The city of São Paulo, for instance, has been governed by three men of Lebanese descent since the 1990s: Paulo Maluf, Fernando Haddad, and Gilberto Kassab. Moreover, the former president Michel Temer is a descendant of Lebanese migrants as well.

Although the most iconic cases of politicians of Lebanese descent are concentrated in the state of São Paulo, examples span the whole country. Illustrating this phenomenon, the Lebanese descendant and Brazilian politician Said Farhat relayed the following anecdote: when the Chief of Staff of the Brazilian military government João Leitão de Abreu asked for a list of candidates for governing the state of Acre, in the Amazon region, Farhat presented him with six names. Abreu looked at the letter with Farhat's suggestions and asked him: "Are you sure these are politicians from Acre? It looks more like a list of Lebanese politicians" (Greiber, Maluf, and Mattar 1998, 387). Indeed, of the six politicians recommended by Farhat, five had Arabic last names. Moreover, the sixth one, Crisarobina Dourato Leitão, was married to a man of Arab descent. In the end, the military regime chose Jorge Kalume for the position—a son of the Arab migrant Abib Moisés. Farhat himself entered politics as Minister of Communication from 1979 to 1985.

As the cases above indicate, Lebanese migrants and their descendants occupy a prominent role in Brazilian politics. Nearly 6 percent of all Brazilian lawmakers during the 2015–2019 term were of Lebanese descent. The figure is particularly surprising given that Lebanese migrants represent a smaller percentage of the Brazilian population. How much lower, however, is unclear, since there is no reliable estimate of the number of Lebanese migrants and descendants living in the country. The official estimates of between 7 million and 10 million people provided by the Brazilian Ministry of Foreign Affairs are largely discredited, for reasons detailed below. Even if they were accurate, Lebanese migrants and their descendants would still comprise no more than between 3.3 percent and 4.7 percent of country's total population. The numbers are probably much lower (Karam 2007, 10–11). Arab migrants and their descendants were also successful in the official politics of other Latin American countries. To name few examples, the presidents Carlos Menem (Argentina), Julio César Turbay Ayala (Colombia), Abdalá Bucaram (Ecuador), Carlos Roberto Flores Facussé (Honduras), and Nayib Bukele (El Salvador) all hailed from Arab migrant families.

This chapter aims to make sense of this apparent over-representation of politicians of Lebanese descent in Brazil. It starts by analyzing the history of their political participation, arguing that the explanation combines four factors: first, Lebanese migrants were particularly engaged in the politics of their homeland even after settling in Brazil and managed to transfer their experience to local Brazilian politics. Second, political participation served as a means of social mobility, through which migrants continued earlier processes of enrichment in commerce and investment in education. Third, Lebanese migrants encountered a favorable environment for pursuing public office in Brazil, as the strongman Getúlio Vargas excited the political participation of minorities during the 1930s as a way of counterbalancing the power of the traditional Brazilian elites. Fourth, Lebanese migrants were spread throughout Brazil, in part as a consequence of their work as peddlers, and, as such, they managed to represent diverse constituencies.

After this historical analysis, this chapter considers the impact of these Lebanese migrants and their descendants on the domestic and foreign policies of Brazil. Given the over-representation of politicians of Lebanese origin, scholars have investigated, for example, whether or not these public officials influence the political decisions taken in Brasília, the capital of Brazil. In a similar vein, the U. S. government researched in 2006 to find out if Arab migrants could shape Brazil's foreign policy *vis-à-vis* the Middle East (U.S. Consulate General in São Paulo 2016). These efforts, both from scholars and policy makers, indicate a recurrent interest in political participation by Brazilians of Lebanese origin.

The last section of this chapter presents a particular case study: the Grupo Parlamentar Brasil-Líbano, a parliamentary caucus that congregates politicians of Lebanese descent. The case study analyzes the caucus' list of members during the term that spanned from 2015 to 2019, in terms of their geographical origin and political affiliation. Politicians of Lebanese descent are present throughout the territory of Brazil and in both the left and the right—they are concentrated, however, in the Southeast and in conservative parties.

This chapter considers "political participation" in its official sense. It analyzes how Lebanese migrants and their descendants participate in official political activity (in the country's Parliament, ministries, and political parties). Therefore, it does not delve into other instances of politics, such as workers' movements. With this choice, it follows the methodology Boris Fausto used in his book *Imigração e Política em São Paulo*. Fausto claims that "official politics" is an important indicator of the relationship between migrant communities and national elites (Fausto 1995, 7–8). He argues, in this sense, that the incorporation of migrants—among them Lebanese—into politics in São Paulo in the 1930s and 1940s evidences a degree of social flexibility (*Ibid.*, 26). That is, it marks the historical moment after which migrants could join the spheres in which political decisions were taken.

The mass Arab migration to Brazil occurred from 1870 until 1930, before Lebanon was a nation-state. Greater Lebanon was only established in 1920, carved out of Greater Syria, with independence declared in 1943 and achieved in 1945. Therefore, calling a migrant "Lebanese" raises all sorts of historical and socio-cultural questions of identity. What makes an individual Lebanese? Would this person be hailing from what is now Lebanon? Who can claim such origins?

In this sense, some authors prefer to use the term "Syrian-Lebanese" or "Syrian and Lebanese," which the migrant community itself adopts (e.g., Duoun 1944 and Truzzi 1997). Others opt for the more comprehensive term "Arab" (Hajjar 1985), although this word does not do justice to the fact that the majority of Arab migrants who arrived in Brazil were either Syrian or Lebanese (Knowlton 1960, 37). In this chapter, the term "Lebanese" is used to refer to the migrants that left the territory that is now known as Lebanon. Whenever it is impossible to establish a precise origin, though, "Syrian-Lebanese" and "Arab" are used.

One of the difficulties in providing definitive answers to the over-representation of politicians of Lebanese descent in Brazil is the fact that, to date, Lebanese migration to Brazil remains understudied. Although Brazil hosts the largest Lebanese diaspora in the world—and by some estimates could have more Lebanese descendants than there are people in Lebanon (Karam 2007, 10–11)—this field receives scant attention. Scholars generally cite the same handful of works and few attempts are currently being made to expand the field. Most recent efforts are being made outside the country, for example, with the work of the U.S. scholars John Tofik Karam (2007) and Stacy Fahrenthold (2019).

The U.S. scholar Clark Knowlton was the first person to work on the issue of Lebanese migration to Brazil from a formal academic perspective, writing his PhD dissertation at Vanderbilt University in 1955 and publishing it in Portuguese in 1960 under the title *Sírios e Libaneses*, now a rare find. Knowlton built upon earlier work produced by some of the migrants themselves after landing in Brazil, who mostly wrote adventurous accounts of their travels and their early experiences upon arrival—while valuable as historical documentation, these works are limited in scope and do not provide broader considerations or analysis of migration (e.g., Kurban 1933 and Duoun 1944). Knowlton's focus was on the spatial distribution of Syrian-Lebanese migrants in São Paulo. Unfortunately, he dedicated only a few pages to official politics.

The next influential work on Lebanese migration to Brazil came thirty years later, with Claude Fahd Hajjar's *100 Anos de Imigração* (1985). Hajjar—a Lebanese migrant herself—did groundbreaking work, given that there were almost no other studies on the subject. Despite the valuable information contained in her text, Hajjar also included only a few insights into official politics. After Hajjar's book, the following relevant attempt to study Lebanese migration to Brazil was made by Oswaldo Truzzi in his *Patrícios: Sírios e Libaneses* (1997). Truzzi was the first and one of the few scholars to delve deeper into the phenomenon of political participation among Lebanese migrants in Brazil. That is one of the reasons why his book is still—deservedly—the most referenced work on Lebanese migration to Brazil. Nevertheless, there is much work to be done to expand upon his two-decades-old work.

After Truzzi, Sergio Tadeu de Niemeyer Lamarão made one of the most remarkable contributions to our understanding of Lebanese politicians in Brazil. He published an article analyzing the last names of Brazilian deputies and senators from 1945 to 1998 (Lamarão 2004). In his study, he found 163 congressmen with Syrian-Lebanese surnames. That made Syrian-Lebanese migrants the second largest ethnic group in terms of political representation after Italians, who had 236 congressmen. Lamarão's work is somewhat limited due to his methods, which are based on last names instead of known origin. It points, nevertheless, to possible avenues of exploration, in its attempt to quantify the phenomenon of the political representation of Lebanese migrants.

HISTORICAL CONTEXT

Arabs began to migrate to Brazil in large numbers during the 1870s, with most of them hailing from present-day Lebanon and Syria. However, given that Lebanon and Syria did not exist at that time as distinct countries—their independence came only in the 1940s—these migrants were at first classified according to various and unsystematic categories like "Turks," "Turk-Arabs,"

"Turk-Asians," "Syrians," and "Lebanese" (Truzzi 1997, 39). It was the classification of "Turks" that stuck during the first decades. Arab migrants found this label particularly aggravating since they had migrated in part to leave behind the economic crisis and the perceived discrimination suffered under the Turkish Ottoman Empire (Kurban 1933, 20). With time, however, the term "Turk" was abandoned, in part as a result of the efforts of the migrant community itself to push for the hyphenated identity of "Syrian-Lebanese."

The story of the Hospital Sírio-Libanês, in São Paulo, is illustrative of this process. Adma Jafet, who had migrated from present-day Lebanon, began to collect funds in 1921 to create what she called the Hospital Sírio. The plans were delayed by World War II and, in the interim, Arab migrants began to reconsider its name. After all, few of the people involved in the project were from what became Syria under the French Mandate. There was pressure from the local Lebanese community to rename it as the Hospital Libanês. Some migrants presented legal claims, a delegation of priests came from Lebanon, and the conflict was only resolved when the institution was inaugurated in 1965 as the Hospital Sírio-Libanês (Greiber, Maluf, and Mattar 1998, 635–636).

There are no accurate statistics of how many Syrian-Lebanese migrants arrived in Brazil, partially due to the above-mentioned inconsistencies in their classification at the ports of entry. To this date, scholars rely upon the estimate that 106,184 people arrived from the Middle East between 1871 and 1942 (Knowlton 1960, 37), most of whom were Christian (*Ibid.*, 57). More recent studies suggest that no more than 150,000 Syrian-Lebanese migrants entered Brazil since 1870 (Pitts Jr. 2006, 3). Regardless of their numbers, it is certain that most of them remained in São Paulo (Truzzi 1997, 30–31).

There is also no precise estimate of the current size of the Lebanese community in Brazil. The Brazilian Ministry of Foreign Affairs claims that between 7 million and 10 million Lebanese and descendants live in the country. However, there is no information regarding how the Brazilian authorities reached that figure. The information could have been drawn from Hajjar's study, which cites the figure of 7,200,000 people of Arab origin in Brazil (Hajjar 1985, 18). Hajjar justifies the number as a projection based on the number of entries, but she does not explain her methodology. It seems unlikely that Brazil hosts between 7 million and 10 million Lebanese and descendants, while only 6 million people live in Lebanon itself. This chapter includes these statistics, nevertheless, because they are a "message" sent by the community, asserting the importance of these migrants in the social formation of the country. In a similar sense, John Tofik Karam writes that "such statistics must not be dismissed as misrepresentations but probed as social facts" given that "maintaining a privileged presence in business and political circles, Middle Easterners have overestimated themselves as a way to strengthen their place in the Brazilian nation (Karam 2007, 11). That is, these estimates may be indications of a particular image projected by the community.

Regardless of their precise numbers, Lebanese migrants have impacted Brazil in several ways. Two of the most prominent Brazilian writers—Raduan Nassar and Milton Hatoum—hail from Lebanese families and their masterpieces—*Lavoura Arcaica* and *Dois Irmãos*—both refer to their Levantine origin. In the region of the 25 de Março street in São Paulo, where most Arab migrants initially lived, one still sees Arabic names and words all around. Another compelling indication of the impact of Arab migration to Brazil is culinary. Sfiha, a traditional meat pie, and kibbeh, a meat croquette, are staples in Brazil, found in any store. The largest Brazilian food chain—called Habib's, with a smiling cheeky genie as a mascot—sells 680 million *sfihas* a year (Meihy 2016, 167).

In addition to these indicators, Syrian-Lebanese are particularly visible in the field of politics. This story begins, in fact, with their earlier engagement with the politics of their homeland. The mass arrival of Lebanese migrants to Brazil coincided with a growing nationalist movement in Beirut and Damascus. It was during these years that the Syrian and Lebanese populations, both in the homeland and abroad, posed a clear challenge to the Ottoman Empire, which had controlled their territories since the sixteenth century. As the Ottoman Empire was replaced by the French Mandate, a nationalist movement gained strength, culminating in the independence of Lebanon in 1943–45.

Scholars still mostly write the history of Arab nationalism from the point of view of what was happening in the homeland (e.g., Hitti 1959 and Provence 2005). They leave behind, however, the intense nationalist debate and activity that was happening in the diaspora. São Paulo was one of the centers of that nationalist movement, with the publication of nationalist newspapers and even the collection of funds to send migrants back to fight against the Ottoman rulers (Fahrenthold 2014).

The story of Antoun Saadeh demonstrates this remarkable flourishing of Lebanese nationalism in the diaspora (Bercito 2019). Born in 1904 in Choueir, Lebanon, he migrated to Brazil in 1921 to join his father Khalil. Together, they edited the publications *al-Jarida* (The Newspaper) and *al-Majalla* (The Magazine). While in Brazil, Saadeh also founded two clandestine nationalist organizations, the Jama'iya al-Shabiba al-Fida'iya al-Suriyya (Syrian Heroic Youth Association) and the Hizb al-Ahrar al-Suriyyina (Party of the Free Syrians). French authorities acknowledged Saadeh's influence both in Brazil and Lebanon. In a letter sent by the French ambassador to Brazil to the French Minister of Foreign Affairs, he named Saadeh as someone to be watched (Hardan 1989, 147).

Saadeh left Brazil and returned to Beirut in 1930. He came back, however, in 1939 and founded the nationalist newspaper *Suriya al-Jadida* (New Syria), through which he promoted the views of his Syrian Social Nationalist Party (SSNP), established in Beirut in 1932 (Schumann 2004, 608). Saadeh's impact in Brazil is still understudied. But anecdotal evidence points to his influence. Hajjar, for example, dedicated her 1985 book on Arab migration to the SSNP. Meanwhile, the Brazilian politician Fernando Haddad—former mayor of São Paulo and runner up for the 2018 presidential election—donated some books authored by Saadeh when he visited his father's village in Lebanon in 2006 (Bercito 2019).

Like Saadeh, many migrants who arrived in Brazil were engaged in politics in their homeland. They "carried sour memories and experiences, usually associated with political issues involving the Turks," writes Truzzi (1997, 149). As time passed and migrant communities became more permanent, the locus of political engagement shifted to their host country, where they began to engage with local politics.

Their political participation in Brazil was also a result of their efforts of integration and social mobility. Some families had become rich through peddling and commerce and had invested their profits in the education of a second generation. Therefore, soon after their arrival, Lebanese migrants and their descendants joined the prestigious liberal professions of law, medicine, and engineering. The trader Faris Nicolau Ansarah was the first Lebanese to graduate from the São Paulo Law School, in 1917 (Truzzi 1997, 139). Moreover, Knowlton claims that Lebanese migrants also invested in politics to protect their businesses from governmental interference (Knowlton 1960, 163).

The late 1930s were a particularly suitable moment for the political ambitions of Lebanese migrants and their descendants. From 1937 to 1945, the Brazilian president Getúlio Vargas sought the support of minorities—among them Arab migrants—to counterbalance the influence of old Brazilian traditional families, who were hostile to his populist government (Fausto 1995, 26 and Hajjar 1985, 159). Hajjar argues that one of the places in which Lebanese migrants had particular success in politics was the western region of the state of São Paulo. It was an area of more recent settlement, she writes, and as such there were no old oligarchies to offer resistance to the political careers of Lebanese migrants, who were more recent arrivals (*Ibid.*, 160).

According to Knowlton (1960), the first Syrian-Lebanese politician in São Paulo was an unnamed deputy mayor of the Ipiranga district elected in 1930. By 1935, there were mayors of Syrian-Lebanese descent in at least four municipalities: Sorocaba, Conchas, Piraçununga, and Presidente Prudente. The number rose to eight municipalities in 1938 and 28 in 1947, mostly in the west of the state (*Ibid.*, 164)—in what seems to reinforce Hajjar's argument of their western geographical distribution.

Truzzi divides the history of Syrian-Lebanese political participation in Brazil in two periods. The first is marked by the presence of graduates from elite universities. The second is characterized by politicians that came from the countryside of the state of São Paulo. With regard to the first period, Truzzi explains the prevalence of college graduates—particularly from the law school—as a result of their familiarity with political activities. He writes:

> The benches of the Law School constituted the preferential barn for leadership recruitment. Those in the community who frequented [such spaces] soon proved to be the individuals with more familiarity with the political medium, those who showed more affinity with such circles. As a result, they were almost automatically accredited to exert the activities of mediating between the migrant community and the São Paulo elites. During at least the first 15 years of political-institutional normality after the Estado Novo period [ended in 1946], this kind of recruitment [. . .] became the norm. Experience with political matters, as well as the prestige brought by the school of law, were crucial. (Truzzi 1997, 152)

According to Truzzi, among the twenty-three Syrian-Lebanese who worked as federal and state deputies from 1947 to 1956, eighteen of them were graduates of the prestigious law school Largo São Francisco. This pattern lasted until 1962, he says, when a second period began.

In this second phase, Syrian-Lebanese politicians were no longer predominantly law students. They came from the countryside of São Paulo, as was the case with politicians like Bady Bassit, Semi Resegue, and Nagib Chaib (Truzzi 1997, 160). Former president Michel Temer, from Tietê, is another example of a Lebanese descendant who began his political career in the periphery. One possible explanation for this pattern is the fact that, working as peddlers, Syrian-Lebanese migrants had acquired prestige and built networks in the countryside of São Paulo. One is also reminded of Hajjar's point that there were no entrenched political elites there to serve as competition.

The political participation of Lebanese and their descendants, however, slowed down for two decades during the Brazilian military dictatorship (1964–1985). During those years, Lamarão writes, the Brazilian Congress ceased to be a privileged space in which migrants and their descendants could convert their economic power into political influence. The number of Syrian-Lebanese lawmakers had multiplied six-fold from the Estado Novo period (1937–1946) until 1962, according to Lamarão, but came to near a halt in 1964. There were only twenty-one lawmakers from Syrian-Lebanese origin from 1967 to 1971 and a mere fifteen from 1971 to 1975, its lowest number (Lamarão 2004).

With the end of the dictatorship in 1985, Lebanese descendants resumed their political work. A large number of corruption scandals involving Lebanese descendants, however, led to a negative image that spread to the whole community. Paulo Maluf, who was governor of São Paulo from 1979 to 1982 and a candidate for the presidency in 1985, became a symbol of corruption—to the point that his followers remarkably would defend his mandate by saying that "Maluf steals, but he at least does something." Maluf was praised for his large-scale projects in particular, like the São Paulo elevated highway Minhocão. To counter this negative stereotype, which associated politicians of Arab with corruption, the community tried to project an image of transparency. It seems, nevertheless, that the battle was lost. According to Montie Bryan Pitts Jr., the scandals related to politicians of Syrian-Lebanese origin served to "reinforce negative stereotypes about the colony in Brazilian society at large" (Pitts Jr. 2006, 26). Pitts Jr. utilizes the word *colony* as a literal translation of the Portuguese term *colônia*, which refers to a group of people of a shared ethnicity. In this sense, he means that the actions of few Arab migrants or descendants strengthened the image of all Arabs "as shrewd and dishonest businessmen who possessed an innate ability to work the system to their advantage and use their cleverness to deceive less crafty Brazilians" (*Ibid.*). Fifteen years after Pitts Jr.'s text, it still seems to be the case, as these stereotypes remain in circulation.

DOMESTIC AND FOREIGN POLICY

The striking number of politicians of Lebanese descent in Brazil is a result of the several factors analyzed above. This includes the social mobility guaranteed by peddling and commerce activities, the investment in education, and the geographic distribution of migrants throughout the countryside (Truzzi 1997, 162). Scholars have brought up other explanations such as the possibility of a coordinated effort among Lebanese migrants to elect members of their community. In other words, some authors have asked: "do Arabs vote only for Arabs?". Knowlton, in his 1960 work, argues that was not the case (Knowlton 1960, 164). Lamarão concurs and adds that Levantine origins did not influence the political careers of elected officials, negatively or positively. Of his thirty-nine interviewees, thirty said that the fact that they descended from Syrian-Lebanese migrants had not impacted their political careers. Moreover, thirty-three said that they did not approve legislation according to their ethnic origins (Lamarão 2004).

Nevertheless, it seems unlikely that the ethnic origin of these politicians had no impact whatsoever in their careers. Truzzi writes that Syrian-Lebanese migrants had a particular interest in the political representation of their community because it served as evidence that their "race" had an inherent value. This consideration takes on additional relevance in this historical context in which Syrian-Lebanese migrants fought for their integration into Brazilian society, combating racist stereotypes that presented them as greedy, unscrupulous, and backward. Through politics, Syrian-Lebanese migrants and descendants worked as mediators between the community and the larger Brazilian society. They were, therefore, "taken as some sorts of extension of the larger family, a resource to which they could appeal in case of necessity" (Truzzi 1997, 167). These considerations suggest that, while Lebanese origin did not completely determine these politicians' careers, it did impact their trajectories considerably.

Moreover, the U.S. scholar John Tofik Karam disagrees with the idea—repeated by Lamarão's interviewees—that the ethnic origin of these migrants did not play a part in their legislative work. The São Paulo lawmaker Hanna Garib, for instance, approved what Karam calls legislation with "explicit ethnic goals." Among such laws was the creation in 1995 of official dates to celebrate Syrian and Lebanese independence from the French Mandate. Other politicians proposed or approved laws during the 1990s that, according to Karam, "changed the name of public streets [and] donated public property for Syrian-Lebanese philanthropic groups" (Karam 2007, 66). For example, in 1995, officials passed a law creating an Islam Square in São Paulo. In 1996, another law called for the institution of a Salim Abeid Square in the same city. São Paulo and Beirut were deemed "twin cities" in 1996. In 2000, lawmakers inaugurated a Marjayoun Square (*Ibid.*, 185). These examples show the active engagement of these politicians with legislative measures—albeit symbolic, naming squares and streets—that connected with their origins.

The impact of the ethnic origin on Syrian-Lebanese politicians is particularly evident in the career of Paulo Maluf. On the one hand, his origin hindered his trajectory, as is evidenced in two anecdotes chronicled by Maluf's biographer, Tão Gomes Pinto. When Maluf was considered for the position of president, during the military dictatorship, the Brazilian general João Baptista Figueiredo allegedly said that "This Turk will not sit on my chair" (Pinto 2008, 11). Likewise, when Maluf was considered for the office of mayor of São Paulo, the publisher of the newspaper *Estado de São Paulo* Julio de Mesquita Filho supposedly told people that the city could not be governed by someone who eats kibbeh (*Ibid.*, 48). These episodes are narrated by Pinto in a quasi-hagiographic biography of Maluf and, therefore, should not be taken at face value. Nevertheless, they gesture to a known, widespread prejudice against Arab migrants in Brazil. Even the fact that the biographer decided to mention these cases points to the importance of ethnicity in Maluf's career.

On the other hand, Maluf was also able to utilize his Lebanese origin to his political advantage. According to Truzzi, Maluf was a successful politician in part due to his strategy of recruiting allies from a common ethnic base, more than from a common political affiliation. He established alliances with other descendants of Syrian-Lebanese migrants to the point that, when he was governor of São Paulo, the joke among the community was that he had established a caliphate in his palace—in 1979, among the twenty-two secretaries of state in his São Paulo administration, five were of Syrian-Lebanese descent (Truzzi 1997, 167). Truzzi describes Maluf's strategy as a process of "conversion," in which he was able to attract other Syrian-Lebanese migrants and descendants to his political project, regardless of their ideologies (Truzzi 1997, 174).

Maluf was not the first Lebanese descendant to achieve political success in Brazil. According to Truzzi, however, he was the first one willing to "reinvest the profits of his political activity into politics itself" (Truzzi 1997, 174). In this regard, he was different from José João Abdalla, one of the first Syrian-Lebanese migrants to hold public office in Brazil. While Abdalla—elected to the municipal assembly of Birigui in the state of São Paulo in 1934—invested his political capital into his business, enlarging his empire, Maluf invested it instead into his political career. That might be one of the reasons why, in spite of having been sought by the Interpol and arrested by Brazilian authorities on charges of corruption, Maluf remains one of the most iconic politicians of Brazil—a political force few would ignore.

While most studies that have dealt with the political impact of Arab migrants in Brazil concentrated on domestic policy, as seen above, there has also been some interest in foreign policy. According to a cable available in the WikiLeaks' archives, U.S. diplomats investigated the potential role of Arab migrants and their descendants in influencing Brazilian foreign policy (Consulado Geral dos EUA em São Paulo 2006). This concern might have been motivated by the administration of the left-wing PT (Workers' Party), which during the 2000s led Brazil to antagonize Israel and lobby for the recognition of Palestine in the United Nations—actions that likely concerned U. S. diplomats. The cable reads:

> Officials often attempt to justify some of their more controversial positions and policies on Middle East matters as a response to the political demands of Brazil's Muslim community. However, neither the Christian nor the Muslim community appears to be keenly interested in the Middle East political scene. This begs the larger question of what is driving the Brazilian government's sometimes controversial and contradictory policies in the Middle East. (*Ibid.*)

Later in the cable, the unnamed author concludes that politicians of Arab descent in Brazil do not form a coherent political bloc. To establish that verdict, diplomats met with three members of the Lebanese community in Brazil: the deputy Ricardo Izar, the editor Raul Tarek Fajuri, and the deputy Said Mourad (one of the few Arab Muslims politicians in Brazil). Mourad still remembers his meeting with the American consul. "She wanted to know who was, after all, the Muslim deputy," he affirms. According to Mourad, the diplomat asked him if, regardless of all the divisions inside the Lebanese community, migrants could still articulate themselves and promote a particular agenda. "I told her that it is like in soccer. Some support Palmeiras, others cheer for Corinthians, but all of us root for the national team during the World Cup," he says, utilizing popular soccer teams in Brazil as a metaphor for the distinct Lebanese communities (Bercito 2021). The cable concludes that politicians of Lebanese descent do not have any tangible influence on Brazil's foreign policy. There is indeed no evidence that these lawmakers are successful in convincing the government in Brasília to make particular geopolitical decisions. Were it that case, these politicians might have been able to stop the current president, Jair Bolsonaro, from diplomatically supporting Israel and alienating his allies in the Arab League.

The case of Bolsonaro's alliance with Israel, however, is an important example of how the Lebanese community in Brazil manages to influence the government through fields other than official, representative politics. Elected in 2018, the far-right President Bolsonaro announced the transfer of Brazil's embassy from Tel Aviv to Jerusalem, following Donald Trump's example. Although the transfer is still under discussion, it has not happened yet. The fact that Bolsonaro has not fulfilled his promise might have been partially the result of the lobbying by Fambras (the Federation of Brazilian Muslims), an association that issues halal certificates for Brazilian meat exports whose founder, Hajj Hussein Mohamed El Zoghbi, migrated to Brazil from Lebanon. Representatives of the Muslim community in Brazil met with government officials to raise awareness of the commercial consequences of creating friction with Arab states, including the loss of thousands of jobs. There was also political pressure from the Arab League, including threats of boycotting Brazilian products in all of its member-states (Bercito 2018).

PARLIAMENTARY GROUP

The Lebanese caucus Grupo Parlamentar Brasil-Líbano (Parliamentary Group Brazil-Lebanon) illustrates some of the trends presented in the sections above. The list of members of the 2015–2019 mandate, for instance, shows how politicians of Lebanese descent are spread throughout every region of Brazil, yet mostly concentrated in the southeastern state of São Paulo. It additionally shows how, although there are left and right-wing politicians of Lebanese origin, most are affiliated to conservative parties. The very fact that these politicians decided to organize themselves in a caucus indicates, furthermore, that they are aware of their numbers and impact—although the author of this chapter found no examples of success in this caucus pushing for particular agendas.

Brazilian politicians of Lebanese descent created their caucus in 1979. Their current leader is Ricardo Izar Jr., a member of the right-wing PP (Progressive Party). His father, Ricardo Izar, had led the group before him. The caucus gathers deputies and senators of Lebanese origin. In the legislature that spanned from 2015 to 2019, there were 35 members, a number that represented 5.9 percent of Parliament (out of 513 deputies and 81 senators). According to Izar Jr., the percentage reached 10 percent in other legislatures, though the author could not confirm the number independently (Bercito 2021). These percentages, however, should not be taken as exact figures of the political participation of Lebanese descendants. Membership is not mandatory, and it might be the case that other descendants decided not to join the group.

According to Izar Jr., the caucus is mostly devoted to fostering commercial relations between Brazil and Lebanon. It makes no attempt to influence Brazilian foreign or domestic policy with regard to the Lebanese community. Izar Jr. himself, however, recognizes the limitations of the Grupo Parlamentar in its stated goal of fostering commerce. He says that the caucus tried, for instance, to promote olive oil imports from Lebanon and palmito exports from Brazil. The plan failed, in part because Brazilian trade agreements depend on Mercosul, a trade bloc in South America, a fact that limits the influence of these lawmakers. "The results of the caucus are usually more in terms of friendship," he says—a field in which it is nearly impossible to measure success, since "friendship" is rather abstract. Meanwhile, the caucus organizes an annual trip of congressmen to Lebanon, where they strengthen ties with officials from the high echelons of power, including the premier and the president.

The list of members (see table 3.1) shows how territorially widespread the political participation of Lebanese migrants and their descendants in Brazil is: politicians of Lebanese descent represent every administrative region of Brazil (see table 3.2), including North, Northeast, Midwest, Southeast, and South. Their geographic distribution, however, is markedly uneven. Out of the thirty-five members of the caucus, nineteen come from the southeastern administrative region—particularly from the state of São Paulo, which is represented by nine lawmakers, or 25 percent of the total number. These numbers, of course, match what we know of the historical processes of Lebanese migration to Brazil. First, Lebanese migrants spread throughout the whole country, more visibly than other groups. Second, they were concentrated in

Table 3.1 Members of the Grupo Parlamentar Brasil-Líbano

Name	Party	State
Arlindo Chinaglia	PT	SP
Arnaldo Jordy	PPS	PA
Beto Mansur	PRB	SP
Carlos Marum	PMDB	MS
Carlos Melles	DEM	MG
César Hallum	PPS	TO
Clarissa Garotinho	PR	RJ
Eduardo Cury	PSDB	SP
Elcione Barbalho	PMDB	PA
Esperidião Amin	PP	SC
Fábio Faria	PSD	RN
Evandro Gussi	PV	SP
Guilheme Mussi	PP	SP
Helder Salomão	PT	ES
Hissa Abrahão	PPS	AM
Jandira Feghali	PCdoB	RJ
Jorge Tadeu Mudalen	DEM	SP
Julião Amin	PDT	MA
Luiz Carlos Hauly	PSDB	PR
Miro Teixeira	PROS	RJ
Marcos Abrão	PPS	GO
Margarida Salomão	PT	MG
Paulo Abi-Ackel	PSDB	MG
Miguel Haddad	PSDB	SP
Patrus Ananias	PT	MG
Paulo Azi	DEM	BA
Ricardo Izar	PP	SP
Ricardo Tripoli	PSDB	SP
Roney Nemer	PMDB	DF
Saraiva Felipe	PMDB	MG
Simão Sessim	PP	RJ
Ciro Nogueira	PP	PI
Simone Tebet	PMDB	MS
Tasso Jereissat	PSDB	CE
Omar José Abdel Aziz	PSD	AM

Source: Information provided by the Grupo Parlamentar Brasil-Líbano.

the economic capital of São Paulo. In this sense, their political representation mirrors their distribution patterns.

In terms of political affiliation, the situation is less predictable. The history of the Lebanese migration to Brazil offers no clear indication as to whether they historically supported conservative or liberal parties. Like other migrant groups, they seem to have spanned the whole spectrum. It was the case during the 2015–2019 legislature (see table 3.3), in which one finds politicians of Lebanese origin affiliated with thirteen different parties. That being said, the list of members of the Lebanese caucus also indicates a concentration around

Table 3.2 Administrative Regions Represented by Members of the Caucus

State	Adm. region	Number
AM	North	2
PA	North	2
TO	North	1
BA	Northeast	1
CE	Northeast	1
MA	Northeast	1
PI	Northeast	1
RN	Northeast	1
GO	Midwest	1
DF	Midwest	1
MS	Midwest	2
ES	Southeast	1
MG	Southeast	5
RJ	Southeast	4
SP	Southeast	9
PR	South	1
SC	South	1

Source: Information provided by the Grupo Parlamentar Brasil-Líbano.

Table 3.3 Party Affiliation and Political Orientation of the Caucus' Members

Party	Political orientation	Number
PT	Left	4
DEM	Right	3
PCdoB	Left	1
PDT	Left	1
PMDB	Right	5
PP	Right	5
PPS	Left	4
PR	Right	1
PRB	Right	1
PROS	Left	1
PSD	Right	2
PSDB	Right	6
PV	Left	1

Source: Information provided by the Grupo Parlamentar Brasil-Líbano.

conservative parties—twenty-three of them are affiliated to right or center-right parties while only twelve are affiliated to left or center-left parties.

Further analysis is required to draw further conclusions about these trends, including a historical comparison with other legislatures to confirm whether this is the rule and not the exception. Moreover, it is necessary to disaggregate these numbers and study them region by region, to verify whether these trends match regional variations in Brazilian politics, regardless of the origin of lawmakers. It would also be productive to compare the Brazilian scenario to the rest of the Latin American region, where Arab migrants and their descendants also had remarkable success in politics, a phenomenon rarely analyzed (Akmir 2009, 44-45).

CONCLUDING REMARKS

When Michel Temer became the president of Brazil in 2016, following the impeachment of Dilma Rousseff, there were some festivities back in Lebanon. Inhabitants of Btaaboura, the village from which his parents had migrated, slaughtered sheep and hired artists to perform belly dance. The main road is now called "Michel Temer, President of Brazil." Alongside these celebrations, there was also ironic commentary on the fact that Lebanon did not have a president at that moment as a result of a political deadlock, while Brazil had a president of Lebanese descent. As I heard multiple times in Lebanon, Temer's rise to power was a welcome indication that, despite the institutional crisis in their country, Lebanese people could do politics successfully. The fact that it had happened in Brasília, and not Beirut, did not seem to invalidate the experience of Temer as a representative of all Lebanese people, not only Brazilians.

Anecdotes aside, Lebanese people as well as Brazilians are aware of the political importance of Lebanese migrants and their descendants in Brazil. When Temer was elected, most of the Brazilian press frequently mentioned the origin of his parents, something rarely done after the election of politicians of Portuguese, Spanish, or Italian descent. Nevertheless, there are few studies on the history of this phenomenon and its political implications. This chapter aimed to further the debate, updating the scant bibliography available and bringing to the debate the specific case of the Lebanese caucus, shedding light on the intersection between ethnicity and politics in Brazil.

REFERENCES

Akmir, Abdeluahed (ed.). *Los Árabes en América Latina: Historia de Una Emigración*. Madrid: Siglo XXI de España Editores, 2009.

Bercito, Diogo. *Brimos: Migração Libanesa no Brasil e Seu Caminho até a Política*. São Paulo: Fósforo, 2021.

Bercito, Diogo. "Nationalism in a New Syria: Antoun Saadeh and the Latin-American Mahjar." *Malala* 7, no. 10 (2019): 70–80.

———. "Governo Palestino Responderá se Brasil Transferir Embaixada em Israel, Diz Negociador." *Folha de São Paulo*, 17 December 2018.

Duoun, Taufik. *A Emigração Sírio-Libanesa às Terras da Promissão*. São Paulo: Tip. Editora Árabe, 1944.

Fahrenthold, Stacy. *Between the Ottomans and the Entente: The First World War in the Syrian and Lebanese Diaspora, 1908–1925*. New York: Oxford University Press, 2019.

———. "Sound Minds in Sound Bodies: Transnational Philanthropy and Patriotic Masculinity in Al-Nadi al-Homsi and Syrian Brazil." *International Journal of Middle East Studies* 46, no. 2 (2014): 259–283.

Fausto, Bóris (ed.) *Imigração e Política em São Paulo*. São Paulo: Sumaré, 1995.

Greiber, Betty L; Maluf, Lina S; Mattar, Vera C. *Memórias da Imigração. Libaneses e Sírios em São Paulo*. São Paulo: Discurso Editorial, 1998.

Hajjar, Claude F. *Imigração Árabe: 100 Anos de Reflexão*. São Paulo: Editora Cone, 1985.

Hardan, Nawwaf. *Saadah fi al-Mahjar*. Beirut: Dar Firk li-l-Abhath wa-l-Nashar, 1989.

Hitti, Philip K. *Syria: A Short History*. New York: The McMillan Company, 1959.

Karam, John Tofik. *Another Arabesque. Syrian-Lebanese Ethnicity in Neoliberal Brazil*. Philadelphia: Temple University Press, 2007.

Kurban, Taufik. *Syrios e Libanezes no Brasil*. São Paulo: Sociedade Impressora Paulista, 1933.

Lamarão, Sérgio. "Identidade Étnica e Representação Política: Descendentes de Sírios e Libaneses no Parlamento Brasileiro, 1945–1998." In Marco de Oliveira (org.). *Guerras e Imigrações*. Campo Grande: Editora Universidade Federal de Mato Grosso do Sul, 2004.

Lesser, Jeffrey. *Negotiating National Identity: Immigrants, Minorities and the Struggle for Ethnicity in Brazil*. Durham: Duke University Press, 1999.

Meihy, Murilo. *Os Libaneses*. São Paulo: Contexto, 2016.

Pinto, Tão G. *Ele: Maluf, Trajetória da Audácia*. Rio de Janeiro: Ediouro, 2008.

Pitts Jr., Montie B. "Forging Ethnic Identity Through Faith: Religion and the Syrian-Lebanese Community in São Paulo". Thesis submitted to the Faculty of Graduate School of Vanderbilt University for the degree of Master of Arts in Latin American Studies.

Provence, Michael. *The Great Syrian Revolt and the Rise of Arab Nationalism*. Austin: University of Texas Press, 2005.

Schumann, Christoph. "Nationalism, Diaspora and Civilisational Mission: the Case of Syrian Nationalism in Latin America Between World War I and World War II." *Nations and Nationalism* 10, no. 4 (2004): 599–617.

Truzzi, Oswaldo. *Patrícios: Sírios e Libaneses em São Paulo*. São Paulo: Hucitec, 1997.

U.S. Consulate General in São Paulo. "São Paulo's Arab Community: Diversity and Divisions Diminish Political Clout." WikiLeaks cable: 06SAOPAULO498_a. March 12, 1973.

Chapter 4

The Arab Community of Cuba
Past and Present
Rigoberto Menéndez Paredes

INTRODUCTION

Contemporary Cuba is the result of numerous migratory processes that began five centuries ago which have led to the current ethnically homogeneous population of over 11 million inhabitants with many origins. The culture that imposed itself in a general way was doubtlessly that of the Spanish metropolis, which was formed first by the groups of Spanish colonizers and immigrants of the period from the sixteenth to the eighteenth centuries, and significantly enlarged by the most numerous migration wave (Spaniards from Asturias, Galicia, Catalonia, the Canary Islands, among others) of the international migration currents of the nineteenth and twentieth centuries. The island was also populated by slaves from several African regions, a process that could be defined as forced migration and that began in the sixteenth century until the nineteenth century. Although there were also French, Italians, Irish, and other ethnic groups in these periods, the Chinese immigrants did not arrive until the nineteenth century, when they became an essential part of the national formation along with the abovementioned ethnic groups. However, other groups not mentioned here were able to have an interesting migratory and ethno-cultural process with wide geographical distribution on the island. Among them, we must mention the immigrants who arrived first from the former Ottoman provinces of Mount Lebanon, Syria, and Beirut, whose territories later on became Lebanon, Palestine, and Syria, with more than 40,000 people approximately reaching Cuba in the period from 1870 to 1957.[*]

---

[*] Apart from these groups, immigrants coming from Egypt, Jordan and Yemen arrived in Cuba, but not so many as the Lebanese, Palestinians and Syrians.

The Arab community of Cuba has been an important pattern in the formation of Cuban nationality, as it is one of the ethnic components that most fluently integrated into the formation of nationality. Together with the Hispanic, Chinese, and Antillean components, Arab migrants managed to establish themselves throughout the Cuban national territory, initially achieving a group of indicators of conservation of their cultural identity as a group through inbreeding marriages, the creation of associations, Ethnic charities and some elements, such as the conservation of traditional Arab cuisine. The previous non-existence of an academic literature that covered these topics is one of the originality points of our research.

The study of the Arab community of Cuba has taken me approximately thirty years of research; it has been developed mainly on the basis of documentary sources (parish archives, migratory documents, censuses, business directories, consular records, and other archival funds), the use of books on migration or parallel studies on Arab communities in America and the use of sources oral. This research has resulted in two published books and dozens of articles. Oral sources (interviews with immigrants and their descendants) have also been important and complementary in carrying out extensive research.

Emitting Societies and Target Areas: Why an Arabic-Speaking Community in Cuba?

Migratory phenomena, regardless of the subjective causes influencing them, are the result of an imbalance between the productive human resources and the profitability level of the emitting societies. That imbalance is supplemented with the existence of a target area that offers attractive conditions to the affected social sectors of the emitting country (Barcia, 2005: 36). Some authors state rightly that international migrations are the result of the conjugation of several elements. On the one hand, there is the imbalance between demographic and economic growth in the country of origin and the possibilities of absorption of labor in the country of destination, on the other hand, the facilities to carry out the migratory displacement and the resources for relocation and settling down of the migrant (Domingo y Viruela. 2001).

Based on such criteria, we must understand the emigration-immigration dialectics that affected several territories in the Middle East as emitting areas and Cuba as the receiving society of Arab migrants, in addition to migrants from all the continents who populated Cuba, adding to its cosmopolitanism in different time periods. The period encompassing the Arab migratory process (1870–1957), which matches the migratory processes in Latin America, was the object of numerous changes in the Middle East. Since it is a long period, we cannot talk about homogeneity of factors, not even about homogeneity of emitting areas. The first waves of Arabic-speaking immigrants in the second half of the nineteenth century happened in the context of a deep economic and political crisis in the Turkish-Ottoman Empire, metropolis in a large part of the Middle East; the present-day Lebanon, Syria, and the occupied Palestine were spread in several provinces (the provinces of Syria and Beirut and the autonomous province of Mount Lebanon), as well as the districts of Tripoli, Nablus, and the independent district of Jerusalem.

The Ottoman government was not able to endure the disadvantageous competitiveness of England and other emerging capitalist countries that since 1840 had free access to the Egyptian and Syrian markets. Thus, there was a decline of the old industrial centers, leading artisans to financial ruin due to the paralysis of growth in the domestic manufacturing facilities of the region. The most affected ones by the crisis, besides the artisans, were agricultural workers, who initially migrated to regional suburbs and later looked for new horizons in other parts of the planet. Demographic pressure factors in Mount Lebanon and other Arabic provinces of the empire were also felt.

A cause of interreligious nature that became a bloody conflict was added to the economic ones. In particular, the war (1840–1860), between the Christian and Druze communities of Mount Lebanon, which resulted in a high number of casualties. The resulting feeling of uncertainty among the people who had lost family members or were exposed to spoliation and killing contributed to the decision of migrating (Menéndez, 2007: 31). We could still add the causes of the repression, first by the Ottoman Empire and later by the government of the Young Turks, on their non-Turkish subjects of the empire, which included the Christian communities of the East Mediterranean territories. The famine was also a cause for migration, as illustrated by Amin Maalouf, who wrote about the massive migration of Lebanese in his book *Origins*:

> [. . .] today we hear that sometimes emigration was caused by the big famine of 1915, which is false, of course, because that movement had already existed for several decades [. . .]. But it grew and took advantage of the horrors of the famine to give the reason to those who had already left, silencing guilt and remorse. (Maalouf, 2004: 259)

Finally, the famine experienced by the population of Mount Lebanon in 1915, in the middle of World War I, generated huge migration waves toward the other side of the Atlantic.

Cuba, as one of the receiving countries in the Latin American space, was also setting an example of international migrations in the nineteenth century, since the period of Spanish rule. It received migrants of many nationalities, including the Arabic-speaking population of the East Mediterranean region, even if these new arrivals were not among the favorite ones of the colonial Spanish government. The wave of Syrian-Lebanese and Palestinian migrants to Cuba occurred in the period from 1870 to 1898,** a wave that was not so large as the ones during the first three decades of the twentieth century, because at that time the island was used as a transit point to other continental destinations (basically the United States, Mexico, Costa Rica, among others).

Cuba became an authentic destination for immigrants during the Republican Period of Cuba (1902–1958). A remarkable decrease in the population, including children, was the result of the War of Independence of 1895, along with a ferocious Spanish repression. An appreciable decrease in the number of inhabitants on the island, and consequently a serious demographic crisis, resulted in the reconcentration policy ordered by the Spanish governor, Valeriano Weyler. In the 1887 census, the Cuban population reached 1,631,700 inhabitants and the statistics of 1899 reported 1,572,800 with a birth rate of barely 6.7 percent. The low birth rates contrasted from the 19.4 percent existing in 1890. Likewise, the deficit of children existing at the beginning of the dependent republic, started in 1902, implied a future deficit of labor that only immigration could fill (Menéndez, 2007: 41–42).

Due to this demographic crisis, the Cuban government promulgated on June 12, 1906 the Law of Immigration and Colonization, which established the creation of a 1-million peso fund to bring seasonal workers who would be destined to the lands given by the owners to lease them. Although no law mentioned or stipulated specifically the entry of Arab migrants, this migratory component influenced the Cuban demographic growth. Thus, for the Arab who migrated to Cuba at the end of the nineteenth century or at the beginning of the twentieth century, the country offered attractions to reside and work in it stably. Amin Maalouf quotes a fragment of a letter sent to his grandfather Botros by the prosperous Lebanese trader Gabriel M. Maluf), who reflects the importance of our country at the beginning of the republican period: "This island, in which we have been given an opportunity, is making progress and will become one of the most important spots of the planet materially, politically and morally" (Maalouf, 2004: 193).

Based on the phrase of the Lebanese trader, some important waves of Arabic-speaking passengers in the twentieth century could be numbered, which widened considerably the migratory process from the Arabic Mediterranean. The wave of 1906–1913 contributed to a total of 3,758 immigrants if we take into account not only those who came from the cultural birth area (Asian Turkey in the documents of the Secretary's Office of the Treasury) but also those who came from other geographic areas (European Turkey, Mexico, USA, South America, England, Haiti, Jamaica, Santo

---

** As far as research goes, the first Arab coming from the Middle East was the "Ottoman" José Yabor, who arrived in the port of Havana in 1870 and declared at customs that he would live in Monte and Figuras, streets in the area that was the main settlement of Arabic-speaking immigrants (Menéndez Paredes, Rigoberto. *The Arabs in Cuba*. Boloña Publishing House, Havana, 2007, p. 38).

Domingo, and other areas) that show an early chained immigration or family claim. About 1,131 immigrants came from the Asian Turkey for 31 percent of the total, followed by Mexico with 638 (17 percent) and the United States with 438 (11 percent), which reflects that Cuba was no longer only a waiting place to enter the countries of the Americas.

Doubtlessly, this migratory wave, probably much more numerous than the one of 1870–1898, took place in more favorable conditions when Cuba opened the doors to international migration in a more transparent and direct way. The Cuban state of the dependent republic[1] was not generally xenophobic; at least it did not show any hostility toward most migrations, including the ones coming from Arabic-speaking territories. In our research, we have only found a case of rejection of the immigrant of reference, but this came from the newspaper *Economic Gazette*, press body that expressed adverse opinions in an editorial:

> At present, the Turk or Arab or Palestinian or Maronite, as you like to call them, continues to enter the island little by little. This element is not convenient at all for the country and our government must take measures to prevent their entry: they do not mix with any other race living in the republic, export all they earn, do not get rooted, do not do any other job or undertaking, wander from one place to another peddling. What benefit can these people bring? (*Economic Gazette*, 15th September 1914: 5)

Thus, one can interpret the previous paragraph as xenophobic and rejecting of Arab migrants. The quotes show that there were many terms that illustrated the heterogeneity of Arab migrations, indicating four nationalities and religious identities. One identity refers to the Turks, who came from the Ottoman conceptualization of the first migratory waves. However, the Arab identity is more accurate, as it stamps the language and the ethnic self-awareness carried by these immigrants. Finally, the Maronite religious identity was the majoritarian confession among the massive Lebanese immigration arriving in Cuba. Beyond this reference to the different Arab migrants, the message is excessively xenophobic and completely inaccurate since Arab migrants did integrate and were rooted into the Cuban social milieu, even with visible promptitude and sense of opening.

In 1920, when World War I was already over, there was another big international migration wave to Cuba, due to the increasing price of sugar and its production. The general number of immigrants grew that year to the top figure of 174, 221 people (Le Riverend, 1974: 567). This migratory boom stimulated the entry of Antillean workers hired as cheap labor. At the same time, the immigration was called spontaneous and free, including by the community in question (Le Riverend, 1974: 566).

Table 4.1 titled Arab immigrants arriving in Cuba (1920–1931), based on the book *Unpublished Memoirs of the 1931 Census*, illustrates the growth in the number of Arabic-speaking immigrants, where the increase was most visible between the years 1922 and 1925. The table shows, among other elements, the problem of classifications often made by the Cuban authorities based on documents, such as a nationality or citizenship, when much of the Arab world was colonized. For instance, it is contradictory that the Lebanese, who were the majority of the migratory block to Cuba in all the periods, appear with a small number and the word "French" between parentheses. This explains that those passengers traveled with documentation of the French mandate dominating Lebanon from 1920 to 1943. Doubtlessly, most of the Lebanese travelers must have been included in the denomination "Syrian," which indicates that they came with documentation of that country, perhaps since Syria was a vast Ottoman province. On the other hand, the denomination "Palestinian" appears for the first time in the statistics, which suggests that these migrants came with documentation of the British mandate in that country.

A considerable group of immigrants originating in the Middle East passed through the Tiscornia Immigration Camp in Havana because there was little solvency and the need to be protected by a family member or welfare organization. The other cause was to be affected by an illness such as trachoma or infectious vision disease, as María Maarawi declared it when interviewed:

> I was born in Rachiin, in Zgarta—María Maarawi narrates—I was very little when my mum brought me by force, because I wanted to stay with my grandmother in town. But my father had been murdered as someone wanted

Table 4.1 Arab Immigrants Arriving in Cuba (1920–1931)

Year	Arabs	Lebanese (franc)	Palestinian	Syrian	Total
1920	45			637	682
1921	45			230	275
1922			2	230	232
1923	14		269	1,059	1,342
1924	15		566	1,373	1,954
1925	43		715	1,037	1,795
1926	2		317	820	1,139
1927	3	22	285	296	606
1928	5	137	164	340	646
1929		154	80	192	426
1930	2	85	35	58	180
1931	1	31	6	22	60
Total	173	429	2439	6294	9337

Source: *Unpublished memoirs of the 1931 census*, Publishing House of Social Sciences, Havana, 1978. Prepared by the author.

to seize his farm and my mother decided to come. We arrived in 1928 on the Champolion ship. We had a stopover in France, lived three months in Marseille, where many fellow countrymen who were travelling with us survived by selling trinkets. When we arrived, we had to stay four days at the Tiscornia Camp, where the Arabs with trachoma were held, or those who had to wait, like us, for a family member to take you out. (Maarawi, 2002)

The research on the books of the Tiscornia Immigration Camp showed the functioning of the migratory network among the Lebanese, Palestinians, and Syrians arriving in Cuba. Most of the applicants were family members of those held or assigned to the migratory quarantine. In some cases, there were members of the Syrian-Lebanese social elite acting as applicants or representing a trading house that guaranteed the immigrant's release. This is the case of Gabriel Maluf, Nicolás Felaifel, or the Daly Brothers firm.

But the stay of immigrants at the Tiscornia Camp also revealed how the Syrian-Lebanese social elite had woven a group of economic and social relations in Cuba. This is also what helped the Spanish healthcare institutions and welfare centers guarantee the release of their confined fellowmen.

Settlements and Trade in Cuba

The main places of settlement of the immigrants were the urban regions of the island, the areas near trading zones, towns with developed sugar industry and cattle raising, as well as rural areas (Menéndez, 1999: 27). The main core of national settlement of the Arabs was the area of Centro Habana in the quarters San Nicolás and Jesús María, which had Monte as the main artery (which we historians call the Arab neighborhood of Monte) and where they had their main shops, charity societies, and the Catholic churches where Christians had their services.

This migratory group was, along with the Spaniards and the Chinese, one of the widest distributions in the country, as there was no head of a province or town that did not have Arab communities. The research that we have conducted in the Register of Foreigners indicates that the main cities had higher concentration of migrants. The figure used for calculations was 3,112 Arabs, who were registered between 1900 and 1955 (see table 4.2, titled main settlements of Arab immigrants (1900–1955)).

When the Arabs settled in the different Cuban territories, they reproduced the same initial occupational code as in the rest of Latin America. Working as peddlers and selling in installments had the advantage of being low-cost and yielding profits quickly. Those who were successful in peddling would rent a local to open shops of textiles and the wealthier ones would open stores for fabric, groceries, and other outlets (Menéndez, 2007: 74).

Table 4.2 Main Settlements of Arab Immigrants (1900–1955)

City or municipality	Amount	%
Havana	763	24.51
Holguín	174	5.59
Santiago de Cuba	120	3.85
Camagüey	102	3.27
Matanzas	95	3.05
Guantánamo	90	2.89
Ciego de Ávila	88	2.82
Santa Clara	83	2.66
Puerto Padre	82	2.63
Cárdenas	74	2.37
Marianao	73	2.34
Guanabacoa	70	2.24

Source: Archive of the General Department of Immigration. *Immigration books.* Prepared by the author.

A sizable amount of the Syrian-Lebanese and Palestinian immigrants developed trade related to textiles, aspect for which they are remembered by part of the Cuban population. This sort of activity provided some of them with capital to fill the material scarcity that led them to migrate. Their success was probably due to the existence of favorable conditions to make profit in the sector: family members of friends from other Arab settlements in the continent were able to supply products to their fellowmen in Cuba with the possibility of selling them to the country's population.

Trade was one of the ways that eventually allowed the insertion of the Arab immigrants from the Middle East into Cuban society, thanks to the establishment of personal relationships with clients who were part of the powerful classes in Cuba. In a general sense, the society gave them recognition and welcomed the Arab immigrant favorably as community members became important links in the socioeconomic structure of the nation. Among the immigrants, who amassed a considerable fortune and social recognition, stood out the Lebanese Gabriel Maluf and Julio Abislaiman, the Palestinian Ibrahim Babun, and the Syrian Badi Kaba.

Religious Composition of the Arabic-Speaking Community

The Arab collective settled in Cuba included representatives of most religious denominations practiced in the Middle East, which exemplified the religious diversity of the region. The largest religious affiliation, with parish priests assisting the community, was the Catholic Maronite, which amounted to 57.6 percent of all the group of Lebanese origin (Menéndez, 1999: 59). The second largest Christian denomination that settled in Cuba was the Greek Orthodox, represented by Lebanese, Palestinian, and Syrian immigrants.

Melkite immigrants or Greek Catholic Lebanese also arrived in Cuba, as well as Protestant Christians. The migratory Muslim collective coming from Lebanon, Palestine, and Syria was a minority, but there were signs of the practice of Islam at individual and family level in the country.

The Maronite community in Cuba was doubtlessly the most established, as five parish priests were sent by the Maronite patriarchate in order to assist the followers of the Maronite church and of other Christian denominations from the Middle East between 1899 and 1960 (Greek Orthodox, Melkite, and others). Among these priests, the most relevant one was Monsignor Jose K. Aramuni, who was very active, not only in the religious environment but also in the social one by interacting constantly with the elite of the community and the Lebanese Society of Havana.

The fact of having a priest during several generations who assembled and encouraged the Maronite community, a public belief that was only practiced in Havana and some other Cuban cities. The parishioners integrated in the different rituals (mass, christening, wedding) led by a priest of their creed, fostering the continuation of the ritual tradition from their original territory. Amelia Zeuk reflected his father Miguel's devotion, a Maronite believer:

> Dad went to mass every day before going to the ironmonger's and when he came back. He was a devotee of Saint Maron; he took us to the church of the same name in Rachiin. He was a very close friend of Father Martinos. He sent my brother Naguib and me to study at religious schools in Havana. (Zeuk, 1998)

Among Christians, just like among Lebanese, Palestinian and Syrian Muslims, there was no generational legacy of the faith to the children in most of the community, except in the case of Maronite Christians. Their affiliation to the Catholic Church made the adaptation process much easier for children who continued their parents' faith. Today, the descendants of Arab origin immigrants are, like the Cuban population in general, followers of different creeds or simply atheists, just like an important number of Cubans.

Associations as a Factor of Preserving Ethnic Identity

As far as associative organizations are concerned, Arab immigrants founded various civil, charitable, and recreational institutions. The founders of these institutions followed the same pattern as other ethnic groups who arrived in Cuba: the constitution of charities, recreational, and cultural societies in order to keep the elements of their autochthonous culture and the solidarity among their members, as well as to help the newcomers. In the 1904–1979 period, there was an intense associative movement that led to a total of thirty-five societies of different nature, where some were included with federative purposes[2] such as the Al Etehad Centre of Cuba (1931), the Syrian-Lebanese–Palestinian Club (1938) and the current Arabic Union of Cuba (1979).[***]

A number of associations were founded, as follows. The first associations created by the immigrants from the Middle East were the Oriental Association (1904) and the Syrian Society (1909), both in Santiago de Cuba, one of the main settlements of these immigrants since the nineteenth century (Menéndez, 2007: 139). Almost a decade later, the first Syrian-Lebanese association founded in Havana was The Syrian Progress. This welfare organization existed already in 1914 and its founding president was the Lebanese Gabriel M. Maluf, an affluent trader from Havana and man of enormous political influence. By the 1920s, as the number of Arab immigrants in Cuba grew, new associations were opened in the country, The Lebanese Society of Manzanillo (1920), The Lebanese Youth of Holguin (1923), the Arab Palestinian Society of Cuba in Havana (1929), and The Lebanese Society of Havana (1930) standing out among them.

The goal of these associations was to encourage assistance for immigrants and preserve cultural codes from the country of origin. They did there all that the Cuban culture and idiosyncrasy could not offer them; speaking their mother tongue, listening to their favorite music, helping a fellowman, or discussing the events in their countries of origin (Menéndez, 2007: 140). Precisely, some of these ethnic groups of social character took a defined stand before the political conflicts affecting their region of origin. An example of this assertion is illustrated in a document issued in 1945 entitled, "The Syrian-Lebanese colony of Cuba before the events of the Near East," which was signed by twelve Syrian-Lebanese associations of the country. The text outlined the opposition of the Syrian-Lebanese associations in Cuba to the military occupation by France in its former territories of Lebanon and Syria. A fragment of such an important document demonstrates the motivation for self-determination and independence that moved the Syrian-Lebanese communities on the island:

> The Lebanese and Syrian colony of Cuba calls the government, the Congress, the public and private corporations, the press and all the national and foreign institutions carrying out their activities in this country to support the just aspirations of the Lebanese and Syrian people and to fulfil the promises of independence made to them, since it is about nothing less than the rights of small

---

[***] To consult the whole list of associations created by the Lebanese, Palestinians and Syrians in Cuba, see: Menéndez Paredes, Rigoberto. "The Arabs in Cuba". In: Akmir, Abdeluahed (coord.) *The Arabs in Latin America*. Siglo XXI Publishing House, Madrid, 2009, pp. 427–428.

nations, conquered by the constant struggle between totalitarianism and democracy, between the eternal conflicts of the progressive and regressive forces of history. (ANC. Source: *Register of Associations*. File 634, dossier 17276)

In this joint statement, the association representatives of the Arabic-speaking communities acted as pressure groups on the Cuban state to achieve their goals. Among the associations signing the document were the Lebanese Society of Havana, the Syrian-Lebanese–Palestinian Club, the Lebanese Youth of Havana, the Lebanese Association of Santa Clara, and the Association of Syrians and Lebanese of Cueto.

The creation of the Pan-Arab Committee of Cuba in 1947 is another important example of how some groups within the Arabic-speaking community behaved like pressure groups before a conflict that affected their countries of origin. It was an interim organization constituted to act as a political lobby in convincing the government of the president, Dr. Ramón Grau San Martín, to vote against the proposal of dividing legally Palestine into two states. It was not a specifically Palestinian association, but a conglomerate of twenty-nine influential members of the Arab community of Cuba. These members were among the social elite of the community, including prestigious doctors and traders of Lebanese and Palestinian origin.

On September 8, 1947, the Committee held a meeting in the local of the Palestinian Centre at 618 Monte Street and drew up a document entitled, "To the government and people of Cuba." It was published on the fourteenth of the same month in *El Mundo*, one of the most important newspapers on the island. It expressed several ideas to explain the Palestinian issue and the unfair decision of dividing the country, mostly Arabic-speaking at the time, into two ethnic states.

The document begins by saying that it is the voice of the whole Arab community expressing themselves in the text, where in some of the fragments they expressly mention were the illegality of the Jewish immigration, the Balfour declaration, and the creation of a Jewish state in Palestine:

> The Lebanese, Syrian and Palestinian Colony of Cuba and its Cuban descendants cannot remain silent anymore to explain the truth of the Palestinian issue to the government and people of Cuba. Although Lebanon, Syria and Palestine, three states which constitutes the same essence in themselves, are far away from Cuba, their nationals and Cuban descendants live and prosper here, closely linked to the Cuban people by identical religious and cultural and family feeling bonds, because there are thousands of homes where the Cuban and Arab blood have mixed; we repeat, although Lebanon, Syria and Palestine are far away, they are small nations like Cuba that arise in the international field facing difficult issues, fighting for the same goals and with the same principles. It can be

Palestine today and tomorrow it can be Cuba. It looks like the time of injustice has not passed yet. (Cuban Pan-Arab Committee..., p.5)

The text of Pan-Arab Committee of Cuba reflects, from its inception, the common stance of the Arabs, as it may be seen in the initial paragraph; some reflections include the origin of the Arab-Jewish conflict in Palestine, which identify among its causes "the economic power of the Hebrew race, its strong unity and international direction, and its activities and political influence in the main countries of the world" (Cuban Pan-Arab Committee..., p.5). Likewise, the document influenced the Cuban vote against the division of Palestine, presenting justifications about why a territorial division in the Holy Land was inappropriate. For instance:

1. Palestine has always been an Arabic country for more than fourteen centuries.
2. Any Jewish connection in Palestine ended more than 2,000 years ago.
3. The Balfour Declaration expressly determined that at no time it would harm the interests or the political status of Palestine.
4. The creation of a new state in Palestine, born from coercion, terrorism, and violence, would set the most terrible and discouraging precedent for humanity.
5. The Arabs will not yield an inch in Palestine.
6. The Arabs demand a solution for Palestine compatible with justice and democracy; that is:
    a) Total end of the Jewish immigration
    b) Total end of the cession of land to Jews
    c) Abolition of the Mandate and the Balfour Declaration
    d) Independence and sovereignty of Palestine (Cuban Pan-Arab Committee..., p.5)

The interpretations given to the Cuban vote against the division were diverse according to the sources. Some specialists in Arab issues in Cuba defend the national reformist position of the government of president Grau San Martin and its economic and political differences with the United States with regards to the vote against the ethnic division of Palestine would show the "independence" of its foreign policy as a bargaining counter to obtain economic benefits, but their other sources refer to a last-minute change of stance in the government and to the anti-Semitic positions of some members of the Pan-Arab Committee of Cuba.[****] (Capestany, 2008)

[****] See López Levy, Arturo. "1949: the right decision". In: https://www.cubaencuentro.com/opinion/articulos/1949-la-decision-correcta-235442

It is not unwise to expose the context of the opposition of Cuba to vote for the division of Palestine, including that of the six abstentions of other Latin American countries that neither wanted to align themselves to the American position nor commit themselves with the Zionist profile. For Amuchástegui and Arias, the vote and the abstentions had nothing to do with the progressive positions of authentic solidarity with the Arabs but with the political and economic position assumed by Cuba's nationalist governments and other Latino-American countries, a stance that contrasted somehow with the interfering attitude of the United States (Amuchástegui y Arias, 1988: 5).

Likewise, there was a difference between the positions of the bourgeois Jewish elite closely linked to the World Zionist Organization and the Arab elites regarding the national reformist governments of Latin America and their pretensions of national development (Amuchástegui y Arias, 1988: 5). This could explain in the case of Cuba, the incidence of the Pan-Arab Committee of Cuba, interim organization that as representative of the commercial and professional Arabic-speaking elite in Cuba acted like a pressure group before the government.

It is true that the Pan-Arab Committee of Cuba did not call itself pro-Palestinian, nor there was a majority of Palestinians among its members. However, Palestinians were among some of the most respectable personalities of the Cuban scene, including the doctors Pedro Kourí and José Chelala Aguilera. Likewise, it is worth mentioning that in Grau San Martín's authentic government, there were politicians of Arabic origin in the Parliament like Primitivo Rodríguez Rodríguez, of whom it is said that played an important role in achieving the Cuban vote (Capestany, 2008). The friendship of some signatories with president Grau should not be ruled out either.

Arab Migration in Cuba and its Uniqueness

Nevertheless, there are other elements that differentiate the evolution of the Arab community in Cuba from those in the rest of the continent, or at least in some of its nations. These factors include a longer history of Arab migration to Cuba, the development of civic associations in Cuban society—some of which were religious.

First, unlike many countries where the migratory waves have included more recent periods (in Argentina there were arrivals in 1946–1947, in Mexico from 1967 to 1973, and from 1975 on, because of the Lebanese civil war), the arrival of Arabs in Cuba has not taken place as the result from the migratory process since the 1950s. This fact affected the community of Arab immigrants in Cuba in terms of its decrease and tendency to natural fall, caused partially by the migration of Middle Eastern people in the largest of the Antilles to other countries from 1960 to 1970.

Another aspect about which the Middle East collectivity was singular was the creation of associations. The religious institutionalization in other nations was visible and strong. For instance, in Mexico, the Lebanese managed to find five Maronite societies: the Maronite Church, the Maronite Association of Mexico, the Maronite Ladies, the World Maronite Association, and the Maronite Youth. In Cuba, however, Maronites were never institutionalized; they managed to organize themselves around a local church and parish priests of the rite without creating a society space. This factor probably contributed, in the case of Cuba, to an easier denominational integration and assimilation.

Similarly, there was no school for the followers of Saint Maron either, compared to Argentina where it did happen (Cazorla, s. f.: 15). The only Arab immigrants who managed to integrate—although late—into a denominational association of their own creed were the Greek Orthodox, as they belonged to the Orthodox Christian Collectivity of Cuba, founded in 1958, along with Greeks and representatives of other ethnic groups.

Concerning the Arab Muslim immigrants, the already mentioned fact that other countries of the Americas had new, more recent waves and that these had significant Islamic components, has influenced the existence of Islamic institutions, aspect not known in Cuba. In Cuba, the identity of the Muslim communities did not reach the development of other receiving areas in Latin America, nor was any mosque built. An Islamic Centre was founded in the capital of Argentina, as well as the Islamic Arab Institute of Argentina (1972) and the Great Mosque of Buenos Aires (1981).

However, the case of Cuba, in the sense of the Islamic practice, has an interesting feature not linked to the migratory process in question: it is a Cuban community of Islamic faith whose members in their totality are not descendants from Syrian-Lebanese or Palestinian immigrants, but Cubans also converted to the Islam by their own will, many of whom are affiliated to the Islamic League of Cuba, organization founded in 2007. Therefore, the Arab migratory group study should not be confused with the current Cuban Islamic community that has no relation to the migratory process studied.

IN CONCLUSION: FROM ARAB COMMUNITY TO CUBAN-ARAB COMMUNITY

The last wave of Arab immigration to our island took place during the first years of the 1950s and consisted of Shiite farmers and traders from South Lebanon mostly in moments when the community had decreased, since in the 1953 census, 2,055 people were registered as coming from different countries of the Middle East (Menéndez, 1999: 78).

The end of migratory waves and the departure of many migrants to other countries after the triumph of the Cuban Revolution in 1959 due to the effect caused by the nationalization of properties. The laws of 1968 for the confiscation of small businesses with the logical impact on the private retail sector forced many of them to leave to different countries of the Americas, Europe, and even some of them returned to their countries of origin.

The remarkable decrease in the community, the signs of ethnic indifference shown by some migrants and the stepwise exodus of many members of this community influenced the assimilation of the migrating collective that became smaller and smaller and does not practically exist nowadays. Today, the Board of Directors of the Arab Union of Cuba, the only social community organization existing today. An Arab-Cuban collective is almost exclusively by first- or second-generation descendants today and covering approximately 60,000 individuals. Therefore, we can conclude that despite the fact that there is no feedback on the process of comparing the Arabs in Cuba (as it has happened in other Latin American countries), the presence of individuals of Arab origin in the country and the conservation of customs of their migrant ancestors have made this group an important component in the formation of Cuban nationality.

NOTES

1. Cuban historiography calls the nation that was established in 1902 as a "dependent republic" after a long period of Spanish colonial domination (1511–1898) and the period of American military occupation (1899–1902). As of 1902, Cuba has its own constitutional government, but conditioned primarily by the so-called Platt Amendment, which legalized the intervention of the United States in the affairs of Cuba from a military, political and economic point of view. Although the said amendment was repealed in 1934, Cuba continued to be a country that depended economically on the United States.

2. For federative purposes we refer to those associations that tried to group immigrants from different backgrounds (Lebanese, Palestinians, Syrians, and other nationalities).

BIBLIOGRAPHY

Amuchástegui Álvarez, Domingo y Arias Castillo, Emilio. "Positions of the Latin American and Caribbean countries at the UNO before the Middle East crisis (1947-1982). Conditioning and variations". In: Collective of authors. *Current issues of the Arab world*. Ciencias Sociales Publishing House, Havana, 1988.

Archive of the General Department of Immigration. *Immigration books*.

Archivo Nacional de Cuba. Fondo *Registro de Asociaciones.*
Barcia, María del Carmen. *Popular strata and modernity in Cuba.* Fernando Ortiz Foundation, Havana, 2005.
Capestany Corrales, Maritza. "Convergences and disagreements between Arabs and Jews from Cuba". In: Raanan Rein (coord.). *Arabs and Jews in Iberoamerica. Similarities, differences and tensions,* Sevilla, 2008. Consulted in: https://www.tau.ac.il/humanities/abraham/publications/arabes_y_%20judios.pdf.
Cazorla, Liliana. *Presence of Syrian and Lebanese immigrants in the industrial development of Argentina.* Los Cedros Foundation, Buenos Aires [s.f.]
Cuban Pan-Arab Committee. "To the Government and people of Cuba." In: *El Mundo,* 14th September, 1947.
Domingo, Concha y Rafael Viruela. "Chains and networks in the Spanish migratory process," 2001. At: http://www.ub.es/geocrit/sn-94-8.htm . *Economic Gazette,* 15th September 1914.
Le Riverend, Julio. *Economic history of Cuba.* Pueblo y Educación Publishing House, Havana, 1974.
López Levy, Arturo. "1949: the right decision". In: https://www.cubaencuentro.com/opinion/articulos/1949-la-decision-correcta-235442.
Maalouf, Amin. *Origins.* Alianza Editorial S.A., Madrid, 2004.
Maarawi, María. Interview done by the author. Havana, 17th June 2002.
Menéndez Paredes, Rigoberto. *Arabic components in the Cuban culture.* Boloña Publishing House, Havana, 1999.
Menéndez Paredes, Rigoberto. *The Arabs in Cuba.* Boloña Publishing House, Havana, 2007.
Unpublished memoirs of the 1931 census, Publishing House of Social Sciences, Havana, 1978.
Zeuk, Amelia. Interview done by the author. Havana, 11th May 1998.

Chapter 5

Exploring the Roots and Identity Politics of the Hadhrami Diaspora in Singapore

Aisha Sahar Waheed Alkharusi

INTRODUCTION

The Hadhramis as a diaspora have received little attention as an object of study, especially as far as the social sciences are concerned (Martin 1974, Warburton 1995). This chapter charts the development and maintenance of targeted policies adopted by the government of the Republic of Singapore in the immediate post-colonial era and its historical impact on the Hadhrami diaspora. It also explores the identity crisis within this community brought about by the conflation of religion and race politics of the city state, resulting in the Hadhrami identity being absorbed into the Malay–Muslim nexus (Hussin 2016). These trends are presented using a theoretical history approach (Romein 1948).

Singapore is a "society of minorities" (Clammer 1985, 170) where Hadhramis are identified as Arab-Singaporeans. Two issues have had an instrumental impact on the sense of identity among the Hadhrami diaspora in Singapore: the multiracialism framework within which the census is conducted, which is known as the CIMO model (Chinese, Indian, Malay, Other), and policies of founding father Lee Kuan Yew's government, namely, the Rent Control Act of 1947, the Land Acquisition Act of 1966, which saw lands held by the Hadhramis compulsorily acquired by the government with little compensation, and the Muslim Law Act of 1966, which regulated Muslim religious affairs and constituted a council to advise on matters relating to the religion as well as establish a *Shariah* (Islamic Law) Court.

The conclusions reached are that given the complex context of multiracial and multireligious Singapore, where colonial and post-colonial constructions of race and race relations endure, Singaporeans of Hadhrami descent engage with their identity in terms of *nasb* (lineage). Additionally, the socio-cultural associations, established by members of the diaspora themselves, have developed into vehicles that play a vital role in retaining the Hadhrami consciousness among the diaspora in Singapore.

Historical Background of Hadhrami Migration to Singapore

Hadhramis migrated to Southeast Asia from the *wadi* (valley) of Hadhramout in eastern Yemen. They were involved in the Arab trading network long before the arrival of the Dutch East India Company in Indonesia and were active on the island before the arrival of Sir Stamford Raffles. The "push factors" for Hadhramis included "perennial problems of famine, wars, limited arable land, unpredictable rainfall and flash floods as well as the lure of lucrative international trade and the Hadhrami's proverbial love of travel" (Martin 1974, Redkin 1995). With a population of almost two million, Hadhramaut hosts 1,300 distinct tribes. Most, if not all of the Hadhramis who migrated to Southeast Asia are descendants of the Ba'Alawi clan or its branches, which include al-sagoff, al-attas, al-aydarus, al-junied, al-qadri, al-yahya, al-shatri, ba-Rukbah (Abdullah 2009, 46). Initially the upper tiers of the tribal hierarchy, the *sada* and *mashayikh,* helped spread Islam (specifically Sufi traditions) and acted as religious advisors and judges to their hosts in the archipelago. The Syeds' and the Shayikhs' superior education propelled them to senior positions across Southeast Asia in colonial times. After settling in Singapore, along with their economic activities they made the island the "pilgrimage transit center" (Talib 1997, 90) for the rest of the Malay Archipelago and established a number of Islamic schools (*madrasahs*) in Singapore.

There is disagreement as to what it actually means to be a Hadhrami (Brehony 2017, 1–15). The Hadhrami identity may be more readily defined, and more acutely felt, in the diaspora than in the homeland, as it transcends status, ethnic origin, the dilution of bloodlines through intermarriage, time, and space (Brehony 2017, 225–233). I ascribe to Iain Walker's take that "Hadhramis are multinational transnationals" and their identity is based on "a deep historical understanding and recognition of belonging that is inscribed in, and performed through daily practice" (Brehony 2017, 164).

For centuries, the Hadhrami diaspora has been a trade diaspora consisting of a "complex network of coastal and island commercial centres, of trade routes and entrepots linking these places with the sea" (Alatas 1997, 26). The Southeast Asian Hadhrami diasporas have created a hybrid distinct culture often referred to as "Arab Indon culture" (Talib 2020). The term diaspora is understood here in the broader sense of its definition which is "dispersal from an original center, collective memory or myth of the original homeland, a feeling of marginality and alienation in the host country, and continual relating to the homeland, physically or emotionally" (Safran 1991, 83ff).

Sociologist Syed Farid Alatas has written extensively on the decolonization of knowledge and academic imperialism and suggested fresh approaches to the study of the history of the Hadhrami diaspora that are more theoretically "self-conscious" (Alatas 1997, 19). He argues that "while there are a small number of works that recognize the diaspora dimensions of Hadhrami immigration, there have been no conceptual attempts to locate the Hadhrami diaspora in the historical context of Indian Ocean trade or in the theoretical context of various historical and comparative perspectives" (Alatas 1997, 19).

The Hadhramis across the Straits settlements, and particularly in Singapore, provided the British with the peaceful conditions in which they could trade—a fact that is little known or recognized in historiographies of the region and its development. The first official residency of a Hadhrami in Singapore was reported in 1820; Syed Omar Ali al-Junied (Talib 1997, 91). He was a wealthy trader and friend of Sir Stamford Raffles (Talib 1997, Alatas 1997). In 1824, the population of Singapore was around 10,500; by 1829, there were thirty-four Arabs with only three Arab women among them (Singapore Department of Statistics). Raffles welcomed the Hadhrami traders across the Straits settlements and encouraged them to settle in Singapore as they had the capital, largely from Indonesia, that the new land desperately needed (Brehony 2017, 1–15). Raffles instructed Singapore's housing committee in 1822: "The Arab population would require every consideration. No situation will be more appropriate for them than the vicinity of the Sultan's residence" (Buckley 1984, 85). This Arab district still exists and is vibrant today.

From first contact to independence in 1965, the Hadhramis contributed instrumentally to Singapore's progress. Syed Omar al-Junied built Singapore's first mosque in 1820. In the later part of the century, Syed Omar's son Syed Ali and grandson Syed Alwi underwrote the building of public wells and public bridges (Aljunied 2013). To recognize their generosity, Aljunied Road, Aljunied MRT station, and Syed Alwi Road were named after them. Along with the al-Junied settlers, the al-Saggoffs were spice traders, known as the "the merchant prince family of the Arabs" (Talib 1997, 94). The "Perseverance Estate," utilized to grow lemongrass, was among the many properties acquired by them. It is today at the heart of the Muslim community in Singapore. Alongside their extensive land ownership and success as merchants, the family was also very civic-minded: Syed Mohamed Ahmed al-Sagoff was the first Arab Municipal Commissioner of Singapore (1878–1898), and Syed Mohamed Syed Omar al-Sagoff was commissioner between 1928 and 1933. From 1963 to 1965, Brigadier-General Syed Mohamed Syed Ahmad al-Sagoff was the Commander of the Singapore Armed Forces. The al-Kaff family arrived in 1852; they too enjoyed lives of considerable opulence. Other notable Hadhramis include Dr Ahmad Mattar, who is known mostly for helping to clean up the Singapore River, entered politics and rose to be, first, Minister for Social Affairs, and then Minister for the Environment (1972–1996).

In the early days of the diaspora's formation, the settlers sought to instill a sense of Hadhrami identity in the next generation so engaged in sending their sons back to Hadhramaut for periods of time (Martin 1974, Talib 1997). This custom maintained their language and Hadhrami culture. Upon their return to Singapore, a place in the family businesses was waiting for them (Mutalib 2016). There had been generations of intermarriage by the time of independence, the product of which were *muwalladin*, who are typically the offspring of mixed marriages who participated more fully in local cultural institutions and practices as they become integrated (Brehony 2017, 1–15). These *muwalladin* were found at the time of independence, and today, in political positions and tend to be part of the civil service elite. As Alatas argues, Hadhrami diaspora communities around the world tend to acculturate and adopt the language and customs of the *mahjar* (host country) but invariably retain certain staples of their origin culture:

> The Hadhrami diaspora provides an interesting case of a transnational community which assimilated into their host societies, but retained their cultural identity. Hadhramis in the diaspora had for centuries married into East African, South Indian and Malay-Indonesian communities without losing the sense of Hadhrami identity, because such identity was neither national nor ethnic, but was based on kinship. The locus of Hadhrami identity was not so much language but *nasab* (lineage). (Alatas 1997, 29)

The keeping of genealogy is typical of tribal societies but is more strictly practiced among the Ba'alawi of Hadthramout. "One major factor that brings about this strictness is because the group can trace their ancestry to the prophet of Islam, Prophet Muhammad and from there the genealogical lineage was established to the first human being, Prophet Adam" (Aljunied 2013).

Post-Independence Policies and their Impact on the Hadhramis

Wills of the nineteenth-century wealthy Hadhramis indicate that elders chose the legal form of family trusts under the English law and translated it to the Islamic private endowment or "*waqaf.*" Whether private or charitable, the *waqaf* bore the family names and gave considerable prestige to the Hadhrami community among the Muslims in Singapore. Before the outbreak of World

War II, Hadhramis owned 75 percent of the land not owned by the British, meaning they owned about 50 percent of the total land area of Singapore (World Business 2007). In 1936, they were the richest group in Singapore in terms of ownership of assets per head (Talib 2020). Almost the entire area of what is today Singapore's Central Business District was once *waqaf* land (Backman 2004, 156). In recent years, different factors have affected the *waqaf* and undermined the status of the community and led to an identity crisis of sorts.

With the coming into effect of the Rent Control Act in 1947, Hadhrami incomes were frozen. The next generation could not rely on the *waqaf* incomes. "The Shayikh Salem Talib family settlement, for example, used to have more than three pages in its audited accounts listing the properties held, but the current accounts have less than one page" (Talib 1997). More than half of the properties were acquired by the government. Zahara Aljunied, the great great grand-daughter of Singapore's pioneer Hadhrami merchant, explains how the "al-Saggoff Perseverance Estate was acquired in 1962 for urban renewal" and how another prime 10-acre (40,000 m²) plot "was donated by the al-Junied family to the Muslim Trust Fund (a *waqaf* created by the al-Saggoffs) to be developed so that the income could be used for welfare projects" (Aljunied 2013). Many such examples of this nature exist and are discussed frequently by the elder Hadhrami Singaporeans with a sense of nostalgia and despair that the youth do not seem to appreciate nor grasp what once was. Much of the property owned by the *waqaf* today compromise three or four-level shop-houses, "many are dilapidated and ready for development, their upkeep hampered by decades of rent controls that were lifted only in 2001" (Backman 2004, 157).

The 1966 Land Acquisition Act also affected Hadhrami land ownership as the post-independence government used a formula that translated to very little compensation in their acquisition of land for state development. Leif Manger notes that "in Singapore, independence signaled the start of a phenomenal economic development that also changed the fortunes of the Hadhramis particularly vis-à-vis the Chinese" (Brehony 2017, 207–224). These two policies eroded Hadhrami wealth and influence. It also brought on an identity crisis because if they were not the elite landowners who were they vis-à-vis the Muslim community, particularly the Malays, and the other minority communities in Singapore?

Furthermore, local *madrasahs* in Singapore, many of which were established by the early Hadhrami settlers, combine secular and religious education. They operated somewhat independently until 1966 with the passing of the Administration of Muslim Law Act; *madrasahs* were henceforth registered and managed by the Majlis Ugama Islam Singapura (MUIS; Islamic Religious Council of Singapore) (Mukhlis 2006). In 2009, the government implemented the Joint Madrasah System (JMS), allowing for a more centralized approach to the dual-learning being offered to the Muslim population and to improve the quality of *madrasah* education as a whole. Three of the six full-time *madrasahs* joined. The *madrasahs* under the JMS focus on different educational pathways: Madrasah Aljunied provides a religious pathway and Madrasah Al-Arabiah, an academic one, while Madrasah Al-Irsyad providing only primary education. The other three—Madrasah Al-Maarif Al-Islamiah, Madrasah Wak Tanjong, and Madrasah Alsagoff Al-Arabiah—continue to offer classes for the primary, secondary, and pre-university levels (Mokhtar 2013).

Although children of the diaspora are allowed to pursue their primary education at one of the *madrasahs*, it was compulsory to sit for the national Primary School Leaving Examination (PSLE). The results of which are published by race and determines the educational career trajectory of students until graduation. Under the Compulsory Education Act, *madrasahs* have to ensure that their students pass the PSLE with an aggregate score higher than the average aggregate score of Malay–Muslim pupils in the six lowest-performing national schools (Mukhlis 2006). This is a reflection of the emphasis on mainstream secular education in Singapore as a means of economic progress. These combination of policies had multiple implications for the Hadhrami community, as how they chose to self-identify in the immediate post-independence era became a multi-faceted decision with profound socio-economic multi-generational consequences, and not merely an issue of identity.

The Census and Conflation of Race and Religion in Singapore

Primary records of the early censuses of Singapore are only available in secondary sources, such as newspapers and books as well as online. Accounts point to Singapore's first census taking place in January 1824. "It recorded a population of 10,683, comprising 74 Europeans, 16 Armenians, 15 Arabs, 4,580 Malays, 3,317 Chinese, 756 Indians, and 1,925 Bugis, and others" (Buckley 1984, 154).

The first systematic census of Singapore as part of the Straits Settlements was conducted in 1871 and showed that 56.2 percent of the population were Chinese, 26.9 percent Malay, and 11.8 percent Indians (Clammer 1998). "This census also had 33 vaguely defined categories, which were streamlined over a decade to 6 main categories (European and American, Eurasian, Chinese, Malays and other natives of the Archipelago, Tamils and other Natives of India, and Other nationalities) housing 47 sub-categories by 1881" (PuruShotam 1998, 61). "From 1921, these 6 categories were further simplified to *Europeans, Eurasians, Malays, Chinese, Indians and*

Others, and in 1931, 70 sub-groups were classified under these 6, blurring the boundaries between race, religion and nationality" (Reddy & Gleibs 2019). The Chinese population has enjoyed a majority in Singapore since 1931, making up approximately 75 percent of society (Singapore Department of Statistics). This demographic make-up is unique to Singapore, as its immediate neighbors in Southeast Asia tend to have Chinese minorities and Muslim majorities.

Arguably Lee Kuan Yew did not hold favorable beliefs about Islam and agreed with the colonial stereotype of the "lazy" Malay and the "industrious" Chinese (Reddy 2016). "The Maria Hertogh racial riots, which took place in December 1950, and the Prophet Muhammad birthday riots in 1964", were used to serve as reminders of the fragility of peace among different ethnic groups (Reddy & Gleibs 2019). Racial and religious conflict characterized the independence period in the mid-1960s; therefore, Yew believed it was important "to forge a collective Singaporean identity among the largely diverse migrant population so as to anchor these migrants to Singapore soil" (Velayutham 2007; Ortmann 2009, 23–46). In pursuing this policy of multiracialism, "the heterogeneity within each ethnicity was collapsed further into simplified categories for ease of administration" (Reddy & Gleibs 2019). A "social formula" was established called the CMIO model: Chinese, Malay, Indian, and Other. The purpose was "to create an egalitarian and inclusive society by integrating the individualized racial groups into a single Singaporean culture" (Barr & Skrbis 2008). This model continues to evolve as the census methodology becomes progressively more sophisticated.

In order to ensure the success of its social policies, the government practices essentialism of the different groups which then influences how people perceive of themselves and think of others (Ackermann 1997). The multiplicity within each category is not acknowledged by the government and "the differences with the categories and between them are minimized, with similarities among one racial category perceived as greater than they actually are" (Reddy & Gleibs 2019). "If you are categorised as Malay, you should be Muslim, and you will develop competency in the Malay language" at school and abide by the racial quota restrictions applied to housing and other public goods and services. In the "collapsing of differences within a category" in this manner, certain groups became invisible (Reddy 2016, 10). This is what has happened to the Hadhrami diaspora.

Hadhramis would technically fall in the Other category as "Arabs"; however, due to "intermarriage between Malay or Indian Muslim men and Hadharmi women, some Malays and Indians have Hadhrami ancestry." People of Hadhrami descent matrilineally were not considered or listed as Arabs because, until 2010, a person's race in Singapore was determined by his father's race. For this reason, the census for the 1970s and 1980s is not believed to reflect the actual number of Arabs in Singapore. Furthermore, "although Singapore's multiracial policy was built upon the foundations of meritocracy and social cohesion, the reality is that uneven focus on individual culture development and unequal opportunities has led to unequal power dynamics between the races" (Chua 2003, 58–77; Mutalib 2012, 31–55).

After independence, educational benefits were granted to ethnic Malays by the state. Due to the erosion of their status and decline in wealth brought about by the battery of government policies, socio-economic considerations meant some Hadhrami families listed the ethnicity of their children as "Malay" to receive these benefits. The case of the Singapore Hadhrami community and its position within Singapore Malay Muslim society came to a head in the 1990s. The Singapore Broad-casting Corporation (SBC) ran a program "Potret Keluarga" (Family Portrait) in which "local Arabs were depicted as part of the Malay community" (Alatas 1997). The program spoke of "Malays of Arab descent" sparking a widespread debate about the identity crisis among the Hadhramis of Singapore, prompting the SBC spokesman to offer assurances to the effect that there was no intention to depict Arabs as part of the Malay community. But this is the status quo and lived reality of the Hadhrami Singaporean: There is an attitude that a "tiny minority" wish to "jeopardize" the process of integrating Arabs into Singapore society by wishing to "set themselves apart from the larger Malay society" (Ismail 1992).

The 2000 Census demonstrates that the father's ethnicity was used to categorize Singaporeans of mixed parentage (Singapore Department of Statistics). In 2003, then Minister for Community Development and Sports, Yaacob Ibrahim, "signalled the state's move from multiracialism to multiculturalism" where Singaporeans were no longer to be hyphenated but rather "cosmopolitan" with each individual possessing "elements and traits reflecting the larger society" (Goh & Holden 2009). Two instances could be seen as catalysts for this change. First, the arrests of Jemmah Islamiah militants in Singapore in 2001 and 2002 which resulted in doubts on the loyalty of Muslims in Singapore, second, the controversy surrounding debates about the *tudung* (headscarf in Malay) in 2002, which involved four Malay Muslim parents calling for the modification of their children's school uniforms to include the *tudung*. Some among the ruling party took issue (and continue to take issue) with the use of the Arabic word "*hijab*" in these debates, extending the grievance to include the use of the Arabic word "*Eid*" rather than the Malay version "Hari Raya" to celebrate the Muslim festivities; correlating such trends to the "Arabization of Islam" (read: Wahabization) in Singapore (Bilahari 2019).

Outside of the technicalities of the racial structures in Singapore, when the issue of religious extremism is explored in the regional or international context, the framing of discussions tend to be either subtly or overtly seeking to test: is the sense of community and identity that has developed among the Hadhrami community in Singapore robust enough to "resist" the challenge of extremism? Will they put their religion above their country in the event of war with Muslim majority neighbors Malaysia and Indonesia? This is something the Hadhrami diaspora must contend with on a daily basis.

With the increasing numbers of Singaporeans of mixed parentage, the Singapore government again evolved its policy allowing them the option of being categorized as mixed ethnicity with "a double-barrel racial option" (Hoe 2010). The results showed "the Chinese as the majority with around 74 percent of the population, the indigenous Malays with 14 percent, the Indians at less than 10 percent and the balance as Other." Here the Arabs are categorized to be "around 7,000, but unofficial estimates place the actual number at around 10,000" (Singapore Department of Statistics 2010). The fact that the number of Hadhramis in Singapore today is not accurate nor reflective of the facts on the ground is the very reason why more nuanced and targeted studies into this diaspora are important and a reconsideration of the essentialized census system is vital for Singapore to sustain its unique model of social organization.

As indicated, among Singaporeans, the Hadhrami in the *mahjar* is a *muwallad* (or what in Malay is called pernakan) or what Sumit Mandal, in his book *Becoming Arab*, calls creole. Essentially, Hadhramis of mixed parentage not living in their ancestral homeland grew up under the influence of Arabic society and educated within the Islamic culture (Brehony 2017, 1–15). This concept of *muwallad* is best used as a means of conceptualizing Hadhrami identity outside of Hadhramaut and in Singapore. Boxberger notes that there is "a conflict between two different facets of Hadhrami identity: their strong identification as Muslims and their identity as a dispersed emigrant community linked to the home-land" (Boxberger 1971, 27). This adds an extra layer of complexity to the identity crisis brought about, first, by the conflation of race and religion and exacerbated by the methodology of the census taking and, second, by the immediate post-independence era policies adopted by the government explored earlier.

METHODS

The data made available by Singapore's Department of Statistics reveals that Singapore has gone through fourteen censuses since its first in 1824. The data was analyzed to frame the trends outlined above coupled with a reliance on describing methods cited in relevant primary and secondary sources. This area demands more critical scholarship.

Celebration of Identity among the Hadhramis of Singapore

Because of the CIMO model and the wide-ranging socio-economic implications brought about by it, a tension exists between the national level and the personal level when it comes to identity. Citizens are encouraged to identify along racial lines and "maintain their uniqueness through the preservation of their individual practices in the private sphere" (Reddy 2016, 13). Members of each group are responsible to maintain the cultural vibrancy of the group, a fact that is all the more salient for the Hadhrami diaspora.

Most Hadhramis in Singapore today, who are fifth or sixth generation, do not speak Arabic and have never visited Hadhramaut (Talib 2020). Yet they have managed, on a personal level, to maintain their distinct identities. This is made possible by deliberate and continued self-identification from one generation to the next, which manifests by still using the title Syed (Sharifa for women) along strict *nasb* guidelines; marriage practices, where overt Yemeni traditions are used despite one or both of the spouses being very much of mixed ancestry and "in their private daily lives through food, language, religion, customs and entertainment" (Sandhu & Wheatly 1989, 563–577). While the community draws from their "home" culture and practices, they have adapted them to the local context, allowing each Hadhrami diaspora to remain distinct from their counterparts abroad (Clammer 1998; Chua 1998, 28–50).

The government actively highlights the need for awareness and development of one's racial heritage as a necessary staple in the public spheres of Singaporean life to help Singaporeans acknowledge and respect the Asia civilizations that have shaped their identity, as well as encourage empathy for Asia's diversity. This priority on internalizing both racial as well as national identity would allow Singaporeans to enjoy an advantage over Western counterparts, as well as rising powers such as China and India, and, importantly for the Malays and Hadhramis, the Islamic countries of Asia. This functions as, in the words of former Minister for Foreign Affairs George Yeo, "knowledge arbitrage" (Crovitz 1993, 18), enabling Singaporeans to engage with their diverse neighborhood as cultural kin familiar and comfortable with their beliefs, customs, idiosyncrasies, and values.

To that end, the Hadhramis were supported when they formed their own association in 1946 which still exists today: The Arab Association Singapore (*Al-Wehda Al-Arabiya Bi Singhafura*), known commonly as *al-Wehda*, which is Arabic for unity. The objective was and remains "to promote and enhance Islamic virtues and education, as well as the use of the Arabic language" (Alwehda n.d.). The idea is to have one entity which "represents" the Arab (Hadhrami) community as a whole around united messages. The profiles of the president, board, and committee members cover the gambit of prominent

Hadhrami families in Southeast Asia. When in 2007 the Foreign Minister of Singapore wanted to visit Yemen, *al-Wehda* invited him to visit Hadramaut as their guest. That visit raised the prominence of the Singapore Arab Association in Hadramaut. Shortly after, Helmi Talib, vice president of *al-Wehda* was appointed as the non-resident ambassador of Singapore to Yemen (Talib 2020).

At the time of the "Potret Keluarga" debate in the early 1990s, a magazine for the community was launched by individuals, *al-Shourouq*, which means "rising of dawn" to imply a beginning of a new era for the Hadhrami community. It published a concept paper outlining the issues and challenges facing the community and called for further participation from the youth (Talib 2020). As times have changed and the circumstances of the Hadhramis have shifted, the diaspora has been able to broaden the notion of identity beyond religion and language to include culture, music, and intellectual activities. This is witnessed in the social enterprise association Arab Network in Singapore, AN@S, which was established in 2010. The association seems to have galvanized the youth as they identify with the spirit of innovation with which it was founded. Activities include "Zumba Love for Refugees in the Middle East" and projects, such as "Educate & Celebrate" (Arab Network Singapore n.d.).

These entities, in different ways, work to organize initiatives that celebrate the Hadhrami identity and its contributions to the formation of Singapore and allow the members of the diaspora to retain a sense of pride in their origin stories and their Hadhrami culture. Most notable is gathering funds for young males to travel to Tarim, and elsewhere in Hadramaut, to echo the cultural and religious education of their ancestors. The recipients of these bursaries tend to be high-performers from one of the *madrasahs*; another subtle encouragement that keeps the religio-cultural link alive. President Khadija al-Attas notes:

> AN@S's work is not meant to be a comprehensive coverage of the Hadhrami community's priorities and activities on the island, but an attempt to represent something more ambitious for the future about the Hadhrami Singaporean experience as a whole. We hope these small activities will resonate with our fellow Singaporeans and perhaps inspire all of us to a better understanding of our multi-faith, multi-racial society, something that should be celebrated and protected.

The activities show that even though their ethnicity is regarded as homogenous in the public arena, there is an unmistakable sense of Hadhrami identity that has beautifully melded with not only the Malay but also Indian and Chinese cultures on the island; the Singapore culture in essence. These are proud Hadhramis but proud Singaporeans too.

In terms of faith, the nexus of religion and Hadhrami identity comes into play in Singapore more specifically with the Ba'alawi Mosque, which is an active center that keeps the Hadhrami culture alive with close interaction with the State via its very prominent, highly decorated imam, Habib Hassan al-atas, himself a personality worthy of study for his work in promoting interfaith dialogue and encouraging tolerance in debates regarding sensitive faultline issues, as well as providing different platforms for socio-economically driven activities. This Hadhrami mosque facilitates the link for the diaspora with Yemen, in a way that assuages any suspicions of the government, as the custodians are well-versed in the "Singapore way" that sets highly regulated boundaries for racial and religious discourse.

Hadhramis in the diaspora, not only in Singapore, are taking an interest in the political future of Yemen, with the war now entering its fifth year. Arguably, more so than the Hadhramis in the homeland, who are preoccupied with survival in an unstable Yemen in which the influence of Hadhramaut has long been weak, particularly as remittances from the Indian Ocean started to dry up. When Hadramaut was besieged by floods in 2008, the community in Singapore rallied to collect funds and representatives went to Hadramaut to provide relief. Recently the diaspora, through the vehicles provided for by *al-Wehda*, AN@S, and the Ba'alawi Mosque, partnered with UNDP in "Yemen Our Home" program to bring solar power to schools in Hadramaut (Talib 2020) and UNHCR to provide relief for Yemeni refugees.

For the most part the Hadhrami diaspora in Singapore appreciate that policies have been designed by the government around the CMIO model and that demanding alteration to accommodate a small mixed ethnicity population will be problematic. The social policy structures have a deep and far-reaching influence on daily life, affecting issues related to housing, education, career prospects, and expressions of faith. Pragmatically, reforming these policies, with all the challenges associated with that reform, will likely have negligible impact in terms of affecting tangible change. Despite this pragmatism, there is a sense that the historiography of the Hadhrami immigration and historiography of the Hadhrami Diaspora (where it can be found) does not meet with the full satisfaction of the *mawaaled*. Especially when compared to other minority groups in Singapore. For example, at many events Singaporean officials, when taking stock of the special relations between Singapore and Israel, extol the contributions of the tiny Jewish community on the island, totaling 300 in number as of 2010 (Singapore Department of Statistics). The earliest Jews in Singapore arrived in the mid-nineteenth century, mostly from Baghdad, then later from Eastern Europe. Singapore's first chief minister David Marshall was of the Jewish diaspora (of Baghdad-Persian descent). The Singapore government's narrative is that their descendants have contributed "out of proportion to their numbers in the country" (Yeo 2019). It is, arguably, an inconsequential matter but it does have a psychological toll on the Hadhrami diaspora (Mutalib 2016), especially as early Hadhrami influences on Singapore are still highly visible across the island.

CONCLUSION AND RELEVANCE

This chapter hopes to contribute to the endeavor of increasing visibility of Hadhrami Singaporeans' lived realities. It has revealed, using a theoretical historical approach, that as the Singapore story took shape, there were, naturally, casualties along the way. The Hadhrami Diaspora in Singapore who enjoyed enormous wealth and prestige at first contact, and for close to a century after, were among such casualties. Despite the obvious flaws inherent in the Singapore racial experiment, by undertaking sustainable educational and socio-economic driven activities by leaders within the community itself, entities such as *al-Wehda* and AN@S and the Ba'alawi Mosque ensure contact and interaction between the homeland and the *mahjar* is constant, keeping the unique Hadhrami identity alive among the diaspora in the multi-cultural multireligious city state.

This chapter also hopes to highlight the potential for richer examinations of this diaspora and their experiences as subjects of history, requiring the attention and scholarship of sociologists, political economists, economic geographers, and psychologists not only anthropologists and historians. Often, the focus in the social sciences has been centered on how individuals and relevant Others identify themselves as members of their racial in-group in multiracial societies. This is why the Singapore example makes for a unique context for research on the Hadhrami diaspora and can be used to further theories on racial identity construction, studies on the psychological impact of race upon an individual's sense of wellbeing (Townsend et al. 2009), attitudes on immigration (Deaux 2006), sense of belonging (Howarth et al. 2013), views on multiculturalism (Verkuyten 2001), experiences of colonization (Fanon 1967), intergroup contact (Ramiah et al. 2015), and racism (Tizard & Phoenix 2002).

REFERENCES

Abdullah, Abudlrahman Tang (2009). *Arab Hadhramis In Malaysia:Their Origins And Assimilation In Malay Society.* In Hassan Ahmed Ibrahim, Ahmed Ibrahim Abushouk (Ed.), *The Hadhrami Diaspora in Southeast Asia: Identity Maintenance or Assimilation? Social, Economic and Political Studies of the Middle East and Asia.* 57–80. Leiden Boston: Brill.

Ackermann, Andreas (1997). "They Give us the Categories and we Fill Ourselves in": Ethnic Thinking in Singapore." *International Journal on Minority and Group Rights* 4: 451–467. Kluwer Law International: Netherlands.

Alatas, Syed Farid (1997). *Hadhramaut and The Hadhrami Diaspora: Problems In Theoretical History.* In W. C.-S. U. Freitag (Ed.), *Hadhrami Traders, Scholars and Statemen in the Indian Ocean 1750s–1960s.* 19–38. Leiden: Brill.

Alattas, Khadija. Interview by Aisha Sahar AlKharusi. Personal Interview. Singapore, Singapore, Oct. 20, 2019.

Aljunied, S. Zahra (2013). "The Genealogy of the Hadhrami Arabs in Southeast Asia – the 'Alawi Family." National Library Board of Singapore.

Backman, Michael (2004). *The Asian Insider: Unconventional Wisdom for Asian Business.* London: Palgrave Macmillan.

Barr, Michael D., and Zlatko Skrbiš (2008). *Constructing Singapore: Elitism, Ethnicity and the Nation-Building Project.* 133–137. Copenhagen: NIAS Press.

Boxberger, Linda (1971). *On The Edge Of Empire: Hadhramawt, Emigration, And The Indian Ocean, 1880s–1930s.* In Abdallah Burja (Ed.), *The Politics of Stratification: A Study of Political Change in a South Arabian Town.* 25–30. Oxford: Clarendon.

Brehony, Noel, Ed. (2017), *Hadhramaut and its Diaspora: Yemeni Politics, Identity and Migration.* London-New York: I.B.Tauris.

Buckley, Charles Burton (1984). *An Anecdotal History of Old Times in Singapore (with Portraits and Illustrations): From the Foundation of the Settlements Under the Honourable the East India Company, on February 6th, 1819, to the transfer of the Colonial Office as part of the colonial possessions of the Crown on April 1st, 1867.* Vol. I. Singapore: Oxford University Press.

Chua, Beng-Huat (1998). *Racial-Singaporeans: Absence after the Hyphen.* In Joel S. Kahn (Ed.), *Southeast Asian Identities: Culture and the Politics of Representation in Indonesia, Malaysia, Singapore, and Thailand.* 28–50. Singapore: Institute of Southeast Asian Studies.

Chua, Beng Huat (2003). "Multiculturalism in Singapore: An Instrument of Social Control." *Race and Class* 44: 58–77.

Clammer, John R. (1985). *Singapore: Ideology, Society, Culture.* Singapore: Chopmen Publishers.

Clammer, John R. (1990). *Religion and Society in Singapore: Ethnicity, Identity, and Social Change.* In C.-A. Seyschab, A. Sievers and S. Szynkiewicz (Ed.), *Society, Culture and Patterns of Behaviour.* 157–182. Unkel/Rhein and Bad Honnef: Horlemann Verlag.

Clammer, John R. (1998). *Race and State in Independent Singapore 1965–1990: The Cultural Politics of Pluralism in a Multiethnic Society.* Brookfield, VT: Ashgate.

Crovitz, L.G. (1993). "Dragon Diaspora: Cultural Links Should Bolster Economic Growth." *Far Eastern Economic Review*, 2 December 1993, 18.

Goh, Daniel, Matilda Gabrielpillai, Philip Holden and Khoo Gaik Cheng (Eds.) (2009). *Race and Multiculturalism in Malaysia and Singapore.* 9; Speech by Yaacob Ibrahim, Minister-in-Charge of Muslim Affairs, at the Wee Kim Wee Center on Cross-Cultural Understanding, Singapore in 2003. London: Routledge.

Hoe, Y.N. (2010). 'Singaporeans of Mixed Race Allowed to "Double Barrel" Race in IC', *Channel News Asia*. Accessed 10 March 2020, http://www.channelnewsasia.com).

Ismail, Abdul Samad, "Melayu versus Arab." *Dewan Budaya* 14, no. 9 (September 1992): 20–21. ISEAS, NLB, NTUNIE, NUS.

Kausikan, Bilahari (2021). "Identity: Religion, Politics, or Something Else?" In Mathew, Mathews and Tay, Melvin (Ed.), *Religion and Identity Politics: Global Trends and Local Realities*. Singapore, Singapore: World Scientific Press.

Mandal, Sumit K. (2017). *Becoming Arab: Creole Histories and Modern Identity in the Malay World* (Asian Connections). Cambridge: Cambridge University Press.

Martin, Bradford G. (1974). "Arab Migrations to East Africa in Medieval Times." *The International Journal of African Historical Studies*, 7; 3.

Mokhtar, Maryam (2013, January 16). The revamped madrasah education system. *The Straits Times*, p. 9. Retrieved from NewspaperSG.

Mukhlis, Abu Bakar (2006). *Between State Interests and Citizen Rights: Wither the Madrasah?* In Noor Aisha Abdul Rahman and Lai Ah Eng (Ed.), *Secularism and Spirituality: Seeking Integrated Knowledge and Success in Madrasah Education in Singapore*. Singapore: Institute of Policy Studies; Marshall Cavendish Academic, 2006. ISEAS, NLB, NTU, NTUNIE, NUS.

Mutalib, Hussin (2012). "Singapore's Ethnic Relations' Scorecard." *Journal of Developing Societies*, 28: 31–55.

Mutalib, Hussin, and Rokiah Mentol, Sundusia Rosdi (Eds.) (2016). *Singapore Malay/Muslim Community 1819–2015 A Bibliography*. vii–xiv. ISEAS Yusof Ishak Institute, Singapore.

Ortmann, Stephan (2009). "Singapore: The Politics of Inventing National Identity." *Journal of Current Southeast Asian Affairs* 28: 23–46.

PuruShotam, Nirmala (1998). *Disciplining Difference: Race in Singapore*. In Joel S. Kahn (Ed.), *Southeast Asian Identities: Culture and the Politics of Representation in Indonesia, Malaysia, Singapore, and Thailand*. 61. Singapore: Institute of Southeast Asian Studies.

Reddy, Geetha. (2016). "Race Rules in Singapore." In J. Lim and T.e Lee (Eds.), *Singapore: Negotiating State and Society, 1965–2015*. (1 ed, pp. 54–75). London: Routledge.

Reddy, Geetha & Ilka H. Gleibs (2019). The Endurance and Contestations of Colonial Constructions of Race Among Malaysians and Singaporeans. *Frontiers in Psychology* 10: 792.

Redkin, O.I. (1995). "Migration in Wadi Amd and Wadi Dawa'an After the World War II: Economic and Cultural Effects." Paper presented at the SOAS Conference "Hadhramaut and the Hadhrami Diaspora, late 18th Century to c 1967", London, April.

Romein, Jan. (1948). "Theoretical History." *Journal of the History of Ideas* 9 (1):53.

Safran, William (1991). "Diasporas in Modern Societies: Myths of Homeland and Return." *Diaspora* 1;1. pp. 83ff.

Sharon Siddique (1989). *Singaporean Identity*. In Kernial Singh Sandhu and Pail Wheatley (Ed.), *Management of Success: The Moulding of Modern Singapore*, 563–577. Singapore: Institute of Southeast Asian Studies.

Singapore Department of Statistics (n.d.). *Census of Population 2010 Statistical Release 2: Households and Housing*, Yearbooks of Statistics Singapore, Singapore Department of Statistics. (https://www.singstat.gov.sg/-/media/files/publications/cop2010/census_2010_release1/cop2010sr1.pdf). Accessed March 2020.

Slama, Martin (2011). "Translocal Networks and Globalisation within Indonesia. Exploring the Hadhrami Diaspora from the Archipelago's North-East." *Asian Journal of Social Science* 39(3): 238–257.

Talib, Ameen (1995). Hadhramis in Singapore, Conference paper for The British-Yemeni Society.

Talib, Ameen (2010, July 9–10). "Sustaining relationships between diaspora and homeland: The case of Singapore Hadhrami", presentation at National and International Academic Conference Innovation And Management For Sustainability, Siam University, Thailand.

Talib, Ameen. Hadramis in Singapore, *Journal of Muslim Minority Affairs*, vol 17 no1 (April 1997): 89–97 (UK).

The Arab Association Singapore (Al-Wehdah Al-Arabiyah Bi Singhafura). https://www.alwehdah.org/ Accessed 1 February 2020.

The Arab Network@ Singapore. (2021). www.arabnetworksingapore.org. Accessed February 1, 2020.

'The World's Successful Diasporas', *World Business*, 3 April 2007. (https://www.managementtoday.co.uk/worlds-successful-diasporas/article/648273). Accessed 20 February 2020.

Velayutham, Selvaraj (2007), *Responding to Globalization: Nation, Culture and Identity in Singapore*. Singapore: Institute of Southeast Asian Studies.

Warburton, David (1995). The Hadhramis, The Hadhramaut And European Colonial Powers In The Indian Ocean. In Gwyn Campbell (Ed.), *The Indian Ocean Rim: Southern Africa and Regional Cooperation*. London: RoutledgeCurzon, 2003.

Yahaya, Nurfadzilah (2009). Tea and Company: Interactions between the Arab Elite and the British in Cosmpolitan Singapore. In Hassan Ahmed Ibrahim, Ahmed Ibrahim Abushouk (Ed.), *The Hadhrami Diaspora in Southeast Asia: Identity Maintenance or Assimilation? Social, Economic and Political Studies of the Middle East and Asia*. 57–80. Leiden Boston: Brill.

Yeo, George "Singapore-Israel ties: 50 years of understanding and helping each other" Article for Today on 12 December 2019. (https://www.todayonline.com/commentary/singapore-israel-ties-50-years-understanding-and-helping-each-other). Accessed 20 January 2020.

Chapter 6

Whither "Integration"? Children's Television, Immigration, and Arab Diasporas in Germany

Christine Singer, Jeanette Steemers, and Naomi Sakr

INTEGRATION DEBATES IN GERMANY

In 2015, Germany accommodated almost one million refugees,[1] the majority of whom were from Syria, Iraq, and Afghanistan (Griebel and Vollmann 2019, 671). A significant proportion of Syrian and other recent immigrants to Germany are children under the age of 18 years. During the first quarter of 2020, children under 4 years accounted for close to 30 percent of the 31,000 asylum applications lodged in Germany, and those aged 5–18 accounted for 21 percent (Bundesamt für Migration und Flüchtlinge 2020). The German public service broadcasters, including the ARD network (Arbeitsgemeinschaft der öffentlich-rechtlichen Rundfunkanstalten der Bundesrepublik Deutschland) and ZDF (Zweites Deutsches Fernsehen) have responded to this development by producing content that deals with the arrival of children who have recently been displaced from the Arab region and elsewhere. Two examples of this content are the eight-part drama series *Dschermeni* (ZDF, 2017), which centers on a multi-ethnic, multi-cultural group of friends, and the reality documentary series *Berlin und Wir* (Berlin and Us, ZDF, 2016–present), which focuses on a group of Berlin-born teenagers and recently displaced teenagers in Berlin. This chapter explores how *Dschermeni* and *Berlin und Wir* represent integration, disintegration—two concepts discussed later—and Arab diasporic communities to an audience of children born in Germany and to those who have recently arrived.

Integration has historically been a contested concept within both policy circles and academia. It has been used to describe the incorporation of immigrants into the host society, especially with regard to educational achievements and labor markets (Garcés Mascareñas and Penninx 2016, 4). Germany has sought to achieve this kind of integration by providing language classes, cultural orientation classes, and job placements for people who are granted refugee status (Hinger 2020, 24). However, asylum seekers from countries classified as "safe" by the federal government often struggle to gain access to integration courses, for they are unlikely to be granted permanent residence (ibid, 24–26). This categorization of immigrants has been interpreted as "organized disintegration" (Täubig 2009, 45–54; Collyer et al. 2020, 2–4), which describes policies that determine who is encouraged to participate in the social life of a host society and who is not.

The recent political discourse on integration in countries across Europe has primarily addressed non-white immigrants and Muslim communities, regardless of how long they have been settled there (Gholami and Sreberny 2018, 244). In Germany, within political debates across the political spectrum, Arab diasporas have been constructed as a homogenous collective frequently referred to as "Muslims," who are thought to contradict German norms and customs (Mattes 2018, 186–87). This idea has fueled a rise in public attitudes that perceive immigrants as a threat to German security and the welfare state (Griebel and Vollmann 2019). Following Germany's 2017 general election, for example, an anti-immigration, Islamophobic political party, Alternative für Deutschland (Alternative for Germany, AfD), became the first far-right party to enter the German Bundestag since the end of World War II.

METHODS AND FOCUS OF THE CHAPTER

This chapter builds on the findings of a recent project that aimed to engage European media professionals who are involved in the production of children's screen content that addresses forced migration, immigration, and ethnic diversity (Children's Screen Content n.d.).[2] The project shared with these practitioners both the findings of an earlier research project on Arab children's TV (Sakr and Steemers, 2017; Sakr and Steemers 2019) and the expert input of Arab professionals working in the field. This chapter draws on insights gained through TV producers' contributions to workshop discussions held as part of the project, in particular a workshop held in Munich in May 2018 as part of the Prix Jeunesse International festival for children's films and television (Steemers et al. 2018).

The chapter begins with a discussion of academic debates surrounding the concept of integration, followed by an analysis of historical and contemporary immigration and integration policies in Germany. It will then briefly consider how German television deals with aspects of immigration and ethnic diversity. Subsequently, the chapter will analyze the ways in which *Dschermeni* and *Berlin und Wir* represent diaspora childhoods, integration, and disintegration, with a focus on Arab children who have recently settled in Germany.

It is argued here that *Dschermeni* and *Berlin und Wir* depict integration as a complex process—rather than a straightforward or linear one—implying that the lives of Arab children recently arrived in Germany are heterogeneous and diverse. The TV programs allude to what Avtar Brah has called the "multi-axial locationality" of diasporic communities (1996, 205) which suggests that diasporas are stratified by means of legal status, ethnicity, age, gender, and class. Simultaneously, the programs address the structures and policies of "organized disintegration" that can be seen to make it difficult for children who have recently settled in Germany to participate in German social life. Furthermore, both TV programs show how German-born children and children recently arrived in Germany form friendships. In this way, they evoke Brah's concept of "diaspora space" (1996, 241–243), discussed later, which describes spaces and experiences that are shared by members of diasporas and the host society. Finally, *Dschermeni* and *Berlin und Wir* propose that German children with an immigrant background can be part of multiple cultures and traditions, suggesting that it is difficult to pinpoint where integration processes begin and end.

THE CONTESTED CONCEPT OF INTEGRATION

The concept of integration has historically presumed homogenous unity within the society of a nation-state, into which non-nationals need to be integrated (Mattes 2018, 188). Schneider and Crul (2010, 1143) distinguish between "successful integration" and "parallel societies" in public policy debates of Western Europe, with the latter group being imagined as culturally bound diasporic communities with few connections to the host society. This notion is rooted within assimilation theory, a concept that has dominated immigrant integration studies in the United States for much of the twentieth century (ibid). Assimilation theory suggests that European immigrants arrived in the United States as clearly identifiable groups, but subsequent generations assimilated by living with, speaking, and thinking like mainstream society (Feldmeyer 2018, 36). This concept has been critiqued widely for positioning one particular group—middle-class people of European ancestry—as the normative society to which non-Europeans should aspire (Gozdziak 2005, 7).

What current debates do not often address is the need for understanding integration as a complex set of cultural, social, and religious practices that affect different diasporic groups in different ways (Gholami and Sreberny 2018, 245). The ability of refugee children[3] to feel at home in Germany, for example, is determined by the need to learn a new language, adapt to a different culture, family disruptions, and experiences of racism (Murray 2016). Avtar Brah's (1996) understanding of diaspora as a "multi-axial" community describes these multiple, intersecting ways of inclusion and exclusion experienced by diasporic individuals. Brah argues that the diasporic experience constitutes a "cartography of the politics of intersectionality" (1996, 14), with power operating through relationships of gender, class, age, and ethnicity (1996, 181–198).

Furthermore, Brah's concept of diaspora space dissects the discursive processes that label immigrants as "other" and host societies as "us." Diaspora space describes encounters, narratives, and spaces where socially constructed boundaries between "natives" and "immigrants" or "diaspora" dissolve (1996, 208–9). This concept problematizes binaries between the categories of "native" and "diasporic" that are often assumed as given, suggesting that both diasporas and host societies are not homogenous groups but heterogeneous collectives.

ARAB DIASPORAS AND INTEGRATION POLICIES IN GERMANY

Before the outbreak of the Syrian civil war, the Syrian diaspora in Germany was a small group of about 30,000 people (Worbs et al. 2020, 197). Today, numbering almost 700,000, they have become Germany's third largest diasporic community (ibid). Yet, immigration to post-war Germany from Arab countries dates back much longer. The first significant wave took place during the 1960s and 1970s, with then West Germany recruiting Moroccan, Palestinian, and Tunisian workers—but also Turks, Italians, and Greeks—to fill labor shortages and maintain the country's economic growth (Kagermeier 2004, 442; Klusmeyer 1993, 85–88). During the 1980s and 1990s, immigration from the Arab region to Germany intensified as a result of the Lebanese civil war (1975–1990), when tens of thousands of Lebanese and Palestinians fled Lebanon and settled in Germany on the basis of German Asylum Law and Political Asylum Law (Rinnawi 2012, 210).

Until the early 2000s, Germany's immigration regime exemplified practices of organized disintegration (Hinger 2020, 21). The federal government did not encourage the settlement of immigrants from the Arab region or elsewhere, with leading politicians claiming that Germany was not a country of immigration (Elrick and Winter 2018, 24). Migrant laborers were deliberately called "Gastarbeiter" ("guest workers") by Germans, and national policies to support them in learning German were absent (Nötzold and Dili 2009, 86–87). Moreover, the children of migrant laborers were unable to obtain German citizenship even if they were born in Germany (Pautz 2005).

Furthermore, during the 1980s, the federal government divided immigrants into asylum seekers with permanent residence status and those with "tolerated" asylum status ("Duldungsstatus", Hinger 2020, 21). The latter referred to asylum seekers whose residency permits were denied but whose deportations were deferred for legal or economic reasons (Leise 2007). Immigrants with an insecure residence status were prohibited from seeking employment and only accepted refugees had the right to work in Germany (Hinger 2020, 21). The German government lifted some of these restrictions during the 2000s, allowing asylum seekers whose application for residence was pending to find employment and private accommodation (ibid). Even so, differential treatment of immigrants has remained up until the present day.

In 2016, Germany ratified the National Integration Bill ("Integrationsgesetz") in response to the 890,000 refugees who arrived in Germany in 2015, and the 476,649 applications for asylum that were submitted during the same year, which came mainly from Syrians, Iraqis, and Iranians (Trines 2019). This bill introduced so-called integration classes that allow asylum seekers to learn German while their claim is pending (Elrick and Winter 2018). Yet, the Integration Bill introduced a division between genuine refugees and immigrants not deemed to be deserving of integration, by introducing the notion of "Bleibeperspektive," that is, the likelihood of settling in Germany (Hinger 2020, 24). This likelihood is judged via refugees' nationality, with applicants from countries that are classified as safe by the federal government seen as unlikely to stay in Germany permanently (ibid). The bill fast-tracks integration measures for those likely to stay while accelerating deportation for those who are not. In doing so, it constructs refugees whose application for asylum is pending as others who do not yet belong to German society (ibid).

This division of refugees into deserving and undeserving of German protection works hand-in-hand with public attitudes and media representations of immigrants. German newspapers across the political spectrum tend to represent displaced women and children as powerless victims of war and persecution, while young male immigrants are often depicted as agents of violent crime (Vollmer and Karayakali 2018). This categorization of refugees as either "good" or "bad" is connected to a discourse of "humanitarian securitization" which constructs young, male, immigrants as undeserving of protection from European nation-states (ibid). This narrative is connected to the rise of anti-immigration and anti-Muslim attitudes in Germany (Griebel and Vollmer 2019), as seen in the rise of anti-immigration group Patriotic Europeans against the Islamization of the Occident (PEGIDA). Horst Seehofer (CDU), the Minister of the Interior, Construction, and Community under Merkel, asserted in a newspaper interview in 2016 that "Islam does not belong to Germany." But, he claimed, law-abiding Muslims living in Germany do belong (BBC 2018). The heterogeneity of Muslim life in Germany has been lost throughout these debates (Mattes 2018).

IMMIGRATION AND GERMAN TELEVISION FOR CHILDREN

On German television, characters with an immigration background are generally the exception, and if they do appear, they often seem stereotyped (Götz 2010, 16). Television programming across Europe is dominated by white characters with fair skin and of northern European descent (Mlapa 2019). Yet, research has shown that children want to see characters with the same ethnic and cultural background as themselves on the screen (Götz 2010, 19). In particular, young people who feel excluded on the basis of their ethnic or cultural identity prefer television characters and narratives that engage positively with aspects of immigration and ethnic diversity (ibid).

In Germany, television programs for and about children with ethnic minority backgrounds are produced and commissioned exclusively by the public service broadcasters, ARD and ZDF, for their joint children's channel, KiKa (Sakr and Steemers 2019, 108–120). Yet, these programs are often not seen by children who have recently settled in Germany. Young refugees from Syria in Germany mostly watch cartoons shown on commercial TV channels, such as Super-RTL and Disney channel, or transnational TV and online news from the region with their parents (Götz 2017, 53), who want to stay in touch with Arab affairs (Rinnawi 2014, 1455).

Dschermeni and *Berlin und Wir* are two examples of German TV programs that do feature children with an immigration background. *Dschermeni* is a fictional drama series aimed at 8–12-year-olds that follows a multi-cultural, multi-ethnic group of children who live in a small German town. The protagonists are Moritz, a white German-born boy; Yassir, a Syrian boy who fled to Germany with his family; Rüyet, a German-Turkish girl who was born in Germany; and Aminata, a Senegalese girl whose family is applying for asylum in Germany. The producers and writing team, from Tellux Films and Sad Origami, made the program with the aim of explaining the arrival of significant numbers of refugees to German children.

Berlin und Wir is a documentary reality series aimed at 11–15-year-olds, which features four teenagers from Syria, Iraq, and Afghanistan who have recently settled in Berlin, and four Berlin-born white teenagers. The director, and the producers from IMAGO TV, gave the children ideas for activities they could carry out together, but they let the young participants decide how to engage with each other, speak freely on camera, and also communicate off camera. In the first series (2016), which was awarded an international Emmy, the teenagers explore whether they can form friendships despite their different backgrounds.

DIASPORA CHILDHOODS AS MULTI-AXIAL EXPERIENCES

Both *Dschermeni* and *Berlin und Wir* represent children's experiences of forced migration and resettlement in Germany as complex and diverse. The programs evoke Brah's understanding of diaspora as "multi-axial experiences" (1996, 10–11), noted earlier, which defines diasporic experiences as multifaceted and diverse. This concept, in turn, destabilizes historical understandings of diaspora as a homogenous collective unified by a common place of origin (Safran 1991).

On the one hand, *Dschermeni* and *Berlin und Wir* reveal the difficulties that can arise from having to adapt to the social life of a host country following experiences of forced migration. In *Dschermeni*, two of the characters, Yassir and Aminata, have applications for permanent residency in Germany pending. Both live in accommodation designated for refugees, an overcrowded hostel, while grieving the loss of a parent. Aminata's mother disappeared during the journey to Europe, which the family undertook by boat. Haunted by the memories of this experience, she is too scared to go to school in Germany or meet other children. Yassir, meanwhile, longs to return to his mother in Syria, but is unable to do so because of the ongoing civil war. *Berlin und Wir* too evokes the challenges that come with having to integrate into a new society. The show introduces Bayan, a Syrian girl who arrived in Germany five months before the production of *Berlin und Wir* began. She is shown to only speak Arabic—but communicates with other members of the group using body language—and struggles with her accommodation, a sport center that hosts hundreds of other refugees. Both TV programs thus emphasize the economic, social, and psychological hardships of many displaced children who are unable to return to their countries of origin but are simultaneously struggling to join in with the social fabric of Germany.

Berlin und Wir shows, however, that some Syrian teenagers have successfully established a new life in Germany. Rashad, a Syrian girl whose family arrived in Berlin three years ago, enjoys living in Germany for she now lives in a flat, is fluent in German, and goes to school. In this way, *Berlin und Wir* works to nuance German mass media representations that tend to essentialize forcibly displaced children as powerless victims (Vollmer and Griebel 2019). The program depicts refugee children as both victims of conflict and as resourceful agents, emphasizing both the hardships and possibilities that can arise from experiences of dislocation (Demos 2013, 3).

THE POLITICS OF INTEGRATION AND DISINTEGRATION

Dschermeni and *Berlin und Wir* portray the heterogeneity of diasporic communities as intersecting with German integration policies in ways that work to include some while excluding others. Both shows emphasize discrimination against immigrants on the basis of their countries of origin, ethnicity, faith, and gender. First, *Dschermeni*'s plot articulates a critique of German immigration laws. Aminata's and Yassir's applications for asylum in Germany are pending and neither knows whether or not they will be able to stay in Germany permanently. When Yassir's friends try to speed up his application for asylum, by visiting a local office for immigration, they learn that the decisions about people's asylum status are made by a different German authority (episode 4). *Dschermeni* thus alludes to the bureaucratic and lengthy asylum processes in Germany, which leave young asylum applicants in limbo, often for a very long time. *Berlin und Wir*, in turn, explains forced family separations that are common in families whose application for asylum is pending, showing how a Syrian girl has been separated from her mother since she fled to Germany with her father.

Dschermeni also addresses those policies that divide immigrant children and their families into "genuine" and "bogus" refugees, discussed earlier. The viewer learns that Aminata's family has pretended to be from Mali upon arrival in Germany, since Senegal is classified as a safe country under German immigration law and asylum seekers from Senegal are likely refused asylum. Aminata worries about the family being deported, especially since her older brother engages in illegal activities, trying to settle the family's debts with the smugglers who helped them escape Senegal. As the series closes, Aminata's brother is arrested and the family is deported because Senegal does not qualify as unsafe. Toward the series' final scenes, we see a tearful Aminata who is about to board a plane that takes her back to Senegal. In this way, the series critiques the impacts of German disintegration policies on the psychological wellbeing and future lives of children caught up in forced migration.

Furthermore, *Dschermeni* makes a point of highlighting public attitudes on immigration, such as racism and perceptions of Islam, which work to construct children with an immigrant background as outsiders of German society. The series opens with a sequence in which two German boys taunt a Syrian boy after school. In a later scene, the same boys racially insult him, as well as a German-Turkish girl, in the classroom. The program thus highlights racist attitudes against children with an immigration background, even if they and their parents were born in Germany.

Berlin und Wir too addresses some of the prejudices immigrant children are facing. Throughout the series, a white German-born girl voices her dislike of the hijab—or head covering worn by some Muslim women—stating, for example, that she sees wearing a headscarf as a "sign of oppression" (episode 6). Yet, her opinion on the hijab provides a starting point for investigating different viewpoints on Islam faith in *Berlin und Wir*. The program shows the heterogeneity of Muslim communities by contrasting the religious views of two Muslim girls, Bayan and Rashad, who practice their faith differently. Rashad explains that she can only dress modestly and states that she intends to wear the hijab when she is older. Bayan, however, experiments with fashion, make up, and wears short skirts. When prompted, she explains: "I don't define my faith via my clothes but my heart" (episode 3).

Hence, both programs highlight governmental policies and public discourses leading to disintegration, presented from the perspectives of children. This focus on disintegration, in turn, complicates historical concepts of integration as a straightforward path leading to the assimilation of immigrants into the host society. Here, integration is depicted as a convoluted and complex process.

DIASPORA SPACE

Dschermeni and *Berlin und Wir* critique discourses and policies that construct refugees and asylum seekers as the "other" and German-born children as "us." Both programs emphasize the importance of what Brah has termed "diaspora space" (1996, 241–43), which refers to those spaces, encounters, and experiences that are shared by members of diasporic communities and a host society. Brah suggests that the notion of diaspora space works to dissolve the seemingly fixed borders between categories of "foreign" and "native" (Brah 1996, 208–9).

Berlin und Wir depicts a vision of diaspora space as described by Brah. The Berlin-born teenagers are shown to participate in the lives of teenagers who have recently settled in Berlin, including exploring environments and activities unfamiliar to them. For example, when Malina, a white German girl, visits Rashad, whose family is Muslim, at home, Malina's body language signals feeling of unease when listening to the call for prayer from a speaker and watching Rashad pray (episode 2). Rashad, in turn, takes part in Malina's football training session—something she has never done before. Over the course of the program, the teenagers establish friendships by regularly participating in shared activities in Berlin. Hence, the program suggests that children with and without immigration backgrounds have many things in common despite differences in nationality, faith, and ethnicity (Singer, Steemers, and Sakr 2019). In the final episode of series 1, the group makes a music video and the teenagers write common public prejudices and racist insults against immigrants and Germans onto a mock stonewall, which they eventually knock down. *Berlin und Wir* thus concludes with a vision of diaspora space that destabilizes binary categories of diaspora and host society.

Dschermeni, like *Berlin und Wir*, constructs diaspora space—that is, shared experiences among children with and without immigration backgrounds—by portraying friendships that develop between children born in Germany and children recently arrived there. Initially, Yassir and Aminata are depicted as excluded from German society, as they have no German friends and spend most of their time in asylum-seeker accommodation. As the series unfolds, however, they develop friendships with two German-born children by spending time together in a hut by a lake, where they engage in shared activities, such as swimming, playing games, and talking about their problems, families, and interests. The lake emerges as a diaspora space where the cultural and ethnic barriers between German-born children and children with immigration backgrounds gradually dissolve and where friendships develop despite national and cultural differences.

By focusing on friendships between children of different nationalities, *Dschermeni* and *Berlin und Wir* affirm that children who have recently settled in Germany belong to German society just as German-born children do, even if their asylum applications are pending. *Dschermeni* and *Berlin und Wir* put forward a vision of integration that is based on social connections, not on one's place of nationality or legal status.

RETHINKING INTEGRATION

The way *Dschermeni* and *Berlin und Wir* treat diaspora space implies that the integration of children newly arrived in Germany requires efforts on the part of both German-born children and newly arrived children, not just the latter. This narrative contradicts the ideas put forward by Germany's Integration Bill, noted earlier, which tend to place the responsibility for successful integration on immigrants (Hinger 2020). In *Dschermeni* and *Berlin und Wir*, both immigrant communities and host communities adapt to each other and create an intercultural basis for mutual adaptation. This implies a multidirectional approach toward integration rather than a linear one.

Some narratives in *Dschermeni* and *Berlin und Wir* challenge the concept of integration as a whole by alluding to Germany's history of immigration. In *Dschermeni*, this history is embodied by Rüyet, a Turkish-German girl born to Turkish-German parents. Rüyet's family background reminds young viewers that immigration and the formation of diaspora communities are not recent phenomena in Germany but are part of the country's history. This discourse challenges traditional theories of integration, which put forward the idea of an ethnically and culturally homogenous host society to which immigrants must adapt. *Dschermeni*'s construction of the German host society as heterogeneous is also underlined by a storyline that focuses on Rüyet's brother, who comes out as gay. While Rüyet accepts her brother's homosexuality, the rest of her family initially rejects it, suggesting that there are multiple viewpoints and values within a given host society. This storyline evokes once again Brah's argument that diasporic communities constitute "cartographies of intersectionality," which are differentiated along the lines of gender, sexual orientation, and cultural customs.

Furthermore, *Dschermeni* proposes that German children with an immigrant background can be connected to different countries, traditions, and languages. The television program addresses the so-called "double frame" of immigration (Bhabha 1996), that is, the "bicultural knowledge" (Demos 2010, 3) that can arise from living in a culture different to one's own. As the drama series develops, Yassir no longer wants to return to Syria because he has made friends in Germany. In episode 4, the camera frames him as he writes two letters to his mother in Syria—one in German and one in Arabic—in which he explains to her that he was initially homesick but has now made friends in Germany and feels happy. Hence, Germany has become Yassir's new home, but he remains connected to his family and culture in Syria. The experience of being connected to different countries and traditions is also affirmed in *Berlin und Wir*, where Rashad goes to school in Germany and is fluent in German, while she embraces the faith and cultural customs of her Syrian family. Hence, both programs challenge concepts of integration which stipulate that immigrants ought to adapt to the host society, suggesting instead that children's experiences of dislocation and resettlement are characterized by multiple forms of belonging.

Rüyet, in *Dschermeni*, also embodies this "bicultural knowledge" that characterizes children born to an immigrant family, for she is depicted as both rooted within Turkish and majority German norms and is, sometimes, torn between the two. She speaks German with her friends and at school and speaks German and Turkish at home. She wears Western clothing, does not wear the hijab, and has both German-born and non-German-born friends. However, she is shown to clash with her grandfather who complains that his daughter-in-law raises her children "too German," meaning too liberal. For example, the grandfather exclaims, in episode 1, that Rüyet is "not a Turkish girl" and tells her: "You're too German for the Turkish and too Turkish for the Germans." Hence, *Dschermeni* reveals the difficulty of determining where integration begins and where it ends when growing up in-between different cultural traditions.

CONCLUSION

Berlin und Wir and *Dschermeni* address the lack of ethnic diversity within German children's television content by featuring a multi-ethnic, culturally diverse cast of German-born children and children recently arrived in Germany. The TV programs share a focus on the heterogeneity of diasporas and refugees from the Arab region, and elsewhere, by highlighting the "multi-axial" (Brah 1996) experiences of recently displaced children. By depicting both the struggles and the opportunities that come with having to settle in a new society, the programs construct forcibly displaced children not simply as powerless victims—a prominent discourse with the German news media—but as both victims of conflict and as resourceful agents. Taken together, *Dschermeni* and *Berlin und Wir* affirm the diversity of diaspora childhoods and the social and cultural transformations that influence diasporas and host societies (see Rastas 2020, 625).

The programs' engagement with the multi-axial character of diasporas, in turn, shows that the integration of forcibly displaced children in Germany is a complex process that intersects with governmental policies, religious identities, social status, gender, ethnicity, and educational achievements. *Berlin und Wir* and *Dschermeni* offer a form of political education for German children, since they introduce young viewers to a critique of German integration policies, presented through the eyes of children. *Dschermeni*, in particular, addresses the ways in which German asylum policies classify immigrants according to their country of origin and construct asylum seekers with uncertain residency status as not yet part of German society. The programs highlight children's personal experiences of policies that work to disintegrate some people while reserving integration for others.

In the way the programs deal with "diaspora space" (Brah 1996), they suggest that recently arrived children, including children from the Arab region, have a lot of things in common with German-born children, and therefore belong to German society just as German-born children do. This focus on friendships between children from different origins destabilizes representations of diasporas and refugees as the other, put forward by German political parties on the right, which argue that people with immigration histories pose a threat to their idea of a supposedly homogeneous, white German society.

The idea of a homogenous host society is further contested by storylines that suggest that it is virtually impossible to pinpoint where integration begins and where it ends, because some children with a family history of immigration can feel aligned to both German society and their parents' country of origin. *Berlin und Wir* and *Dschermeni* thus raise questions about the future relevance of the concept of integration in grasping the complex experiences of children with a family history of immigration. Chancellor Merkel herself has recently admitted that integration is a problematic concept, when she noted that black Germans continue to be asked "where they are from," even those who are from third or fourth generation immigrant families (Seibert 2020).

Finally, *Dschermeni*'s and *Berlin und Wir*'s emphasis on diaspora space can be said to redefine integration as a fluid concept that is determined not only by someone's legal or economic status but primarily by the ability to feel "at home" and to participate in the social fabric of a society. Both programs construct integration as an open-ended process, rather than a predictable or linear one, whereby both diasporic communities and host society are expected to adapt to each other and create a new, intercultural basis for mutual identification and solidarity.

NOTES

1. A refugee is someone who has been recognized under the United Nations' 1951 Refugee Convention as "someone who is unable or unwilling to return to their country of origin owing to a well-founded fear of being persecuted for reasons of race, religion, nationality, membership of a particular social group, or political opinion" (UNCRC n.d., "What is a Refugee?"). An asylum seeker is someone who is seeking international protection but whose claim for refugee status has not yet been determined (UNCRC, n.d., "Asylum Seekers").

2. The project "Collaborative Development of Children's Screen Content in an Era of Forced Migration Flows: Facilitating Arab-European Dialogue" (2017–18) was funded by the UK's Arts and Humanities Research Council (AHRC), Grant Ref AH/R001421/1.

3. Unicef (2019) defines refugee and migrant children as children below the age of 18 years.

The Arts and Humanities Research Council (Grant No. AH/R001421/1) supported the research in this article.

REFERENCES

BBC. 2018. "Islam Does Not Belong to Germany." *BBC News*, March 16, 2018. https://www.bbc.com/news/world-europe-43422770.

Bhabha, Homi K. 1996. "Unsatisfied: Notes on Vernacular Cosmopolitanism." In *Text and Nation: Cross-Disciplinary Essays on Cultural and National Identities*, edited by Laura Garcia-Moreno and Peter C. Pfeiffer. Columbia, SC: Camden House.

Brah, A. 1996. *Cartographies of Diaspora: Contesting Identities*. London: Routledge.

Bundesamt für Migration und Flüchtlinge. 2020. "Aktuelle Zahlen (03/2020)." Bundesamt für Migration und Flüchtlinge. https://www.BAMF.de/SharedDocs/Anlagen/DE/Statistik/AsylinZahlen/aktuelle-zahlen-maerz-2020.html?nn=284722.

"Children's Screen Content in an Era of Forced Migration: Facilitating Arab-European Dialogue – A Project Funded by the AHRC." n.d. Accessed May 28, 2020. https://www.kcl.ac.uk/research/euroarabchildrensmedia.

Collyer, Michael, Sophie Hinger, and Reinhard Schweitzer. 2020. "Politics of (Dis) Integration – An Introduction." In *Politics of (Dis) Integration*, edited by Sophie Hinger and Reinhard Schweitzer, 1–18. IMISCOE Research Series. Cham: Springer International Publishing. https://doi.org/10.1007/978-3-030-25089-8_1.

Demos, T. J. 2013. *The Migrant Image: The Art and Politics of Documentary During Global Crisis*. Durham ; London: Duke University Press Books.

Elrick, Jennifer, and Elke Winter. 2018. "Managing the National Status Group: Immigration Policy in Germany." *International Migration* 56 (4): 19–32. https://doi.org/10.1111/imig.12400.

Feldmeyer, Ben. 2018. *The Classical Assimilation Model*. Routledge Handbooks Online. https://doi.org/10.4324/9781317211563-4.

Garcés-Mascarenas, Bianca, and Rinus Penninx. 2016. "Introduction: Integration as a Three-Way Process Approach?" In *Integration Processes and Policies in Europe*, edited by Bianca Garcés-Mascarenas and Rinus Penninx, 1–18. IMISCOE Research Series. Springer. http://dx.doi.org/10.1007/978-3-319-21674-4_2.

Gholami, Reza, and Annabelle Sreberny. 2019. "Integration, Class and Secularism: The Marginalization of Shia Identities in the UK Iranian Diaspora." *Contemporary Islam* 13 (3): 243–58. https://doi.org/10.1007/s11562-018-0429-7.

Götz, Maya. 2010. "Black, White, or Turkish?" *Televizion* 23: 16–19.

Götz, Maya, Melanie Baxter, and Anne Pütz. 2017. "Settled in Germany?" *Televizion* 30: 50–54.

Gozdziak, Elzbieta M. 2005. "New Immigrant Communities and Integration." In *Beyond the Gateway: Immigrants in a Changing America*, edited by Elzbieta M. Gozdziak and Susan Forbes Martin, 3–17. Lanham: Lexington Books.

Griebel, Tim, and Erik Vollmann. 2019. "We Can('t) Do This: A Corpus-Assisted Critical Discourse Analysis of Migration in Germany." *Journal of Language and Politics* 18 (5): 671–697. https://doi.org/10.1075/jlp.19006.gri.

Hacket, George. n.d. "5 Facts about the Muslim Population in Europe". *Pew Research Center*. Accessed March 11, 2020. https://www.pewresearch.org/fact-tank/2017/11/29/5-facts-about-the-muslim-population-in-europe/.

Hellgren, Zenia. 2015. "Immigrant Integration as a Two-Way Process: Translating Theory into Practice." *Interdisciplinary Research Group on Immigration: Working Paper Series* 23: 30.

Hinger, Sophie. 2020. "Integration Through Disintegration? The Distinction Between Deserving and Undeserving Refugees in National and Local Integration Policies in Germany." In *Politics of (Dis)Integration*, edited by Sophie Hinger and Reinhard Schweitzer, 19–39. IMISCOE Research Series. Cham: Springer International Publishing. https://doi.org/10.1007/978-3-030-25089-8_2.

Kagermeier, Andreas. 2004. "Marokkanische Migration Nach Deutschland: Charakteristika Und Perspektiven." In *Die Arabische Welt Im Spiegel Der Kulturgeographie*, 442–447. Mainz: Zentrum für Forschung zur Arabischen Welt.

Klusmeyer, Douglas B. 1993. "Aliens, Immigrants, and Citizens: The Politics of Inclusion in the Federal Republic of Germany." *Daedalus* 122 (3): 81–114.

Leise, Eric. 2007. "Germany to Regularize 'Tolerated' Asylum Seekers." Migration Policy. April 5, 2007. https://www.migrationpolicy.org/article/germany-regularize-tolerated-asylum-seekers.

Mattes, Astrid. 2018. "How Religion Came into Play: 'Muslim' as a Category of Practice in Immigrant Integration Debates." *Religion, State and Society* 46 (3): 186–205. https://doi.org/10.1080/09637494.2018.1474031.

Mlapa, Manda. 2019. "Children's Television Is Primarily White." *Television* 32: 2, 18–19.

Murray, John S. 2016. "Meeting the Psychosocial Needs of Child Refugees During Resettlement in Germany." *Issues in Mental Health Nursing* 37 (8): 613–618. https://doi.org/10.1080/01612840.2016.1175039.

Nötzold, Katharina, and Sirin Dilli. 2009. "Media and Migration in Germany." In *Media and Cultural Diversity in Europe and North America*, edited by Claire Frachon and Virginie Sassoon, 86–101. Paris: Institut Panos and KARTHALA Editions.

Oltmer, Vera, and Jochen Hanewinkel. n.d. "Integration and Integration Policies in Germany." Bundeszentrale für Politische Bildung. Accessed April 9, 2020. https://www.bpb.de/gesellschaft/migration/laenderprofile/262812/integration-and-integration-policies-in-germany.

Pautz, Hartwig. 2016. "The Politics of Identity in Germany: The Leitkultur Debate:" *Race & Class*, June. https://doi.org/10.1177/0306396805052517.

Rinnawi, Khalil. 2012. "'Instant Nationalism' and the 'Cyber Mufti': The Arab Diaspora in Europe and the Transnational Media." *Journal of Ethnic and Migration Studies* 38 (9): 1451–1467. https://doi.org/10.1080/1369183X.2012.698215.

Safran, William. 1991. "Diasporas in Modern Societies: Myths of Homeland and Return." *Diaspora: A Journal of Transnational Studies* 1 (1): 83–99. https://doi.org/10.1353/dsp.1991.0004.

Sakr, Naomi, and Jeanette Steemers. 2017. *Children's TV and Digital Media in the Arab World: Childhood, Screen Culture and Education*. London and New York: I.B.Tauris.

Sakr, Naomi, and Jeanette Steemers. 2019. *Screen Media for Arab and European Children: Policy and Production Encounters in the Multiplatform Era*. Basingstoke: Palgrave Pivot. https://doi.org/10.1007/978-3-030-25658-6.

Schneider, Jens, and Maurice Crul. 2010. "New Insights into Assimilation and Integration Theory: Introduction to the Special Issue." *Ethnic and Racial Studies* 33 (7): 1143–48. https://doi.org/10.1080/01419871003777809.

Seibert, Steffen. 2020. "Wie Lange Muss Sich Eigentlich Jemand Fragen Lassen, Ob Er Oder Sie Integriert Sei?" Twitter. March 2, 2020. https://twitter.com/RegSprecher/status/1234521286958821377.

Singer, Christine, Jeanette Steemers, and Naomi Sakr. 2019. "Representing Childhood and Forced Migration: Narratives of Borders and Belonging in European Screen Content for Children." *Jeunesse: Young People, Texts, Cultures* 11 (2): 202–24. https://doi.org/10.1353/jeu.2019.0023.

Steemers, Jeanette, Naomi Sakr, and Christine Singer. 2018. "Children's Screen Content in an Era of Forced Migration: Consolidated Report on an AHRC Project for Impact and Engagement." London: King's College London. https://kclpure.kcl.ac.uk/portal/files/102210294/Consolidated_Report_FinalSV_221018.pdf.

Täubig, Vicki. 2009. *Totale Institution Asyl: Empirische Befunde zu Alltäglichen Lebensführungen in der Organisierten Desintegration*. Weinheim: Juventa.

Trines, Stefan. 2017. "Lessons from Germany's Refugee Crisis: Integration, Costs, and Benefits." World Education News and Reviews. May 2, 2017. https://wenr.wes.org/2017/05/lessons-germanys-refugee-crisis-integration-costs-benefits.

Unicef. 2019. "Latest Statistics and Graphics on Refugee and Migrant Children." Unicef. 2019. https://www.unicef.org/eca/emergencies/latest-statistics-and-graphics-refugee-and-migrant-children.

United Nations High Commissioner for Refugees. n.d. "Asylum-Seekers." UNHCR. Accessed April 10, 2020a. https://www.unhcr.org/asylum-seekers.html.

———. n.d. "What Is a Refugee?" UNHCR. Accessed April 10, 2020b. https://www.unhcr.org/what-is-a-refugee.html.

Vollmer, Bastian, and Serhat Karakayali. 2018. "The Volatility of the Discourse on Refugees in Germany." *Journal of Immigrant & Refugee Studies* 16 (1–2): 118–139. https://doi.org/10.1080/15562948.2017.1288284.

Wieviorka, Michel. 2014. "A Critique of Integration." *Identities* 21 (6): 633–641. https://doi.org/10.1080/1070289X.2013.828615.

Worbs, Susanne, Nina Rother, and Axel Kreienbrink. 2020. "Demographic Profile of Syrians in Germany and Aspects of Integration." In *Comparative Demography of the Syrian Diaspora: European and Middle Eastern Destinations*, edited by Elwood D. Carlson and Nathalie E. Williams, 197–235. European Studies of Population. Cham: Springer International Publishing. https://doi.org/10.1007/978-3-030-24451-4_9.

Chapter 7

Maghrebis in France

From "Arab Immigrants" to "Muslims"

Imène Ajala

The Maghrebi diaspora in France includes primo-migrants from Algeria, Tunisia and Morocco, and their descendants. Algeria and Morocco are the main countries of origin representing, respectively, 31 percent and 20 percent of Muslims in France, while Tunisian origin accounts for 8 percent (Institut Montaigne 2016, 15). Bernard Godard and Sylvie Taussig's estimates in absolute numbers show the following repartition: 1.5 million Algerians, 1 million Moroccans, and more than 400,000 Tunisians (Godard & Taussig 2007, 454).

The Maghrebi diaspora as an ethnic minority is based on four factors of unity: geographical, historical, demographic, and sociological. The geographical unity stems from the situation of Morocco, Algeria, and Tunisia in the North of the African continent. The historical unity refers to their past as former territories of French colonialism. Immigration from Algeria is more ancient than immigration from Morocco due to the different status of the Algerian territory under French colonial rule, considered as administrative units (*départements*) until Algeria's independence in 1962 (Bidet and Wagner 2012). On the contrary, Moroccan immigrants resulted from recruitments carried out by French companies in need of workforce (Bidet and Wagner 2012). Immigration from Tunisia was also close in type to the Moroccan labor migration. The demographic unity precisely refers to the Maghrebi migration status, representing first a labor migration before turning into permanent migration. Finally, the sociological unity is to be found in the economic and social exclusion affecting a majority of the migrants from the Maghreb and their descendants (Bidet and Wagner 2012; Institut Montaigne 2016).

Despite these unities, there are a number of lenses through which the Maghrebi diaspora has been apprehended. Identity is multi-layered and some referents become more relevant than others for self-identification and mobilization as a community. This chapter thus explores the shift in the mobilization and perception of French Maghrebis from Arab immigrants to Muslims while questioning the reality of this latter label in terms of religiosity and the political responses it has entailed. Religion has indeed increasingly become a marker of identity and the principle around which attempts of mobilization have taken place.

The first section retraces the concerns and perceptions of Maghrebis as Arab immigrants. Then, the second section analyzes the emergence of the Muslim label through which Maghrebis have started identifying themselves and through which they have become more and more perceived and depicted. The third section deconstructs the realities of the Muslim label in terms of religiosity thanks to a range of national polls and surveys. Finally, the last section examines the governmental perspective on Maghrebis as Muslims and the top-down attempts at domesticating Islam in France.

MAGHREBIS AS ARAB IMMIGRANTS

French Maghrebis constitute a postcolonial minority. After World War II, the need for labor drove immigration from North Africa. A turning point occurred in 1974, when the oil crisis led to the suspension of immigration through administrative bills leading to a drop, more restrictions and more importantly, to a conceptual shift as "the economic crisis made it possible for considerations of identity and integration to gain ascendance over a need for labor" (Schain 2008, 60). The consecration of the right to family reunification in the governmental decree of April 29, 1976 also contributed to the emergence of integration issues. Indeed, immigrant workers, who were initially supposed to go back to their home countries, turned into permanent settlers, bringing along their families. Attempts to encourage immigrants' return, starting with Algerians, failed (Institut Montaigne 2016, 34). The project of returning to one's homeland after sufficient savings thus turned into a myth. Still, this myth of return was expressed through an attachment to the homeland materialized by remittances, periodical returns for holidays, and economic investments, for instance in real estate (Bidet and Wagner 2012).

The first waves of primo-migrants from North Africa were not perceived according to their alleged religion but through the ethnic or nationality lens. Thus, North-African immigrants were perceived as "Arabs" and primarily as workers. As a result, from the 1950s to the 1970s, the primary concerns of Arab immigrants mostly related to residency rights (Geisser & Kelfaoui 2001: Laurence & Vaïsse 2006, 6: Institut Montaigne 2016). The names of the movements emerging during that period are in fact explicit. The Movement of Arab Workers, for instance, created in 1972 or the Association of Maghrebi

Workers born in 1982 (from the previous Association of Moroccan workers which emerged in 1961) include ethnicity as the variable of identification. The term "workers" refers indeed to the socio-economic identification and reflects the agenda of these organizations focused on the struggle for workers' rights. This agenda included contesting the exclusion of undocumented migrants, asking for work permits, organizing strikes, demanding better wages and working conditions, and fighting against discrimination and racism (Aissaoui 2006). Therefore, the history of North-African immigrants was first intimately related to the history of workers (Green 2002) and the class lens was crucial.

The mobilization shifted from the emphasis on working conditions to identity issues as new generations born in France, claiming their Frenchness contrary to their parents attached to a mythical return to the homeland, started to be more visible (Samers 2003, 355). At the national level, the Left paved the way for the creation of ethnic organizations, after a law was passed in October 1981 abrogating the necessity for foreigners' associations to have an authorization from the Ministry of Interior. This facilitated the emergence of youth movements denouncing racial discrimination, calling for a better integration and acting as mediators (Schain 2008, 107). In 1983, the March for Equality and Against Racism represented a symbol in this regard (Samers 2003, 355; Fondation Jean Jaurès 2019). The narratives claiming civic rights and anti-discrimination were based on a discourse mobilizing Republican values to argue in favor of a "right to be different" (Samers 2003, 355). Traditional agents of integration, such as trade unions, were actually losing influence (Schain 20008, 83). As a result, associations established themselves as mediators between immigrant populations and other social and political actors and emerged as ethnic lobbies mobilizing on the basis of national origin or religion (Schain 2008, 107). Moreover, as integration issues grew heavier with periodic urban riots, the involvement of the state agencies grew as well, creating the need for ethnic interlocutors (Schain 2008, 81).

To conclude, whether it concerned working rights for primo-migrants in the first stage or an anti-discrimination and anti-racism agenda in the second stage with the shift to permanent migration and the emergence of second generations, religion was still confined to the private sphere, as it was for labor primo-migrants (Samers 2003, 355). Maghrebis were Arab workers, North Africans or Arabs. How did they become Muslims?

MAGHREBIS AS MUSLIMS

At the end of the 1980s and early 1990s, a shift emerged whereby the religious referent became the lens through which immigrants and the second generations were perceived (Silvestri 2007), supplanting integrationist claims based on secular narratives such as the right to difference promoted during the 1983 during the March for Equality. In other words, there was a "transformation of the 'Arab immigration problem' into a 'Muslim problem'" (Bayrakli, Hafez and Faytre 2019, 145). The "Muslim citizen" claiming for the right to a Muslim identity and its expression emerged as the new archetype (Geisser & Kelfaoui 2001: Laurence & Vaïsse 2006, 6: Institut Montaigne 2016).

The growing visibility of Islam on the international scene in the 2000s is considered as the time of a "religious and identity-based awakening in the whole Muslim world" (IFOP 2019), but this Islamic revival had already started in the 1970s and the 1980s. This revival was characterized by several international events and phenomena with a deep impact on the political landscape of the Middle East and North Africa but also on Islam in the West: they include for instance the Iranian Revolution of 1979, the emergence of Islamism, the Algerian Civil War, and the Gulf War (Blanchard 2016). In Europe, events, such as the Salman Rushdie Affair, stirred Muslims' mobilization. In France, the first "Headscarf Affair" in Creil, when three female students were expelled from secondary school (France 24), ostensibly symbolized the challenge to secularism and revealed how French authorities were poorly equipped to deal with Islam as a referent for a minority (Samers 2003, 357).

This international context placed Global Islam on the international scene, and with it, the associated idea of a global ummah, in other words, the "global community of the faithful," which includes all Muslims, plugged into transnationalism (Salvatore 2004, 1015: Silvestri 2007, 169: Césari 2009). While primo-migrants have been dreaming of returning to their homeland countries, generations born in France could not indulge into the myth of returning to a country they barely knew. However, at the same time, their foreign origins always seemed to inspire "otherness" in the French context. Consequently, the ummah became a focal point for feelings of belonging which took the form of a growing distance from North-African countries in favor of a transnational mode of identification instead (Leveau 2004). While the primo-migrants continued showing attachment to their country of origin in the context of the myth of return, generations born in France have progressively detached themselves from the homeland link in favor of a Muslim self-identification to the global ummah (Salvatore 2004, 1015: Silvestri 2007, 169: Césari 2009). Though 77 percent of the French with immigrant origins declared themselves as very or quite close to inhabitants of the homeland for example (Brouard & Tiberj 2006a, 122), there seems to be a generational divide where 43 percent of second-generation Muslims (born in France) declared themselves as "not really close" or "not close at all" to the people of the homeland (Brouard & Tiberj 2006a, 123).

Brouard and Tiberj also note in their study that "French Muslims' closeness to French citizens prevails" as "less than 30 percent of people from African or Turkish immigration declared a higher closeness to people of the family homeland(s) than to French people in general" (Brouard & Tiberj 2006a, 125). This also impacted modes of mobilization. For instance, while primo-migrants built associations constructed on the basis of national or regional origins and close to (or on the contrary, built in opposition to) homeland countries, second- and third-generations have preferred independent networks (Frégossi 2009, 45). In other words, there has been a deterritorialization of the identity of origin in favor of a more abstract, but also more religious sense of identity. This is particularly enhanced by the internet and the social media revolution favoring the emergence of digital transnational communities.

Indeed, the move from immigrants to long-term residents and then citizens has resulted in growing and diversified forms of mobilization (Silvestri 2007). Frégossi distinguishes three forms of mobilization for European Islam: religious, socio-political, and identity-based (Frégossi 2009, 42). Religious mobilization puts forward Islam as faith and practice with an emphasis on its ritual dimension, through the mosque, for instance (Frégossi 2009, 42). It can be structured around the cult and, in that case, includes a process of national institutionalization to establish legitimacy vis-à-vis public authorities and be on an equal footing with other religions' national representations (Kastoryano 2006; Frégossi 2009, 42). Otherwise, it can be structured around spirituality with groups upholding their interpretations of religion through different expressions, such as the Salafis, engaging in a counter-society and denouncing all other expressions of Islam or orthodox reformists, such as the European Council of Fatwa and Research aiming at creating an Islamic jurisprudence adapted to Muslim minorities living in secular countries (Frégossi 2009, 45). Religious mobilization can also be based around associations. The goal is then to defend a particular vision of Islam and its dogmatic, spiritual, and cultural content in order to favor the emergence of Islamic awareness in the community (Frégossi 2009, 44).

Socio-political mobilization highlights the idea that the Islamic faith involves an ethical perspective encouraging an active contribution to society as a whole which is not limited to fighting for Muslims' rights. The pillars of the Muslim socio-political mobilization are the contestations against assimilation and liberal globalization (Frégossi 2009, 51). Younger generations are the most active in this type of mobilization whereby they can show that their religious identity is not separate from but rather is attached to their citizenship. Nonetheless, this type of contestation is not necessarily peaceful. Terrorist cells affiliated to Al-Qaeda and the so-called Islamic State are a case in point. The rise of fundamentalism internationally has also affected

Maghrebis in France in the context of economic, political, and social vulnerability (Institut Montaigne 2016, 31).

In identity-based mobilization, Islam serves more as a cultural rather than as a religious reference. In the French context, this refers to as secular mobilization that condemns any official acknowledgment of Muslim particularism in the name of universal citizenship and denounces the French Council of the Muslim Faith (CFCM) as a neo-colonial instrument (Frégossi 2009, 53–4).

To conclude, the Muslim label has replaced the ethnic or homeland nationality label in the international context of an Islamic revival. Coupled with the common experiences of economic and social marginalization characterizing Arabs in France, the feeling of belonging to the ummah led to a growing number of Muslims openly identifying themselves as believers and increased identity assertiveness in younger generations (Dargent 2003, 19: Laurence & Vaïsse 2006, 82: Godard & Taussig 2007, 29; Institut Montaigne 2016). However, does applying the Muslim narrative to the whole Maghrebi community reflect the level of religiosity that such a label could imply? This is what the next section investigates.

A FRAGMENTED PICTURE OF RELIGIOSITY

The uniform label of Muslims to designate Maghrebis in France could theoretically lead to the assumptions of a homogeneous pattern in terms of religiosity. However, the strong individualization of practices, especially with second-generation Muslims born in France (Roy, 2004: Salvatore 2004, 1021: Césari 2009, 153) makes the growing religious self-identification and reaffirmation of Muslim identity depicted in the previous section very plural and very relative. As an example, the results of the survey carried out by Institut Montaigne confirm the diversity of religious views and practices and reveal that French Muslims who adhere to a strict view of religion only constitute about 15 percent of all French Muslims, including non-Maghrebi communities (Institut Montaigne 2016, 18). The five prayers every day and the attendance to the mosque are the usual criteria to distinguish practicing believers from non-practicing believers (IFOP 2008, 10). Three categories stand out. First, secularized individuals, some of who renounced their religion and where people belonging to higher-echelons of society are overrepresented, represent 46 percent of French Muslims (Institut Montaigne 2016, 18). Second, people with ambivalent views in favor of a strong expression of religiosity but who still accept secularism (condemning the niqab and polygamy for instance) represent 25 percent (Institut Montaigne 2016, 18). Finally, the most *problematic* group made of Muslims who are in a position of rejection vis-à-vis the French state with an overrepresentation of young, low-skilled, and unemployed people, counting for 26 percent of Muslims in France (Institut Montaigne 2016, 18). Precisely, about 27 percent of French Muslims believe sharia laws should prevail over Republican laws, with differences according to the time spent in France. This figure reaches 18 percent for interviewees born in France but 41 percent for new immigrants who recently arrived (Fondation Jean Jaurès 2019, 55–56). When considering people between 18 and 50 years old who grew up in a Muslim household, beyond Maghrebis, 28 percent are engaged in a dynamic of secularization compared to their parents, 57 percent experience religiosity similar to their parents while 15 percent develop a greater religiosity than their parents, leaving Simon and Tiberj (2008, 5) to conclude that the dynamic of religious reinforcement characterize Muslims, contrary to waves of secularization impacting the general population. This is confirmed by the study of Institut Montaigne noting that the group "most far-removed from religion has few members among the new generations" (Institut Montaigne 2016, 17).

Another significant factor is the economic and social class. French Muslims enjoying a higher socio-economic status are overrepresented in the first group and underrepresented in the last group, suggesting that the most integrated people at the economic level are the most likely to stay away from radical approaches of religion (Institut Montaigne 2016, 20). Religious practice is also intertwined with the homeland link. It thus declines with the time spent in France (Godard & Taussig 2007, 29). People declaring themselves without religion are also the least connected to the country of origin.

Besides, some results are surprising and suggest than Islam seems to be used as a foundation for rebellious views rather than as a source of spiritual attachment leading to a strict religious practice (Institut Montaigne 2016, 21). This rebellion is expressed in a context of tensions in the debate on the integration of Maghrebis now claiming their religiosity. The dominant perception of Islam in France concerns indeed its assumed incompatibility with a successful integration into French society. As do most Europeans, the French believe removing public signs of religiosity is necessary for integration (Gallup 2009, 21). In fact, only 32 percent of French people think Muslims are well-integrated into society (IFOP 2016). It thus seems one cannot be French and Muslim at the same time, and the two identities are seen as incompatible. In fact, 61 percent of French people believe that Islam is not compatible with the values of the French society and 78 percent think that French secularism is in danger (Europe 1).[1] Adida, Laitin, and Valfort partly attribute the failure of Muslims' integration to a prevalent anti-Islam sentiment (Adida, Laitin & Valfort 2016). As an example, the visibility of Islam through the Islamic veil or the construction of mosques triggers negative responses (63% of French people think Islam is too influential and too visible and 52% oppose the construction of mosques). Other indicators about the visible signs of Islam confirm this trend: 63 percent of French people oppose the wearing of the veil in the public space, 88 percent oppose it in public schools, and 77 percent are hostile to the existence of political parties or trade unions referring to Islam (IFOP 2016). Indeed, the French philosophy of integration based on assimilation rejects any recognition of groups on an ethnic, cultural, or religious basis (Bertossi 2007, 8). Moreover, the centralized and secular fabric of the institutional landscape resting on the 1905 Law strictly separating the state and religion are not favorable to the expression of minority politics, especially religious (Poutignat & Streiff-Fenart 1995, 9: Bertossi 2007, 8: Statham and Tillie 2016, 180).

Islam then becomes a tool of contestation in the context of a "denial of Frenchness" felt by young Maghrebis (Institut Montaigne 2016, 31). The common experiences of racism, discrimination, and deprivation partially explains this re-islamization process, whereby young people are in search for an identity beyond the "family Islam" of their parents (Laurence & Vaïsse 2006, 90). However, religious identity as such is not necessarily more pronounced: rather, it refers to cultural and religious traditions (Laurence & Vaïsse 2006, 87). Affiliation to Islam is thus more symbolic than political (Ayhan 2006, 11) and contributes to give a statement about identity. For instance, 60 percent of Muslims have a distant or non-existent relationship with the mosque and over 40 percent of Muslims think that eating halal is one of the five pillars of Islam, which is not the case (Institut Montaigne 2016, 22–25). Other indicators point to cultural more than religious behavior, such as fasting (Ramadan), and the non-consumption of alcohol which constitute the most shared practices (IFOP 2008). The conformity to halal food also stands out as a common practice as 57 percent of French Muslims only eat halal sweets and 48 percent claim checking the composition of the food they buy to check there is no pork or animal gelatin (Fondation Jean Jaurès 2019, 20). The wearing of the veil, despite its disproportionate coverage in the media, is a minority practice that essentially concerns practicing believers (IFOP 2009). Therefore, these indicators confirm again tailored practices of religiosity (Roy 2002: Godard & Taussig 2007, 220: Institut Montaigne 2016).

Having said that, other indicators clearly show the importance of the religious norms and paint a more complex picture. Though the majority of French Muslims (70 percent) state that they are able to practice their religion freely in France, other figures reveal specific demands to adjust the secular framework: as an example, 37 percent of French Muslims believe the secular framework should adapt itself to Muslim practice while 41 percent believe the opposite (Fondation Jean Jaurès 2019, 34). Moreover, 59 percent oppose the law forbidding the niqab in public spaces that was passed in 2010 while they were only 33 percent in 2011 to express this was a bad thing (Fondation

Jean Jaurès 2019, 31). Furthermore, approximately 68 percent of French Muslims think girls should be able to wear their veil at school (Fondation Jean Jaurès 2019, 57). With regard to work, 49 percent believe that employers should adapt to their employees' religious obligations (Fondation Jean Jaurès 2019, 57).

Finally, what stands out is a mosaic of different practices, all approached via the single and simplifying term of Muslims. Governmental initiatives to capture this single community contributed further to reinforce the use of the Muslim label to approach the Maghrebi diaspora.

A CONTESTED AND WEAK INSTITUTIONALIZATION

While the Maghrebis have mobilized around nationality, ethnicity, and then religion, with grassroots initiatives, top-down attempts at homogenizing Muslims as a single community progressively emerged in the context of this transformation. The state-driven creation of Muslim councils fitting the pattern of religion–state relations for purposes of "domestication" and establishment of a "moderate" Islam are not specific to France (Silvestri 2007; Bayrakli, Hafez and Faytre 2019). Mostly driven by security concerns related to radicalization, this type of process aims, from the part of governments, to establish community leaders serving as interlocutors: The problem is such agenda often results into artificial bodies that seldom reflect the plurality of the different Muslim sensitivities and often experience acute crises of legitimacy (Silvestri 2007: Frégossi 2009, 44; Savage 2004, 41: Bayrakli, Hafez and Faytre 2019).

French Islam is mainly organized at the local level (Godard & Taussig 2007, 40: Institut Montaigne 2016, 68) with 2,450 mosques counted in 2015 (Institut Montaigne 2016, 69). From 1960 until 1989, the management of Islam related issues by countries of origin, or "Consular Islam," was prevalent (Institut Montaigne 2016, 56; Alouane 2019; Bayrakli, Hafez and Faytre 2019). Historically, French secularism and the belief that these migrants perceived as temporary workers would return to their homelands encouraged French authorities to delegate all issues related to Islam to foreign regimes; this was especially done through consulates and embassies (Samers 2003, 355; Laurence & Vaïsse 2006, 113: Zehgal 2005, 4). A paradigm shift questioning these foreign financial and ideological influences progressively emerged, forced by integration challenges but most importantly, the emergence of Islamic radicalism and security threats (Laurence & Vaïsse 2006, 138). From the 1990s onward, an era of crisis opened for Consular Islam with the emergence of new generations born in France and detached from these foreign forms of Islam (Institut Montaigne 2016, 33).

The first step of this plan to establish a domesticated and moderate French Islam was the creation of a Council for Deliberation (CORIF) in 1990 under the then Minister of Interior Pierre Joxe. This set in motion consultations resulting in the establishment of a framework of agreement, whereby French Islam reaffirmed loyalty to the Republic and establishing the voting procedures and status of the French Council of the Muslim Faith (CFCM) (Laurence & Vaïsse 2006, 148: Zehgal 2005, 6; Bayrakli, Hafez and Faytre 2019). On December 9, 2002, the three big federations (Great Mosque of Paris) (GMP),[2] Union of Islamic Organizations in France (UOIF),[3] and the National Federation of Muslims in France (FMNF)[4] signed an agreement on the composition of the CFCM (Zehgal 2005, 9). The first CFCM was elected in April 2003 (Laurence & Vaïsse 2006, 149) and comprised regional councils dealing with religious issues so as to represent Islam as a cult, not Muslims, thus discarding any lobbying ambition (Institut Montaigne 2016, 64). In 2012, a restructuring of the institution took place with three federations (the Gathering of the Moroccans of France (RMF), the Coordinating Committee for Turkish Muslims of France (CCMTF)[5], and the GMP) (Institut Montaigne 2016, 61).

The CFCM has been mostly prominent in issues related to the certification of halal meat, the organization of the pilgrimage to Mecca and the nomination of Muslim chaplains in prisons (Laurence & Vaïsse 2006, 155). In 2015, another governmental initiative emerged to build a larger space of dialogue for French Islam and resulted in the creation of a Foundation for Islam in France, in August 2016, to centralize funding for mosque buildings, supervise imam training, and manage contributions from the halal industry and worshippers (Institut Montaigne 2016, 62; Bayrakli, Hafez and Faytre 2019).

The CFCM has not been judged successful in its mission due to deep divisions along ethnic, national, and ideological lines along with a lack of coordination, investment, and material facilities (Godard & Taussig 2007, 180; Bayrakli, Hafez and Faytre 2019, 149). It has in fact been largely discredited, turning into "a stage for endless power struggle," where "rivalries between the different countries of origin were reproduced" (Institut Montaigne 2016, 61). The control exerted by foreign influences is still prevalent: lots of imams are sent from abroad (Alouane 2019) and only 20 percent have French citizenship (Institut Montaigne 2016, 71). Institut Montaigne reveals that "only a third of Muslims are aware of the CFCM, and among this third, only 12 percent feel that they are well represented by this institution" (Institut Montaigne 2016, 61). In total, only 9 percent of Muslim respondents say they feel CFCM represents them (Institut Montaigne 2016, 25). Indeed, the Council gives a highly visible community role to practicing Muslims but leaves aside younger generations, as well as secular Muslims[6] (Laurence & Vaïsse 2006, 160).

Therefore, it is safe to say that the influence of Islamic political organizations over Muslim populations is limited in general (Laurence & Vaïsse 2006, 3: Institut Montaigne 2016).

As of 2019, additional initiatives had been emerging against the monopoly of the CFCM, namely, the platform "The Muslims." Headed by French Muslim activist Marwan Mohammad, previously the head of the Collective against Islamophobia or the Muslim Association for an Islam of France, carried by Hakim el Karoui under the impulsion of the French President Emmanuel Macron. "Reforming Islam" has thus often represented a common ambition for all French governments since the end of the 1980s, but it never materialized into a successful and inclusive project. This contributes further to trap Maghrebis in the "Muslim" label (Fellag 2014), regardless of their religiosity.

CONCLUSION

As a conclusion, this chapter retraced the evolution of identification and perceptions of the Maghreb Diaspora in France, first rooted in nationality and ethnicity, before being rooted in religiosity. The figure of the Arab immigrant worker of the 1970s who was mostly concerned with residency rights and visas and the young Arab of the 1980s who mobilized in associations against racism and discrimination have been progressively replaced by the figure of the Muslim citizen claiming for the right to a Muslim identity and expression of this identity (Geisser & Kelfaoui 2001: Laurence & Vaïsse 2006, 6). As the Muslim label progressed, a concomitant movement took place at the level of the state in the midst of heavy geopolitical changes connected to Islam on the international scene: top-down initiatives in search for a Muslim interlocutor culminated in the creation of a CFCM, a largely failed and ill-equipped institution mired by divisions reflecting the heterogeneity of an elusive "Muslim community" that French authorities have dreamed to capture in one representative body. This heterogeneity is reflected again in a plurality of understandings and ritualization of the Maghrebi experience of Islam in France. Though estimates sometimes reveal contradictory findings, the picture that stands out is a multitude of compositions in the spectrum between secularism and radical Islam. The patterns of religiosity of Maghrebis in France reveal a fragmentation of discourses and practices, whereby different ways of asserting Islamic identity take form. Conservative attitudes on gender relations, the halal food standard as a sign of belonging, a more frequent religious practice compared with the French whole population, and the support for the veil stand out as common denominators (Institut Montaigne 2016, 29). Again though, the Islamic discourse itself is not homogenous, and different ways of asserting Islamic identity take form (Haddad, Smith and More 2006, 149).

NOTES

1. Europe 1. 27 October 2019. *61 pour cent des Français pensent que l'Islam est incompatible avec les valeurs de la société française.*
2. The Great Mosque of Paris (GMP) is the oldest institution and is strongly tied with the Algerian government which has been in charge of its finances since 1982. It is perceived as a moderate institution which theologically promotes the reconciliation of Islam and Western values: it meets regularly with Jewish groups and was cooperative with the 2004 law banning outward signs of religion in schools (Laurence & Vaïsse 2006, 103).
3. The Union of Islamic Organisations in France (UOIF) is a strong grassroots force founded in 1983 and affiliated to the Muslim brotherhood. Its relative success comes from efficient networking at the grassroots level on the one hand and its rooting in transnational networks on the other hand (Zehgal 2005, 5). UOIF also targets the categories of Muslim population through a compartmentalized strategy visible in the different associations: *Jeunes musulmans de France* (Young Muslims of France), *Étudiants musulmans de France* (Muslim Students of France), *Ligue française de la femme musulmane* (French League of the Muslim Woman), *Association des imams de France* (Association of French Imams) (Institut Montaigne 2016, 46). It is also the French branch of the Federation of Islamic Organizations in Europe. UOIF is especially notorious for its annual gathering in Le Bourget, attracting 300 people in its first edition in 1983, 100 000 in 2006 and 200,000 by 2016 (Institut Montaigne 2016, 49). The organization name has changed to "French Muslims" in 2017.
4. The National Federation of French Muslims (FNMF) was founded in 1985 and is under Moroccan influence: some of the members are also members of the Moroccan Justice and Development party (Laurence & Vaïsse 2006, 105). The Gathering of Muslims in France (RMF) was created in 2006 by dissidents of the FNMF.
5. The Coordinating Committee for Turkish Muslims of France (CCMTF), founded in 2000, is close to the Turkish government. For the first time in 2017 and till June 2019, a representative from the CCMTF became the President of the CFCM, Ahmet Ogras.
6. In reaction to the CFCM, talks about a representative organisation for secular Muslims had been initiated by then Minister of the Interior Dominique de Villepin (Laurence & Vaïsse 2006, 161). Examples of these associations include the French Council of Secular Muslims (CFML), the secular convention for equality of rights and participation of Muslims of France (CLE) or the French secular Muslims' Movement (MMLF)(Frégosi 2008, 392). These secular groups highlight cultural and ethnic aspects of the belonging to Islam and do not claim any religious practise. These secular groups claim to speak on behalf of the "silent majority" (Laurence & Vaïsse 2006, 99) and started to emerge around the end of the nineties (Godard & Taussig 2007, 91). Politically, they are rather situated on the right and have been especially supported by Sarkozy (Zehgal 2005, 6). However, they are very fragmented and share different ideological views as to Islam reform (Frégosi 2008, 413).

REFERENCES

Adida, Claire L., David D. Laitin and Marie-Anne Valfort. 2016. *Why Muslim Integration Fails in Christian-Heritage Societies*. Harvard University Press.

Aissaoui, Rabah. 2006. "Le discours du Mouvement des travailleurs arabes (MTA) dans les années 1970 en France. Mobilisation et mémoire du combat anticolonial." *Hommes & Migrations* 1263 (Setembre-Octobre): 105–119.

Alouane, Rim-Sarah. 2019. "Islam, made in France? Debating the Reform of Muslim organizations and foreign funding for religion." May 1, Brookings. https://www.brookings.edu/blog/order-from-chaos/2019/05/01/islam-made-in-france-debating-the-reform-of-muslim-organizations-and-foreign-funding-for-religion/.

Ayhan, Kaya. 2006. "Les Français musulmans: enquête sur une rébellion républicaine." *Revue européenne des migrations internationales* 22 (3): 135–153.

Bayrakli Enes, Farid Hafez, and Léonard Faytre. 2018. "Engineering a European Islam: An Analysis of Attempts to Domesticate European Muslims in Austria, France, and Germany." *Insight Turkey* 20 (3): 131–156.

Bertossi, Christophe. 2007. "Les Musulmans, la France, l'Europe : contre quelques faux-semblants en matière d'intégration." *Migrations et citoyenneté en Europe* (mars). Fondation Friedrich-Ebert, Institut Français des Relations Internationales.

Bidet, Jennifer and Lauren Wagner. 2012. "Vacances au bled et appartenances diasporiques des descendants d'immigrés algériens et marocains en France." *Tracés* 23: 113–130.

Blanchard, Pascal. 2016. "The Paradox of Arab France." *The Cairo Review of Global Affairs*. June. https://www.thecairoreview.com/essays/the-paradox-of-arab-france/.

Brouard, Sylvain & Vincent Tiberj. 2006. *Français comme les autres? Enquête sur les citoyens d'origine maghrébine, africaine, et turque*. Paris: Presses de Sciences-Po.

Dargent, Claude. 2003. "Les musulmans déclarés en France: affirmation religieuse, subordination sociale et progressisme politiques." *Les Cahiers du CEVIPOF* 39 (février): 1–43.

Fellag, Nora. 2014. "The Muslim Label: How French North Africans Have Become "Muslims" and not "Citizens." *Journal on Ethnopolitics and Minority Issues in Europe* 13 (4): 1–25.

Europe 1. 2019. "61 pour cent des Français pensent que l'Islam est incompatible avec les valeurs de la société française." 27 October, 2019.

Fondation Jean Jaurès/IFOP. 2019. "Etude auprès de la population musulmane en France, 30 ans après l'affaire des foulards de Creil." https://jean-jaures.org/sites/default/files/redac/commun/productions/2019/0923/etude_ifop_le_point_jean_jaures.pdf.

Frégosi, Franck. 2008. *Penser l'islam dans la laïcité*. Paris: Fayard.

Frégosi, Franck. 2009. "Formes de mobilisation collective des musulmans en France et en Europe." *Revue internationale de politique comparée* 16 (1): 41–61.

Gallup. 2009. *The Gallup Coexist Index 2009: A Global Study of Interfaith Relations*. Muslim West Facts Project. London: Coexist Foundation.

Geisser, Vincent & Schérazade Kelfaoui. 2001. "Trois générations de militantisme politique sous la Vème République: l'activiste immigré, le beur civique et l'électeur musulman." *La Médina* Printemps.

Godard, Bernard & Sylvie Taussig. 2007. *Les Musulmans en France : courants, institutions, communautés : un état des lieux.* Paris: Robert Laffont.

Green, N. (2002). "Religion et ethnicité: De la comparaison spatiale et temporelle." *Annales. Histoire, Sciences Sociales*, 57e année(1), 127–144. doi:10.3917/anna.571.0127.

IFOP. 2009. "1989–2009: Enquête sur l'évolution de l'Islam en France." August.

IFOP. 2016. "Regards croisés sur l'Islam en France et en Allemagne." 29 April, 2016.

IFOP. 2019. "Les musulmans en France 30 ans après l'affaire des foulards de Creil."

Institut Montaigne. 2016. "A French Islam is Possible." http://www.institutmontai gne.org/res/files/publications/a-french-islam-is-possible-report.pdf

Kastoryano, Riva. 2006. "French Secularism and Islam: France's Headscarf Affair." In *Mulituclturalism, Muslims and Citizenship*, edited by Tariy Modood, Anna Triandafyllidou and Ricard Zapata-Barrero, 57–69. New York: Routledge.

Laurence, Jonathan & Justin Vaïsse. 2006. *Integrating Islam.* Washington DC: Brookings Institution Press.

Leveau, Rémy. 2004. "Flux migratoires, imaginaires sociaux et importation des conflits dans l'espace euro méditerranéen." Sciences-Po Paris. https://liberalarts.utexa s.edu/france-ut/_files/pdf/resources/leveau.pdf

Poutignat, Philippe & Jocelyne Streiff-Fénart. 1995. *Théories de l'ethnicité.* Paris: Presses Universitaires de France.

Roy, Olivier. 2002. *L'islam mondialisé.* Paris: Le Seuil.

Salvatore, Armando. 2004. "Making Public Space: Opportunities and Limits of Collective Action Among Muslims in Europe." *Journal of Ethnic and Migration Studies* 30 (5): 1013–1031.

Samers, Michael E. 2003. "Diaspora unbound: Muslim identity and the erratic regulation of Islam in France." *International Journal of Population Geography* 9 (4): 351–364.

Savage Timothy M. 2004. "Europe and Islam: Crescent Waxing, Cultures Clashing." *The Washington Quarterly* 27 (3): 25–50.

Schain, Martin A. 2008. *The Politics of Immigration in France, Britain, and the United States.* New York: Palgrave Macmillan.

Silvestri, Sara. 2007. "Asserting Islam in the EU: actors, strategies and priorities." In *L'espace public européen à l'épreuve du religieux,* edited by François Foret, 159–177. Bruxelles: Université Libre de Bruxelles publications.

Statham, Paul and Jean Tillie. 2016. "Muslims in their European societies of settlement: a comparative agenda for empirical research on socio-cultural integration across countries and groups." *Journal of Ethnic and Migration Studies* 42 (2): 177–196.

Withol De Wenden, Catherine. 2003. "Multiculturalism in France." *International Journal on Multicultural Societies* 5 (1): 77–87.

Zehgal, Malika. 2005. "La constitution du Conseil Français du Culte Musulman: reconnaissance politique d'un Islam français?" *Archives de sciences sociales des religions* 129 (janvier-mars): 97–113.

Chapter 8

Arab Youths' Sense of Belonging to Canada

Integrated and Hyphenated Identities

Bessma Momani and Nawroos Shibli

INTRODUCTION

Internationally regarded for its commitment to multiculturalism and one of the most ethnically diverse countries in the world (Daily Hive 2019; Morin 2013), Canada is home to 7.5 million people born outside the country—representing almost 22 percent of the national population—who hail from over 200 countries from around the world, cumulatively speaking almost 215 languages (Statistics Canada 2017e, 2017c, 2017b). While the majority of Canada's newcomers have origins in Asia, including the Middle East, Arabs are among one of the largest visible minority communities in Canada and represent the second fastest growing racialized group. Arabs in Canada have a population that has nearly doubled between 2006 and 2016 to 523,235 due to increased rates of immigration (Chui and Anderson 2013; Galloway, Bascaramurty and Maki 2017; Statistics Canada 2017a). As of 2016, 81 percent of Canada's self-identified Arab population were concentrated in provinces of Ontario and Quebec, primarily nestled in cosmopolitan city areas like Montreal, Ottawa-Gatineau, and Toronto (Chui and Anderson 2013; Statistics Canada 2017d). Aside from representing one of the largest and fastest growing ethnocultural groups in the country, Canadians of Arab descent are also among the youngest with a median age of 30.2 years old (Chui & Anderson 2013), compared to a national average of 40.8.

The increased presence and high immigration rates of Arabs in Canada, coupled with a relative understudy of this group (Eid 2007, ix), makes research of their experiences ever more necessary. Moreover, as crisis in the Middle East saw millions of Arabs and Muslims take part in mass global migration from the region into Western countries, notably into Europe, cultural reductionists have questioned Arabs' integration, identity formation and sense of belonging to Western values and nations. The rise of home-grown terrorism and migration of Arab or Muslim youth to the Middle East to join terror organizations, like ISIS, has revived policy debates about whether Arabs, and by extension Muslims, feel that they belong in Western societies or whether they feel marginalized (see Lyons-Padilla et al. 2015). While this narrative has been adopted by particularly right-wing and populist discourses across Europe, it has often seeped into common public discourses about this growing ethnocultural community in Western societies (See Betz, 2013). To respond to this broader socio-political debate, Arab youth were surveyed across Canada to get a clear sense of how they navigate their identities between their ethnocultural roots and their sense of belonging as members of the Canadian community. Specifically, in 2016, we conducted a Canada wide survey (n = 973) and asked participants questions about their views about their identity, their sense of belonging, means of cultural connectedness to homelands, and life in Canada.

Analyzed through the lens of transnationalism we examine the acculturation process or how Canadian-Arab youth navigate cultural and psychological change in their relationship to larger society (see Berry 2005). We find that some of the factors that influence the balance between maintaining their ethnic Arab identity and adopting a civic Canadian identity include age, familial relationships, connections with country of origin, consumption of Arab media, language proficiency, experience with discrimination, and other socialization factors and practices. Highlighting the empirical illustrations of acculturation, this chapter will expand the discussion beyond these frameworks by asking how to mitigate this tension between ethnic identity and civic/national identity. We utilize mixed methods to illustrate the complex personal decisions and voices of Arab youth within Canada.

Findings of the survey showed that Arab-Canadian youth born inside and outside of Canada have a hyphenated nature of self-identity, strong sense of belonging to Canada, and overall happiness and comfort living in Canada. In the four categories of acculturation, Canadian youth of Arab heritage are deemed to be well-integrated. Enriched by additional qualitative focus group data undertaken in June and July of 2016, research findings demonstrate that Arab-Canadian youth are a conscious young community who strategically negotiate their personal identities in a hybridity of Eastern, cultural (Arab) and Western/civic (Canadian) identity. Moreover, this transnationalism contributes to their sense of belonging in multiple communities, including what many respondents considered a cohesive, welcoming, multicultural Canada.

SENSE OF BELONGING IN DIASPORA COMMUNITIES

Populist-nationalist discourse that has dominated public and media spaces has tended to question the ability of Arabs, and more broadly visible minorities of Muslim faith (albeit the two are not mutually exclusive), to integrate in many Western societies. While reviewing and critiquing those cultural reductionist views are not the focus of this chapter, we posit that contemporary academic literature provides an alternative understanding of diaspora communities' sense of belonging and identity based on the general framework of transnationalism. Of course, an important part of whether people feel that they belong is how they frame their loyalty to a nation-state. Bradatan et al. (2010, 172) note how historically there has been a tension or conceptual contradiction with the idea that a person has citizenship, or what they frame as "a set of rights and duties of an individual toward a certain country" and of transnationalism which is a perhaps a cultural attachment or identity connection to multiple countries.

Although the term diaspora is often used to describe Arab settlement in the Western world, we find Arab-Canadians embody the idea of transnational citizenship which connotes strong connections to homeland while simultaneously holding strong civic values to being Canadian. As noted by Schiller et al. (1995, 48), transnational connections of diaspora communities involve keeping multiple networks of social relations. Transnationalism, according to Jonathan Fox (2005), also captures a long-term global trend and reality of how diaspora communities are building relationships while they pursue political and social equality, rights, and privileges. Fox's (2005, 171) use of the term "transnational citizenship" captures the concord of both "citizenship," which is about given rights from a constitution or set of laws, and "participation," which is the act of seeking one's rights through activities like voting or volunteering. Ethnocultural minorities use their transnational connections not only to aid diaspora communities to hold on to ties to home countries but also to help bridge their sense of belonging into their new home countries (see Finn, Opatowski, and Momani 2018).

With transnationalism, ethnocultural minorities are less likely to discard the socio-cultural identity of their origin country. As they use modern technologies to stay connected to homelands, they also keep their identity as they navigate a sense of belonging to their new country. Instead of transnational communities abandoning their old identities, they form hyphenated identities, mix their cultural practices in new societies, and contribute to the broader notions of multiculturalism (see Clarke et al. 2007). As Cheng (2005, 146) noted:

> When immigrants travel frequently, both physically and symbolically, back and forth between a host society and a homeland, there emerges a new sense of

locality that transcends the polarity between the place of origin and the place of residence. This locality is the sense of simultaneously belonging to more than one place. I call it a transnational, multilocal sense of belonging. (Cheng, 2005)

Much of this transnational identity formation is due to globalized media, rapid advancement in communication technologies, and shared common spaces such as ethnocultural media in the new homeland (see Tufte 2001, Pocius 2000, and Momani 2015).

In Canada, where multiculturalism is celebrated and immigrants are seen as part of a mosaic rather than participating in an "American melting pot," there is an understanding and social acceptance that ethnocultural minorities will hold on to some of their cultural practices while contributing to Canadian society in meaningful ways (see Jedwab 2014). As Tupuola (2006, 303) notes transnationalism suggests that diaspora communities will hold multiple cultures, lingos, and styles as they navigate in their new home. As Dib et al. (2008) find, moreover, Canada's official 1971 multicultural policy is not about creating ethnocultural enclaves nor is meant to encourage separate identities from the broader Canadian identity. On the contrary, as multiculturalism expands in common spaces where people of diverse ethnocultural backgrounds interact and meet across Canada, so does ethnocultural communities' "sense of shared citizenship and collective experiences" (Dib et al. 2008, 161). As Berry and Huo (2016, 254) elucidate,

> Inherent in this multicultural vision is the acceptance of the view that individuals can be proud of and feel attached to both their heritage cultures and to Canada. The underlying notion is that an individual may hold many identities, know many languages, and develop many cultural competencies, and thereby participate in many cultural communities, without any serious psychological incompatibilities among them. (Berry, 2016)

A better means of understanding social integration of new immigrants in an age of transnationalism is not in the question of dropping home cultural practices or ethnocultural identities rather it is in the concept of "sense of belonging" or an attachment to one's community or "feeling at home" in the new country (Berry 2005, 700–701). Rather than looking for an end process of "assimilation," transnationalism looks for forms and means of immigrant adaptation (see Portes 1999, 228). Of course, Canada's official multicultural policy permits newcomers to not shed their ethnocultural identity in order to be perceived as "Canadian." Sense of belonging, then, is a more appropriate frame to try and determine new Canadians' experiences with social integration.

To categorize or measure sense of belonging and acculturation, scholars have conceptualized four different classifications: transnationals who showed a strong sense of belonging to only Canada were *assimilated*, those who have strong belonging to both were *integrated*, those who have weak sense of belonging to both identities were *separated*, and those who showed mixed belonging were *marginalized* (see Rudmin, 2003). Why do some groups integrate while others are marginalized? Case studies of transnational Canadians and their sense of belonging, identity, and question of adaptation are mixed, and quite dense, with many case studies showing no conclusive explanation for why some communities adapt or are marginalized more than others (see Satzewich and Wong 2011). However, in a large dataset of 7,000 immigrants to Canada, Huo et al. (2018, 1627) found that the vast majority do have a strong sense of belonging to Canada, and although where people come from is important, equally relevant is what entry status (refugee versus economic migrant) they came to Canada with and their experiences in Canada with employment and discrimination. Hence, knowing the source country of migration is not enough to determine a sense of belonging; experiences in Canada are just as relevant.

The question of youth adaptation in Canada is of empirical importance because of the policy expectation that immigrants' sense of belonging among youth who are children of immigrants and grow up in Canada is more likely to be positive and that youth ought to demonstrate stronger promise of feeling that they belong. To this end, Berry and Huo (2017, 33) examined the sense of belonging of 3,000 second-generation Canadians and found 75 percent were integrated, 15 percent assimilated, 6 percent separated, and 5 percent remained marginalized. To dig deeper, in a study of Canadian youth originally from Hong Kong, Chow (2007, 512) found that sense of belonging was high among those who achieved socio-economic success, made friends in Canada, had positive academic and work experiences free of discrimination, and that they were also happier and more likely to have a deeper sense of belonging to Canada. Moreover, in a study of Canadian youth that compared both non-immigrant and immigrant sense of belonging and acculturation processes, Lee and Hebert (2006, 517) found that both groups had strong identification to Canada. Immigrant youth often leveraged their right to equality, such as through the Charter of Rights and Freedom, as a means of identifying what it means to be Canadian (Lee and Hebert, 497).

MIXED METHODS: NATIONAL SURVEY AND FOCUS GROUPS

Trying to research transnationalism and sense of belonging is often a challenge. How does one know that an individual truly feels like they belong? Is it in one's actions, feelings, and emotions or in outside observation? Our mixed-method approach of both surveys and focus groups is, in our opinion, a best practice in determining our research question (see Satzewich and Wong 2011, 6). This chapter derives its findings from a national survey questionnaire distributed in twelve major cities across Canada in 2016, comprised forty-seven questions, both qualitative and quantitative, ranging from the topics of campus life, education, and professional development, to questions of political participation and civic engagement, identity and transnational connections, and general demographic questions. The survey questionnaire garnered responses from 973 participants and was conducted in English and French.

With the intention of recruiting a random and diverse set of Arab youth which reflected the general demographic makeup of the heterogenous Arab population in Canada, and to avoid selection bias, canvassing for survey respondents took place in popular social spaces frequented by Arab youth including university campuses, ethnic Arab grocery stores, restaurants, shisha lounges, and cafes. Here, project organizers wore t-shirts advertising the survey and offered a financial incentive (a $25 Visa card) in exchange for participation. This method of public advertisement and recruitment garnered a significant number of responses. Our focus on Arab youth limits our study to two primary age groups, those aged 18–24 and 25–29, which, excluding those survey responses which did not specify an age group, narrows our sample size down to 879 respondents, with over 40 percent belonging to the former age group.

In addition to the data collected through the survey, this study also gathered qualitative data in focus groups held in Ottawa and Montreal (where Arabs represent the second largest visible minority group in each city) to augment our quantitative findings and to capture other dimensions of the intended research and validate the survey findings. Utilizing this quantitative and qualitative mixed-methods approach allowed both a broad survey of Arab youth across Canada as well as in-depth analysis to hone in on questions and issues that needed further elucidation (Ivankova, Creswell, & Stick, 2006). Twenty focus groups which lasted roughly sixty to ninety minutes in duration were held in each city, with approximately seven to ten participants per session, resulting in the participation of 100 youth per city, with a cumulative total of 200 focus group discussants. Participants were recruited through a bilingual social media strategy targeting Arab youth under 30 years of age on platforms including Facebook and were motivated to participate with the offer of dinner and gift certificates to popular retailers. These group discussions were conducted in both English and French in accordance to participants' linguistic preferences and/or capacity. Other than age, no personal or demographic details were collected from our focus group discussants which remain anonymous due to privacy and research ethics restrictions.

Organized as a social event to generate open discussion and convened in a mix of both English and French, focus group participants were asked four questions regarding their connectivity to Arab culture around the world: their relationship to the Middle East writ large; the frequency and means of their consumption of Arab media, literature, art, film, etc.; the Arab cultural values they embraced and wished to retain; and the compatibility of their Arab identity with their Western one.

FINDINGS

Using a Likert scale, the pan-Canadian survey contained three key questions: (1) How do you self-identify: Arab, Canadian, Canadian-Arab, or Arab-Canadian? (2) How would you rate your sense of belonging to Canadian society? and (3) How would you rate your comfort and happiness living in Canada? Taken together with the focus group discussions, two themes revealed that Arab youth embrace fluid, hyphenated identities and indicated both strong sense of belonging and high level of comfort and happiness within Canadian society. Hence, we argue using Rudmin's (2003) categorization, Arab-Canadian youth are indeed *integrated* in Canadian society.

When asked how one self-identified, over half of the survey respondents endorsed a hyphenated identity. Of the youth respondents, 23 percent identified as Canadian-Arab and 29 percent as Arab-Canadian, whereas only 28 percent identified as solely Arab, and just 5 percent as solely Canadian. This suggests that those who identified as Arab-Canadian more strongly associated first with their ethnic identity and then their national one, while the opposite is true for those who identified as Canadian-Arab where their national identity as Canadian takes precedence. The results highlight the importance of maintaining one's cultural roots and ethnic heritage among Arab youth in Canada.[1] This is in keeping with how multicultural identities in Canada are often celebrated and seen in harmony with keeping one's ethnocultural identity.

A cross-sectional analysis indicates that one's place of birth can provide some insight into the differences among survey respondents who subscribed to a hyphenated identity. The data gathered suggests that there is a relationship between being born outside of Canada and choosing to first identify with their Arab ethnocultural identity. Those who identified as Arab first, selecting "Arab" or "Arab-Canadian" as their preferred category of self-identity, were overwhelmingly born outside of Canada, with 83 percent and 62 percent, respectively, born elsewhere and arriving to Canada as immigrants. Similarly, the majority of respondents who identified first with a national Canadian identity before their cultural Arab one—that is, 69 percent of those who identified as Canadian and 61 percent as Canadian-Arab—were born in Canada.

This indicates that, for these youth, there is a connection between place of birth (in or outside of Canada) and the degree of their connection to their cultural identity and their national one, at least in terms of how they choose to self-identify to the aforementioned categories. In this vein, many focus group respondents who were born outside of Canada and had spent a portion of their formative years living in their country of origin expressed that it was easier to connect with and retain their Arab culture, identity, and values due to their deep attachments, especially if they maintained an active relationship with their country of origin by visiting often and keeping in touch with familial relatives and friends. As one respondent explained: "I personally am still connected with the Middle East because I go there every year and have family there, and friends; I do have a connection with the country. So that makes it harder to detach."[2] Another suggested that their place of birth impacted their level of connectivity toward the predominantly Arab Middle East, and thus to identifying as Arab: "Connection wise, I don't feel as connected, as I probably should be just because I was born here, but if I was born in the Middle East, I would probably feel more connected."[3] Another respondent held a similar point of view:

> I definitely have some connection; I have my whole family there pretty much. So, there is a connection there. For someone who was born and raised abroad for eleven years, now as I grew up I realized that a lot of things I am still connected by—I grew up in that community and grew up with the mentality or the state of mind that you develop there, so it's not easy to get away from that. So, like even though I've been here for the past 8–9 years, I've gained a lot of different knowledge and opened my mind more. But I still have some of that mentality, it's just how I was born.[4]

Indeed, many focus group respondents explained that their connections to their ancestral lands and culture was not only impacted by their geographic distance and country of birth but also by other factors including their consumption of Arabic media, music, and television, their upbringing within an Arab household, their level of interaction and connectivity to family and friends living abroad in their home country, as well as the ethnocultural makeup of their social circles and friend groups, which in part affected their consumption of Arabic media including the news, music, television series, and internet programs available through satellite TV or online video platforms such as YouTube. This was expressed by several focus group participants: "Me, personally, I don't really listen to Arab media until recently, that is, because my friends influenced me. I became friends with more Arab people. Before that I had nothing to do with Arab media. I was too whitewashed now that I think about it."[5] Another participant echoed a comparable sentiment, similarly highlighting the influential power associated with one's social group: "I like when you surround yourself with people who are more cultural and aware of 'Arabness;' I feel like I have become more aware of my 'Arabness.' So, when you surround yourself with more people like that and open yourself up to that."[6]

Indeed, many Canadian-Arab youth noted their consumption of Arab music, radio, television shows, talk shows, and to a lesser extent, news:

> I will go online. . . . and watch talk shows every once in a while, or like comedy skits. But one thing I have noticed that will always be is Arab music. As much as I listen to English, Western music, I will always kind of go back to Arabic music because it was what I was raised on; it's just very different and sometimes you need that little dose of it.[7]

Others described similar preferences: "I watch a lot of series, and a part of watching Arab shows is just to keep some type of Arabic language in the daily life, because I speak English with almost everyone I know, and everyone speaks it. So, I like to just have shows [on] every now and then to hear the different dialects and keep in touch with the culture."[8] Such sentiments were echoed frequently by Arab youth who consumed media as a conduit with which to nourish ties to their traditional cultural roots:

> I do miss my country, and the people and the accent so I do find myself watching shows from that country so I can see and be surrounded and listen to that accent and feel more connected in that sort of way. Because personally I barely find Jordanians here, or Palestinians from my nationality, so I don't really hear the accent. I do find myself listening to songs and watching shows with that accent just to feel more connected.[9]

That the majority of the youth surveyed also indicated frequent communication with people in their home countries using digital platforms and social media, such as Skype, Facebook, FaceTime, Viber, WhatsApp, Instagram, and Snapchat, and more traditional methods, such as phone, email, and text message, underscores the importance of media and technology in maintaining transnational connections. As one focus group participant put it: "We need to keep up with what's going on in our cities. Otherwise, we lose that connection."[10]

Arab youth also used these mediums to preserve their Arabic language skills, something that many participants agreed represented an essential part of their cultural heritage and a practical tool with which to navigate life within their homes and in their home countries when visiting. As one respondent put it, "Yes, language really matters; it facilitates. No matter what we do outside, when we come home, that's what we find: our Arabic."[11] Arabic was also perceived as a universal link across the diverse ethnocultural Arab world and a critical element of Arab identity: "I feel like with the language, it's a source of relation between our culture and us. I feel if the ties . . . [to] the language are dead, we have little connection with the Arab world, what prides us as Arabs. It's what makes us proud to be Arabs and connects our identities."[12] Thus, the Arabic language was viewed as not only important in retaining this connection to their culture but also in their ability to connect with and feel a sense of belonging in their/their parents' country of origin. Though our survey data does not capture the relationship between fluency in Arabic and how one self-identifies, it is clear that retention of or fluency in Arabic generally serves to strengthen Arab youths' connection to their Eastern Arab roots. Many respondents shared their desire to speak, learn, or improve their Arabic language skills because they believed that their mother tongue was a critical part of their identity.

This is not to say that the affinity toward their Arab roots and cultural identity conflicts with their sense of belonging in Canadian society. As such, we posit that Arab-Canadian youth are not marginalized or separated, but quite integrated. Indeed, the cultivation of ethnic ties, especially within ethnocultural community organizations, has been proven to have a positive effect on the integration of immigrants and newcomers within host societies by mitigating negative experiences, finding comfort in shared experiences, and establishing new connections within their ethnocultural community which can then extend into the wider community (see Jurkova 2014; Guo and Guo 2011). As table 8.1 reveals, Arab youth felt a strong sense of belonging to the country, with a combined 66 percent of respondents feeling "extremely 'at home' in Canada" and "moderately 'at home' in Canada." When taken in conjunction with self-identity, the "extremely 'at home' in Canada" category was overrepresented by respondents who subscribed to hyphenated identities, Canadian-Arabs and Arab-Canadians at 39 percent and 28 percent, respectively.

When the divisions within the self-identity categories are analyzed in isolation, however, an interesting trend appears regarding which group overall felt the most "at home" in Canada: the youth who identified as Canadian first felt the most "at home" in Canada. The breakdown is as follows: 46 percent of Canadians felt "extremely at home" while 48 percent felt moderately so; 53 percent Canadian-Arabs felt "extremely at home;" 30 percent of Arabs-Canadians felt "extremely at home" though 41 percent felt moderately; and approximately 17 percent of Arabs felt "extremely at home," while 29 percent felt moderately, and 36 percent felt only "somewhat at home" in Canada. Regardless, there seems to be a relatively healthy sense of comfort and happiness among Arab youth in Canada.

Table 8.1 Self-Identity, Sense of Belonging, and Level of Happiness in Canada

How do you self-identify?	1 (completely uncomfortable and unhappy)	2	3	4	5 (completely comfortable and happy)	NA	Grand Total
Arab	**4**	**15**	**59**	**88**	**84**	**1**	**251**
How would you rate your sense of belonging to Canadian society?							
Extremely "at home" in Canada			3	8	32		43
Moderately "at home" in Canada	1	1	9	37	26		74
NA		1			1		2
Not at all "at home" in Canada	1	1	2	1	1	1	7
Slightly "at home" in Canada		9	17	6	3		35
Somewhat "at home" in Canada	2	3	28	36	21		90
Arab-Canadian	**2**	**9**	**32**	**106**	**102**	**2**	**253**
How would you rate your sense of belonging to Canadian society?							
Extremely "at home" in Canada			1	14	61		76
Moderately "at home" in Canada	1		9	61	33		104
NA			2			2	4
Not at all "at home" in Canada	1	2		1			3
Slightly "at home" in Canada		2	4				7
Somewhat "at home" in Canada		5	16	30	8		59
Canadian	**1**			**27**	**20**		**48**
How would you rate your sense of belonging to Canadian society?							
Extremely "at home" in Canada	1			5	16		22
Moderately "at home" in Canada				19	4		23
Somewhat "at home" in Canada				3			3

(Continued)

Table 8.1 Self-Identity, Sense of Belonging, and Level of Happiness in Canada (*Continued*)

How would you rate your comfort and happiness living in Canada from 1-5? (where 1 = completely uncomfortable and unhappy living in Canada, and 5 = completely comfortable and happy living in Canada)	1 (completely uncomfortable and unhappy)	2	3	4	5 (completely comfortable and happy)	NA	Grand Total
Canadian-Arab	2	2	21	50	123	1	199
How would you rate your sense of belonging to Canadian society?							
Extremely "at home" in Canada			4	7	94		105
Moderately "at home" in Canada		2	6	33	26		67
NA						1	1
Not at all "at home" in Canada	2						2
Slightly "at home" in Canada			2	2			4
Somewhat "at home" in Canada			9	8	3		20
NA	1	3	2	6	7	31	50
How would you rate your sense of belonging to Canadian society?							
Extremely "at home" in Canada				1	5		6
Moderately "at home" in Canada				4	1		5
NA						31	31
Slightly "at home" in Canada	1	1	1				3
Somewhat "at home" in Canada		2	1	1	1		5
Other	1	5	10	29	30	3	78
How would you rate your sense of belonging to Canadian society?							
Extremely "at home" in Canada			2	1	15	2	20
Moderately "at home" in Canada		2	1	17	11		31
NA						1	1
Not at all "at home" in Canada	1						1
Slightly "at home" in Canada			3	3			6
Somewhat "at home" in Canada		2	4	8	4		19
Grand Total	11	34	124	306	366	38	879

Though a brief cross-table analysis suggests that place of birth (whether one was born in Canada or not) seems to have little to no bearing on whether one feels a positive sense of comfort and happiness in Canada, self-identity indicates comparable patterns as outlined above—that Arab youth with hyphenated identities rate their level of comfort and happiness quite high. Arab-Canadians and Canadian-Arabs represent over two-thirds of those who rated their comfort and happiness at 5 on the Likert scale which indicates complete satisfaction. Excluding surveys which indicated "Other" or "N/A" in their responses (n = 747), 68 percent of Arabs, 82 percent of Arab-Canadians, 98 percent of Canadians, and 87 percent of Canadian-Arabs signaled that they were very or completely comfortable and happy living in Canada (see table 8.1).

Taken together, these findings underline that Arab youth actively prioritize their ethnic heritage and cultivate connections to their cultural identity, and despite this—but more likely, because of this—they not only feel a strong sense of belonging to Canadian society but also a healthy sense of comfort and happiness. It is clear that through their local and transnational relationships, facilitated through the use of information technology and media communications, they are able to retain expand their connections with important features of Arab culture, including their mother tongue, while also embracing the values of Canadian society—among them, belief in the value of multiculturalism in Canada which supports hybridized self-identities. As one respondent aptly stated:

> Yes, Arab identity is very compatible with Western identity because Western identity is actually a broad concept, so, as long as you respect other people you can be yourself and act according to your Arabic identity and still fit in the Canadian society. Western society is very open and inclusive so you can be yourself and still be part of the Western world in some way.[13]

Another respondent shared similar sentiments whereby combining both cultures was perceived as the ideal:

> I think cultures are beautiful, so I think our culture is so beautiful! We have amazing values and amazing people but we also can learn so much from this culture here and Canadian society and values. If we can put them both together, just imagine! I strongly believe in what we have to offer but I also believe in what Canada can teach us. And to mix them together, we can produce something so powerful.[14]

Despite discussions about Arab culture writ large, it is important to recognize, as several focus group respondents do—that Arab culture is not monolithic;

it is diverse, distinct, and exists across various geographic, national, social, and political plains at various community levels. This was emphasized by a respondent when they noted that, "There is a huge difference between North African Arabs and Middle Eastern Arabs. I feel more detached from North Africans because of the dialect, the food, the traditions"[15] These nuances were also discussed by others in the focus groups. "When we think about Arabs," one participant mused, "we think of it as an umbrella term. We don't see it that way; it's so specific and personal, everyone interprets their 'Arabness' in their own way depending on how their parents raised them . . . It all depends on your experience with culture and how you identify with yourself."[16] Indeed, as this respondent alluded, there are countless iterations of what it means to be or identify as Arab and how this is culturally manifested on a personal scale. In this vein, it is critical that discussions of pan-ethnic Arab identities be had with these complexities in mind.

In the Canadian context, reference to Arab youth in Canada, as in this chapter, encompasses individuals originating from a wide array of countries around the world, ranging from the Middle East, North Africa, and Asia. Reflecting the overall diversity of Canada's population, the demographic makeup of Arab youth and their countries of ancestry are similarly diverse. When asked "What is the country of your family's ancestry?" survey respondents (n = 780, with 99 missing responses) selected all options that applied, resulting in a plural picture of Arab youth origins. Of the twenty-eight countries reported, Lebanon (20.9 percent; n = 184), Palestine (12.4 percent; n = 109), Morocco (9.3 percent; n = 82), Syria (9 percent; n = 79), Egypt (8.2 percent; n = 72), Iraq (7.5 percent; n = 66), Jordan (5.9 percent; n = 52), Algeria and Yemen (4.6 percent; n = 40), Libya (3.1 percent; n = 27), and Saudi Arabia (2.6 percent; n = 23) were the most frequently cited. This highlights the pluralistic and polylithic nature of "Arabness" that focus group participants discussed, particularly in terms of country of origin; it also confirms that the youth at the focus of this chapter identify with a multitude of nationalities.

A significant portion of the youth who participated in this study agreed that strictly choosing between their ethnocultural Arab identity and their Western Canadian identity, as if part of a zero sum equation, was not natural; instead, for these Arab youth, their identities embodied an ever-changing, fluid mixture of perceived positive values, personal experiences, and cultural practices from both their country of origin/ancestry and their current country of residence. This flexibility made it easier for them to comfortably lay down their roots in Canada while embracing their ethnocultural ties. An unfortunate side effect of this duality, however, is the sense of homelessness that can accompany straddling various countries, cultures, and languages. One participant described this: "You feel [like] a visitor in your own home country; while you're born here, you also feel as not necessarily an immigrant, but you're not Canadian-based like as a real Canadian because you have background and another origin than other people here."[17] Another added the following, but with a more positive outlook: "When I go to Morocco, people are like, 'where are you from?' And . . . here in Canada, they're like 'where are you from?' . . . . So, it's just perfectly completed. . . . I always try to take the best from like Arab identity and best of Western and try to have a mix of both as much as I can."[18] As highlighted above, it is this same hybridity across cultures that allows Arab youth to constantly shift and reconfigure their self-identities to suit their experiences and allow them to identify with and explore the best of both worlds.

DISCUSSION AND CONCLUSION

Findings from our pan-Canadian survey and focus groups of 200 youth, in two major cities, showed that most Canadian youth of Arab descent viewed themselves as a hyphenated identity: either Arab-Canadian or Canadian-Arab. The identity that came first was often explained by whether they were born in Canada or outside of Canada. Nevertheless, a minor few saw themselves as Arab only or as Canadian only. Their connection to Arab homelands was often due to the consumption of Arabic media, music, and television, supporting the theoretical arguments in favor of viewing immigrants to Western countries today as highly influenced by transnationalism. When asked about their sense of belonging, youth also noted how their sense of belonging to Canada was strong and robust and that their life in Canada was generally a happy and comfortable one. Our findings concur with academic investigation to ethnocultural youth in Canada who have a strong sense of attachment to Canada while still wanting to maintain their cultural identity. In Rudmin's (2003) classification, we find Arab-Canadian youth as integrated in Canadian society; however, we add that this is also due to positive features of Canadian society and multicultural policies that allows them to feel happy in Canada.

This chapter sought to critically engage with how diaspora communities are perceived to belong in a globalized world of transnational identities. Far too long, studies of immigrants sought to suggest that immigrants' attachment to home country culture was a negative process of acculturation. In other words, people who immigrate and hold on to culture and identity of home countries are not adapting to their new country and are therefore not integrating effectively, or not loyal to their new country. This has tended to simplify the diaspora experience and fail to account for the use of modern informational technologies that help people to bridge their new societies. Rather than viewing identity formation as a zero sum game where one cultural identity must be abandoned to retain a new one, or what is referred to assimilation, our findings confirm the growing view that people's sense of belonging is complex, and in the age of transnationalism, there are new means of relating to places of origins and culture that are not in competition. As a number of other studies have also shown, children of immigrants in Canada are also transnationals who form their identity in the West as a hybrid. Somerville (2008) found that Indo-Canadians who are children of immigrants also feel like they belong: "they feel Indian, yet also Canadian," (p.23). These follow similar findings in Canada's second-generation Somali community (Tiilikainen, 2017) and Habesha communities (Goitom, 2017). A large study also found that many of those children of immigrants in Canada who have these transnational identities have higher levels of life satisfaction and mental health than those that do not have multiple identities (Berry and Hou, 2019). The question of whether this transnational identity will abate is still too early to tell, as we are in the moment when Canadian children of immigrants are of age to take advantage of strong connectivity that allows transnationalism to flourish. Lastly, it is inconclusive, but transnational identity among second-generation youth may also be influenced by external events (Levitt and Glick-Schiller, 2004), it could "ebb and flow" (Somerville, 2007) or it could be dependent on socio-economic factors of how advantaged or disadvantaged the community is in their country and overall social mobility (Zhou, and Bankston 2016). These questions are well beyond the scope of this chapter, but merit further investigation. Nevertheless, our study finds that Canadian youth of Arab heritage are integrated. They are relatively happy in Canada, have a strong sense of belonging, and want to retain many aspects of their Arab culture that is often mediated through connectivity and technology.

The role of the media in enabling transnational connectivity, intercultural integration, and the retention of ethnocultural ties cannot be understated. It is well-documented that television, for instance, contributes to the socialization of adolescent immigrants in their new host country whereby they adopt the dominant society's values through a process of recognition, evaluation, and acceptance (Tan et al. 1997, 94; Dong, Gundlach, and Phillips 2006, 66). Youth who identify with a bicultural, hybrid, or transnational identity—that is, those who are more integrated—are more likely to recognize and accept Western values represented in television broadcasts they have watched which implies that bicultural youth actively learn Western values through media, especially where they lack interpersonal connections to aid the integration process, while still preserving their own cultural values (Dong, Gundlach, and Phillips 2006, 72). These trends speak to the significance of the media as an instrument of socialization and value adoption among ethnic immigrant populations in host country environments.

In this vein, McKelvy and Chatterjee's (2017, 23) study on the impact of internet media on the integration of immigrant Muslim women in the United states found that communication media not only helped these women learn and embrace the language of the host country but also eased the adoption of certain social norms. The consumption of media helped them to "maintain and strengthen their connections with friends and family in their homelands . . . [which] could possibly make the adaptation to a new culture less stressful" especially since the same social media and communication technology facilitated the development of new relationships in the host country (Mckelvy and Chatterjee 2017, 23). As the results of our study on Arab youth in Canada similarly suggest, media plays an important role in striking a balance between what Berry (1997, 12) refers to as "a high degree of contact and participation" with the dominant society and "a high degree of cultural maintenance" of one's original ethnocultural heritage.

Interestingly, the acculturation and identity formation processes negotiated by immigrants and second-generation persons in reaching integration can not only be strongly influenced by and precipitated through the use of media (Mckelvy and Chatterjee 2017, 24) but also the type of media that is consumed (i.e., host country media targeting the national population, Arab media from the countries of origin, and ethnic media related to and directed at particular ethnic minorities within the broader immigrant group) (Hmida, Ozcaglar-Toulouse, and Fosse-Gomez 2009, 530). Hmida et al.'s (2009, 530) study of the role of the media in the acculturation experiences of the Arab Maghrebin immigrant population in France posits that integrated immigrants were more likely to consume the most diverse media: in this case, integrated Maghrebins absorbed "French media (because they feel affected by what goes on in France)," at the same time that they consumed "Arab media (in order to stay in contact with the Arab-Muslim culture) and ethnic media (because they have to face problems specific to them)." Of note here is that there is also a generational consideration when it comes to evaluating one's level of acculturation based on the type of media consumed; for instance, first-generation Arab speakers' intake of French media and the second-generation's consumption of Arab or ethnic media could potentially indicate one's achieved level of acculturation (Hmida, Ozcaglar-Toulouse, and Fosse-Gomez 2009, 530). Still, what these studies emphasize, and what our research substantiates, is that immigrant youths' degree of acculturation and sense of belonging is affected by a myriad of factors including transnational media which has served to nurture hybrid, dual, or bicultural identities.

The idea of holding multiple identities, being integrated, and still having a strong sense of belonging to a new country is possible. It helps that in

Canada, there is a greater recognition that cultural differences are an asset to broader multicultural policies. Certainly, in this populist-nationalist age where right-wing views of immigrants is one of xenophobia and doubt at their ability to integrate, or in their demand for complete assimilation, this study is ever more prescient. Moreover, the right-wing populist view that Arabs living in the West can only be marginalized and hence lead to radicalization is similarly debunked by the evidence presented. Transnationalism has certainly challenged our understanding of diaspora identity and concepts of loyalty and attachment, but our study confirms that Arab youth in Canada have less confusion about their place in Canadian society that is often assumed in popular public debate.

NOTES

1. We intentionally did not include how Arab is defined because, as mentioned throughout the chapter and as is echoed by many of the respondents, ascribing to the label is a personal, intimate issue of how one self-identifies and we did not wish to restrict our definition beyond what the survey stipulates which is whether one's family has ancestral ties to any of the twenty-two traditional Arab speaking countries across the MENA (see page 142). Beyond this, we - and our respondents - consider Arab an umbrella term which is nuanced and complex. To more strictly define what is Arab and what is not is to do a disservice to those who identify as such and those who struggle with their ethnic identity; as Finn and Momani (2019, 37) state, "many youth self-identify as Arab, but many others do not, even though they are Arab descendants." The question of nationalities is similarly discussed, albeit briefly, on page 142.
2. Focus Group Respondent, Ottawa, June 2016.
3. Ibid.
4. Ibid.
5. Ibid.
6. Ibid.
7. Ibid.
8. Ibid.
9. Ibid.
10. Focus Group Respondent, Montreal, July 2016.
11. Ibid.
12. Focus Group Respondent. Ottawa. June 2016.
13. Ibid.
14. Ibid.
15. Focus Group Respondent, Montreal, July 2016.
16. Focus Group Respondent, Ottawa, June 2016.
17. Focus Group Respondent, Montreal, July 2016.
18. Ibid.

REFERENCES

Berry, J. W. 1997. Immigration, Acculturation, and Adaptation. *Applied Psychology* 46 (1), 5–34.

Berry, J. W. 2005. Acculturation: Living Successfully in Two Cultures. *International Journal of Intercultural Relations* 29, 697–712.

Berry, J. W. and Hou, F., 2016. Immigrant Acculturation and Wellbeing in Canada. *Canadian Psychology/Psychologie canadienne* 57 (4), 254.

Berry, J. W. and Hou, F., 2017. Acculturation, Discrimination and Wellbeing Among Second Generation of Immigrants in Canada. *International Journal of Intercultural Relations* 61, 29–39.

Berry, J. W. and Hou, F., 2019. Multiple Belongings and Psychological Well-Being Among Immigrants and the Second Generation in Canada. *Canadian Journal of Behavioural Science/Revue canadienne des sciences du comportement* 51 (3), 159.

Betz, Hans-Georg. 2013. "Mosques, Minarets, Burqas and Other Essential Threats: The Populist Right's Campaign against Islam in Western Europe." In Ruth Wodak, Majid KhosraviNik, and Brigitte Mral, (Eds.) *Right-Wing Populism in Europe: Politics and Discourse.* London: Bloomsbury Academic, 71–88.

Bradatan, Cristina, Adrian Popan, and Rachel Melton. 2010. Transnationality as a Fluid Social Identity. *Social Identities* 16 (2), 169–178.

Cheng, H. L. 2005. Constructing a Transnational, Multilocal Sense of Belonging: An Analysis of Ming Pao (West Canadian Edition). *Journal of Communication Inquiry* 29 (2), 141–159.

Chow, H. P., 2007. Sense of Belonging and Life Satisfaction among Hong Kong Adolescent Immigrants in Canada. *Journal of Ethnic and Migration Studies* 33 (3), 511–520.

Chui, Tina, and Thomas Anderson. 2013. Immigration and Ethnocultural Diversity in Canada. Ottawa. https://www12.statcan.gc.ca/nhs-enm/2011/as-sa/99-010-x/99-010-x2011001-eng.pdf.

Clarke, S., Gilmour, R. and Garner, S. 2007. "Home, Identity and Community Cohesion." In M. Wetherell, M. Lafleche and R. Berkeley, (Eds.) *Identity, Ethnic Diversity and Community Cohesion,* London: Sage, 87–101.

Daily Hive. 2019. "Canada Named One of the Most Diverse Countries in the World." Daily Hive. 2019. https://dailyhive.com/toronto/canada-most-diverse-countries-ranking-2019.

Dib, K., Donaldson, I. and Turcotte, B., 2008. Integration and identity in Canada: The importance of multicultural common spaces. *Canadian Ethnic Studies* 40 (1), 161–187.

Dong, Qingwen, Dean Phillip Gundlach, and John C. Phillips. 2006. The Impact of Bicultural Identity on Immigrant Socialization through Television Viewing in the United States. *Intercultural Communication Studies* 15 (2), 63–74.

Eid, Paul. 2007. *Being Arab: Ethnic and Religious Identity Building among Second Generation Youth in Montreal.* Montreal & Kingston: McGill-Queen's University Press.

Finn, Melissa, Michael Opatowski, and Bessma Momani. 2018. Transnational Citizenship Capacity-Building: Moving the Conversation in New Directions. *International Political Sociology* 12 (3), 291–305.

Fox, Jonathan. 2005. "Unpacking 'Transnational Citizenship.'" *Annual Review of Political Science* 8 (1), 171–201.

Galloway, Gloria, Dakshana Bascaramurty, and Allan Maki. 2017. "Canada Getting More Diverse as Immigration, Indigenous Population Increase." The Globe and Mail. https://www.theglobeandmail.com/news/national/census-2016-highlights-diversity-housing-indigenous/article36711216/.

Goitom, M., 2017. "Unconventional Canadians": Second-Generation "Habesha" Youth and Belonging in Toronto, Canada. *Global Social Welfare* 4 (4): 179–190.

Guo, Shibao, and Yan Guo. 2011. Multiculturalism, Ethnicity and Minority Rights: The Complexity and Paradox of Ethnic Organizations in Canada. *Canadian Ethnic Studies* 43 (1), 59–80.

Hmida, Manel, Nil Ozcaglar-Toulouse, and Marie-Helene Fosse-Gomez. 2009. "Towards an Understanding of Media Usage and Acculturation." In *Advances in Consumer Research*, 36. Urbana: Association for Consumer Research, 524–531.

Hou, Feng, Grant Schellenberg, and John Berry. 2018. Patterns and Determinants of Immigrants' Sense of Belonging to Canada and Their Source Country. *Ethnic and Racial Studies* 41 (9), 1612–1631.

Ivankova, V., Creswell, J. W., & Stick, S. L. 2006. Using Mixed-Methods Sequential Explanatory Design: From Theory to Practice. *Field Methods* 18: 3–20.

Jedwab, Jack. 2014. *The Multiculturalism Question: Debating Identity in 21st Century Canada.* Montreal: McGill-Queen's University Press.

Jurkova, Sinela. 2014. "The Role of Ethno-Cultural Organizations in Immigrant Integration: A Case Study of the Bulgarian Society in Western Canada." *Canadian Ethnic Studies* 46 (1), 23–44.

Lee, Jennifer Wenshya and Yvonne M. Hébert. 2006. "The Meaning of Being Canadian: A Comparison Between Youth of Immigrant and Non-Immigrant Origins." *Canadian Journal of Education* 29 (2), 497–520.

Levitt, P. and N. Glick Schiller. 2004. ConceptualizingSimultaneity: A Transnational Social FieldPerspective on Society. *International Migration Review* 38 (3), 1002–1039.

Lyons-Padilla, Sarah, Michele Gelfand, Hedieh Mirahmadi, Mehreen Farooq, and Marieke Egmond. 2015. Belonging Nowhere: Marginalization & Radicalization Risk among Muslim Immigrants. *Behavioral Science & Policy* 1 (2), 1–12.

Mckelvy, Lawanda, and Karishma Chatterjee. 2017. Muslim Women's Use of Internet Media in the Process of Acculturation in the United States. *Qualitative Research Reports in Communication* 18 (1), 18–26.

Momani, Bessma. 2015. *Arab Dawn: Arab Youth and the Demographic Dividend They Will Bring.* Toronto: University of Toronto Press.

Morin, Rich. 2013. "The Most (and Least) Culturally Diverse Countries in the World." Pew Research Center. 2013. https://www.pewresearch.org/fact-tank/2013/07/18/the-most-and-least-culturally-diverse-countries-in-the-world/.

Portes, Alejandro, Luis E Guarnizo, and Patricia Landolt. 1999. The Study of Transnationalism: Pitfalls and Promise of an Emergent Research Field. *Ethnic and Racial Studies* 22 (2): 217–237.

Rudmin, F.W., 2003. Critical History of the Acculturation Psychology of Assimilation, Separation, Integration, and Marginalization. *Review of General Psychology* 7 (1): 3–37.

Satzewich, Vic, and Lloyd Wong. 2006. *Transnational Identities and Practices in Canada*. Vancouver: UBC Press.

Schiller, Nina Glick, Linda Basch, and Cristina Szanton Blanc. 1995. From Immigrant to Transmigrant: Theorizing Transnational Migration. *Anthropological Quarterly* 68 (1) (January 1, 1995), 48–63.

Somerville, K. 2007. "Life Cycle Events and the Creation of Transnational Ties among Second Generation South Indians" Chapter 20 In L. Tepperman and H.Dickinson (Eds.), *Sociology in Canada: A Canadian Sociological Association Reader*. Canada: Oxford University.

Somerville, K., 2008. Transnational Belonging Among Second Generation Youth: IDENTITY in a Globalized World. *Journal of Social Sciences* 10 (1): 23–33.

Statistics Canada. 2017a. "Canada Census Profile, 2016 Census." Catalogue No. 98-316-X2016001. https://www12.statcan.gc.ca/census-recensement/2016/dp-pd/prof/details/page.cfm?Lang=E&Geo1=PR&Code1=01&Geo2=&Code2=&SearchText=Canada&SearchType=Begins&SearchPR=01&B1=All&TABID=1&type=0.

———. 2017b. "Census in Brief: Linguistic Diversity and Multilingualism in Canadian Homes." 2017. https://www12.statcan.gc.ca/census-recensement/2016/as-sa/98-200-x/2016010/98-200-x2016010-eng.cfm.

———. 2017c. "Immigrant Population in Canada, 2017 Census Population." https://www150.statcan.gc.ca/n1/pub/11-627-m/11-627-m2017028-eng.htm.

———. 2017d. "Immigration and Ethnocultural Diversity Highlight Tables - Visible Minority (Arab), Both Sexes, Age (Total), Canada, Provinces and Territories, 2016 Census – 25% Sample Data." Catalogue No. 98-402-X2016007. https://www12.statcan.gc.ca/census-recensement/2016/dp-pd/hlt-fst/imm/Table.cfm?Lang=E&T=41&Geo=00&SP=1&vismin=8&age=1&sex=1.

———. 2017e. "The Daily— Immigration and Ethnocultural Diversity: Key Results from the 2016 Census." https://www150.statcan.gc.ca/n1/daily-quotidien/171025/dq171025b-eng.htm.

Tan, Alexis, Leigh Nelson, Qingwen Dong, and Gerdean Tan. 1997. Value Acceptance in Adolescent Socialization: A Test of a Cognitive-Functional Theory of Television Effects. *Communication Monographs* 64 (1), 82–97.

Tiilikainen, M., 2017. "'Whenever Mom Hands Over the Phone, Then We talk': Transnational Ties to the Country of Descent Among Canadian Somali Youth." *Migration Letters* 14(1), 63–74.

Tufte, T. 2001. "Minority Youth, Media Uses and Identity Struggle: The Role of the Media in the Production of Locality." In K. Ross and P. Playdon (Eds.), *Black Marks: Minority Ethnic Audiences and Media*33–48. Aldershot; Ashgate.

Tupuola, A.M., 2006. "Participatory Research, Culture and Youth Identities: An Exploration of Indigenous, Cross-Cultural and Trans-National Methods." *Children Youth and Environments* 16(2), 291–316.

Zhou, M. and Bankston III, C.L., 2016. *The Rise of the New Second Generation*. John Wiley & Sons.

Chapter 9

Mahjari Musicians

The Recorded Sounds of Arab Americans in the Early Twentieth Century, 1912–1936

Richard M. Breaux

On March 15, 1956, a short inconspicuous story appeared in the Brooklyn's *Caravan* newspaper, an English-language periodical by, for, and about Arab Americans. The article's title simply read, "Alexander Malouf." There was no particular reason to pay much attention to the story. There was no accompanying photograph and no grand pronouncements. The United States-born children or grandchildren of an Arab immigrant may have missed the article completely and a researcher in the twenty-first century could miss the story in a search, because the surname "Maloof" is misspelled "Malouf." The author of the piece unceremoniously wrote, "Mr. Maloof was a pioneer manufacturer of Arabic records, an accomplished pianist, and headed the Conservatory of Music in Englewood."[1] The brevity of the story belies the fact that at the height of his career, Alexander R. Maloof became a composer without peer. He wrote and published more music for Arabic- and English-speaking Arabs in the United States than any Arab American in the music business from 1899 to 1956. Maloof published his first pieces of music around the same time Ameen Rihani began writing for Arabic-language newspapers in the United States like *Al-Hoda*.[2] Also, Maloof published additional songs at the same time Kahlil Gibran had his first art exhibition and, coincidently, wrote *Al-Musiquah* in 1904 and 1905.[3] Lastly, Maloof recorded his first piano solos in 1913, two years after Rihani published *The Book of Khalid* with illustrations by Kahlil Gibran and the same year future Pen League founder, Nasib Arida, established *Al-Funun* magazine, edited by Mikhail Naimy.[4] Maloof's piano solos "A Trip to Syria" and "Al-Ja-Sa-Yer" represent the first known commercial recordings of music by an Arab American in the history of recorded sound.[5] One of his compositions rose to such prominence that it competed for the coveted spot of the National Anthem of the United States, and he founded one of the first and most prolific Arab American-owned record labels during the early Mahjari Era. The combination of Maloof Phonograph Records and A.J. Macksoud Phonograph Company were to Arab American music in the 1910 and 1920s what the Pen Club was to Mahjar or the Arab American literary movement during the same time period.

Alexander Maloof and Abraham J. Macksoud embodied the spirit of economic and cultural self-determination in the U.S. arm of the Arab diaspora. Their creative and entrepreneurial endeavors entertained and affirmed the cultural identities of countless Arab immigrants to the United States and Arab Americans. From their businesses, based in the mother colony that was Washington Street's Little Syria neighborhood in lower Manhattan, New York City, the influence reached across the United States into our largest cities, our smallest townships, and wherever Arabs settled and put down roots in these United States. The Maloof and Macksoud record labels introduced us to some of the previously little known pioneers of Arabic-language music in the United States.[6]

This chapter explores Arab American cultural self-determination in music industry through an examination of the lives of Alexander Maloof and Abraham J. Macksoud. For most of his life, Alexander Maloof toiled as a music composer, songwriter, pianist, record label owner and seller, and music teacher. By contrast, A.J. Macksoud's worked as phonograph record importer, seller, and record label owner. His was a family of businessmen who opened and operated a host of businesses in New York's Little Syria. Before we examine the establishment of Alexander Maloof's Maloof Deluxe Oriental Phonograph Record Company, Abraham J. Macksoud's Macksoud Phonograph Records, and the artists that performed on these and a few other independent record labels in the 1920s, the lives of Alexander Maloof and A.J. Macksoud in the context of the recording industry in the Middle East, Arab immigration to, and Arab music in, the United States are necessary.

RECORDED MUSIC FOR THE MASHRIQ, MAGREB, AND MAHJAR

To understand the uniqueness of the record labels and musicians highlighted in this chapter it is important to distinguish between music made by and for the Mashriq, Maghreb, and Mahjar. Musicians and record labels produced the earliest commercially available Arabic music in cities like Cairo and Beirut for the expressed purposes of entertaining listeners in the Mashriq countries where northeast Africa, western Asia, and the eastern Mediterranean converge like Egypt, Lebanon, Syria, Jordan, Palestine, Saudi Arabia, Iraq, Yemen,

Bahrain, Qatar, Oman, and the United Arab Emirates. Most people in the first two of three waves of Arab immigrants to the United States (1870s–1940s, 1940s–1960s) hailed from a core of these known as Bilad Al-Sham or Greater Syria—Lebanon, Syria, Jordan, and Palestine. The predominantly North African countries west of Egypt—Libya, Algeria, Morocco, Tunisia, Mauritania, and Western Sahara constitute the Maghreb. The Mahjar represents both place and time—the destinations to which Arabs immigrated and the Mahjari Literary Movement from approximately 1911 to 1940.

Determining a precise beginning or end to the Mahjari Literary Movement can be complicated given the life-span of those writers, poets, and visual artists that were a part of groups like the Pen League. Existing literature acknowledges that the so-called Nadha period and the Mahjari period overlap a few years but is less clear about where one ends and the other begins. If we consider the careers of Afifa Karam, Kahlil Gibran, and Ameen Rihani, we can argue the Mahari Literary Movement began with the earliest published short-stories and poems in Arabic-language newspapers in the 1890s. Moreover, if we consider the years these authors published their first work in English or Arabic, the period gets narrower. Furthermore, Gilbran died in 1931, Karam died in 1924, and Rihani in 1940.

The Mahjar Era vs. The Middle Period of Music

Much has been written about the Mahjar and the Mahjar literary movement that included writers and poets Kahlil Gibran, Ameen Rihani, Abraham Rihbany, Mikahil Naimy, and Afifa Karam; Mahjari musicians—the instrumentalists, singers, record company founders, and owners who replicated and created the recorded sounds of old world and the diaspora on 78 rpm records receive far less attention.[7] Heretofore, the lives, struggles, successes, and setbacks, Arab American musicians in the 1910s, 1920s, and 1930s faced appear in passing, if at all in the existing literature. Ethnomusicologist A.J. Racy has thoroughly and painstakingly documented the history of early Arabic music on 78 RPM records manufactured for the Mashriq and, to a lesser extent, the Maghreb.[8] Similarly, Anne K. Rasmussen has published pioneering research about Arab American musicians who performed and recorded during what she labels "the middle period," "the night club scene," and "contemporary times." This chapter, however, examines the musicians and recorded music of Arab immigrants to the United States and Arab American musicians during the "early years."[9]

The existing literature about Arab American music treats recorded music, record labels, and recorded singers and musicians as largely a monolithic group and makes reference to musicians in the middle period as old timers; in this chapter, these are complicated to conceptualize more specifically what record labels operated during the early versus the middle period, what singers and musicians recorded in the early versus middle period, and those whose careers defy periodization because they recorded, publicly performed, and remained active across the early, middle, and night club eras of Arab American music.[10]

In her reissue retrospective of Arab American music ethnomusicologist, Anne K. Rasmussen notes that Arab Americans created their own labels including "Maloof, Macksoud, Mar'ouf, Star of the East, Abdel Ahad, Cleopatra, Nilephon, Metrophon, Arabphon, Golden Angel, and al-Chark/Orient."[11] The names of these labels are familiar to record collectors and people who purchased them years ago; while Rasmussen does an excellent job of highlighting so-called "old timer" musicians of the middle and night club eras, she does little to distinguish early era from middle era record companies, labels, and to a lesser degree musicians from each other. Stanley Rashid identified fewer, but many of the same record labels, such as "Macsoud, Malouf, Maarouf, Ash Shark, and Alamphone." Rashid, one of two sons of record seller and producer, Albert Rashid, rightly remembered that Maloof and Macksoud represented older Mahjari labels that also produced piano rolls in the early twentieth century.[12]

Record Sellers and a Music Composer in Mahjar Era

Suzanne Macksoud gave birth to Abraham J. Macksoud in August 1878 in Greater Syria, within one year of Thomas Edison's invention of the tinfoil phonograph and some two years after the Centennial International Exposition in Philadelphia in 1876. According to Linda K. Jacobs, several of the Middle Eastern merchants, likely from Beirut, Aleppo, and Damascus, erected booths outside the official Turkish Pavilion. Among the more popular of these was the Palestine bazaar set up by "Nachley & Bros., Jerusalem" where fairgoers bought carved wooden objects, such as cigar boxes, rosaries, and crucifixes.[13] While Syrians lived in the United States before and after this time, Jacobs does not attribute large-scale Arab immigration to the United States to the world's fairs in Philadelphia and Chicago but rather to the combination of the silk market collapse, the exponential population growth in Beirut, and the lure of wealth to be made, pushed, and pulled people from the Near East to United States and other countries in the Americas.[14] New York's Little Syria emerged to replace a neighborhood largely inhabited by Irish immigrants along the Washington Street, Rector Street, and Greenwich Street area, but had not fully come into the full measure of its future influence.

Meanwhile, back in Zaleh, Greater Syria (now Lebanon), Abraham and Hanna Maloof witnessed the birth of Alexander, their second of six children in 1884 or 1885.[15] The Maloofs immigrated to the United States in 1892 or

1894 and settled at 90 Amity Street in the heart of Brooklyn, New York's slightly more affluent Syrian community.[16] In four to six years, Joseph, Suzanne, Abraham J. Macksoud, and the rest of their household joined their relatives, mostly cousins, to the United States.[17] By the early 1900s, the Macksoud Brothers grew their businesses and contacts shrewdly making deals and opening up small businesses in Little Syria. In between the time of Alexander Maloof and A. J. Macksoud arrived in New York with their families, the inventor and entrepreneur, Emile Berliner improved on his Gramophone and developed the flat disk record instead of the wax cylinder record associated with Edison. Recorded music in the United States came to be dominated by the Big Three: Edison (1896), Columbia (1887), and Victor (1901). The Columbia Phonograph Company traces its origins to 1887, although it had connections to the Edison and North American Phonograph Company until 1894.[18] Maria Lisme and Khalil Zacharia recorded the first widely known Arabic music for an audience in the United States on September 25, 1893, for the 1893 World Columbian Exposition in Chicago.[19] We don't know for sure whether these were commercially available, which they likely were not. Although the 5-inch, then 7", 9", and later 10-inch disk record contained a recording on only one side of the disk initially, its design proved to be more durable and easier to store. It was adopted as the industry standard by the time Columbia Phonograph Company and the Victor Talking Machine Company recorded and pressed disk records in 1901.

Most early music on phonograph disks recorded in Arabic for the Mashriq was recorded in Cairo, Beirut, and Damascus. The pioneering work of A.J. Racy tells scholars that signs of the phonograph's popularity emerged in Cairo, Egypt, and Beirut in the 1880s and 1890s.[20] General home use of recording and playback technology did not reach the point of broad distribution until the mid-1890s. According to Racy, London's Gramophone Company (c.1898) likely recorded in Egypt before any other around 1903 or 1904.[21] Gramophone with its company's well-known winged cherub scribe logo, sent employees to Egypt to record early Egyptian, Syrian, and Lebanese singers including Yusuf al-Manyalawi, Dawud Husni, Ibrahim al-Qabbani, Sayyid al-Safti, and Abd al-Hayy Hilmi.[22]

In addition to records on the Gramophone label, the German-based Odeon label similarly recorded musicians like Abd al-Hayy Hilmi, Salamah Hijazi, and Sulayman Abu Dawud. Founded in 1903, evidence suggests Odeon began recording in Egypt by 1905. A.J. Racy asserts that Odeon recorded a significant amount of religious music—Arab Christian and Muslim.[23]

Baidaphon, earlier Baida Records, operated as one of the first Mashriq-focused labels to record Arab musicians owned by Middle Easterners—the Baida cousins.[24] Jibran, Farajallah, Brutus, Michel, and another cousin also named Jibran established Baidaphon in 1906 and within a year the family opened a storefront on Martyrs Square in Beirut.[25] The only other early Mashriqi-targeted label to record artists and press records before 1910 seems to have been Mechian, owned and operated by an Egyptian Armenian named Setrak Mechian. Fewer Mechian disks seemed to have taken and survived the trans-Atlantic journey when compared to Gramophone, Odeon, and Baidaphon records.

There is no primary or secondary source evidence that Alexander Maloof or A.J. Macksoud composed, recorded, or sold any Arabic music prior to immigration. Maloof's would be music composed and recorded for mainstream non-Arab Americans and/or the U.S.-based Mahjar; Macksoud first sold music recorded for the Mashriq to Arab immigrants and Arab Americans, then music recorded in Egypt and Beirut for the Mahjar, and finally music by Mahjari musicians for the Mahjar. As early as 1900, Alexander Maloof, then only 15 or 16 years old, composed and published his first piece of music, "Only Mother's Picture."[26] For his first venture into composing, Maloof teamed up with songwriter George Marguard. By 1903, Maloof composed and published the sheet music for "A Robin's Serenade;" he also performed in one of his first concerts at the Torrington, Connecticut YMCA, in June of the same year. Some 300 listeners attended.[27] The opening of Henius Music Studios brought Maloof and Joseph Henius, the former National Conservatory of Music and Italian Grand Conservatory member, together to teach piano and composition in Brooklyn.[28]

A.J. Macksoud opened his 80 Greenwich Street record store in Little Syria by 1909 with inventory of mostly Baida (later Baidaphon), Odeon, and Columbia records; no known person of Arab ancestry had recorded in the United States yet.[29] As a marketing strategy, Macksoud had dealer stickers designed to affix to the labels of the records he sold. Dealer stickers, for his first location, were oval-shaped with red-ink-printed-on-white and read, *A.J. Macksoud 80 Greenwich St. New York.* These were usually placed strategically on a label so as not to obscure any song titles, performer's name, or identifying matrix, take, or catalog numbers.[30] Whether Macksoud sold sheet music remains unclear, but advertisements suggest that he later stocked piano rolls in addition to records.[31] Alexander Maloof, busily working in his own right, composed and published two more songs by 1910, "Nowhere" and "Empire State Barn Dance."

Maloof, Arab American Musicians, and Macksoud and the Politics of Race during the Mahjar Era

While all this happened, a series of court cases on the question of race transformed the lives of Syrian Americans and Syrian immigrants in the United

States. The 1790 Naturalization Act had long affirmed the practice of limiting naturalized U. S. citizenship to people identified as racially white. Up until this point, Syrian immigrants (technically all people from what is today Syria, Lebanon, Jordan, and Palestine) identified by immigration, census, and judicial authorities as racially white became naturalized citizens after the requisite five years of residency. In 1909, both in California (*Shishim*) and Georgia (In re *Najour* 174 F 735), the courts ruled that Syrians were white, and therefore eligible for naturalized citizenship.[32] But not everyone agreed with these ruling, in the same year U.S. Census Bureau administrators and government employees, charged with administering naturalization, questioned the whiteness of Syrian immigrants causing a ripple effect in some parts of the country.[33] With legal precedents set, the case ruling that Tom Ellis in re *Ellis* 179 F. 1002 appeared to be a foregone conclusion, but three years later, the decision in the *Shahid* 205 F. 812 changed that. In the *Shahid* case, the courts ruled Syrians were Asian, not white. As Asians, Syrians could no longer become naturalized U. S. citizens and some who had already gone through this process had their citizenship and their rights threatened with revocation. Ironically, Alexander Maloof became a naturalized citizen in 1912.[34]

The same year, Maloof became a naturalized citizen, A.J. Macksoud moved around the corner to a bigger space at 89 Washington Street; he also expanded his operation to include record reissuing. It seems that Macksoud may have also opened a second location at 52 Broadway, but for how long? We don't know.[35] At his 89 Washington Street store, Macksoud also began to duplicate low stock items and duplicate them with his own Macksoud label affixed. Macksoud's first label displayed a man on a camel riding toward two pyramids, with a palm tree, sun, and the address 89 Washington Street, New York, at the label's top.[36] Today, this is a much rarer label to locate.

Syrian immigrant and Syrian American fraternal organizations, churches, and community groups recognized Alexander Maloof's talents and began to book him for recitals, concerts, and other engagements. Between 1911 and 1914, Maloof was showered with a host of predictable and unforeseen opportunities. Gigs at the Damascus Masonic Lodge in Brooklyn and an agreement to score the all-Syrian cast performance of "The Iron Master" at Brooklyn's Academy of Music kept Maloof busy and fairly compensated. Reportedly, some 1,000 Syrians in Brooklyn and Manhattan bought tickets for the play.[37] On July 24, 1913, and September 16, 1913, Alexander Maloof made history when he recorded his "A Trip to Syria" #17443-A and "Al-Ja-Za-Yer," #17443 B for the Victor Talking Machine Company.[38] No Arabic script appeared anywhere on the record label, yet Victor categorized the songs as "Syrian."[39] Although not the first commercial record marketed exclusively to an Arabic-speaking audience in the United States, it was the first known recording by an Arab American produced in the United States.

Based on the fact that Maloof did not record with Victor again until 1926 music historians assume sales tanked.[40] An alternative interpretation of the records sale numbers suggest Victor did a poor job of marketing to the Arab immigrant populations in the United States, opting to market Maloof to English-speaking listeners as a crossover musician. One year after Maloof recorded the two sides for Victor, he composed and published, along with E.T. Paulli, his breakout sheet music hit, "The Egyptian Glide" in 1914. The Lebanese, immigrant singer Nahim Simon became Victor's and Columbia's success story; however, we know very little about Simon. Sources suggest he used the revenue from his success to travel between mandate-controlled Lebanon and the U.S. through the 1920s.[41] Others who recorded for Columbia and/or Victor in the 1910s included the Maronite priest Rev. George Aziz.

Maronite churches in Buffalo, New York, West Scranton, Pennsylvania, Cleveland, Ohio, and Birmingham, Alabama operated under Aziz's leadership, and he remained well-known for his splendid singing voice. Birmingham, Alabama's Saint Elias Maronite Church procured Aziz's service as pastor for two separate tenures—1920–1923 and 1929–1934. According to Saint Elias Church history, during his first tenure, Father Aziz "rewrote the music and Arabic phonetically so the choir and parishioners could fully participate in the Liturgy."[42] Increasingly, second generation U.S.-born Arab Americans may have spoken and understood spoken Arabic but were less likely to read Arabic script. The generational changes and assimilation, especially in smaller communities that did not take in newer waves of Arab immigrants, no longer read handwritten or printed Arabic. By providing transliterated Arabic, younger people could hold onto traditions that many smaller communities of Syrian and Lebanese Americans eventually lost. Aziz died during a return trip to Lebanon in 1936.[43] Over the course of his life, he only commercially recorded the two Christmas songs for Columbia E Series 1867, # 39380/#39381 – Sabeho Elrab b/w Samawty Yabatoulatt on May 15, 1914 and one song "Lebanon" #6891 on Alexander Maloof's label in the 1920s.[44]

The U.S. courts finally settled the issue of naturalization for Syrian immigrants in the case of George Dow. Initially, using the "common knowledge" argument as basis for its decision, the courts ruled that Syrian were not racially white and could longer become naturalized citizens. Syrian Americans and Syrian immigrants in the United States mobilized their global resources and called on scholars, journalists, ministers to donate their collective financial and intellectual capital to the case. Rev. Khalil A. Bishara stands out as one of those Syrian Americans who lent his research to the case. He published, *The Origin of the Modern Syrian* in 1914 with backing from *Al-Hoda* founder and publisher, Naoum Mokarzel. In the English edition of the work, Bishara aligned Syrians with the biblical "Moses, Elijah, Hannibal, Amos, Paul, Peter, and John."[45] Although Bishara, added the Prophet Mohammed in the

Arabic edition of the text, he omitted such references to Islam and its prophetic founder in the English edition. In the end, the court ruled Dow, and by extension Syrians, white.[46]

During the years Syrians in the United States fought to maintain their path to citizenship, Alexander Maloof's song "America Ya Hilwa" or "For Thee, America" competed to become the National Anthem of the United States. In 1912, the U. S. Congress had not yet voted to adopt the "Star-Spangled Banner" as the nation's official national anthem. Maloof, a budding composer with a number of published songs under his belt, collaborated with Elizabeth Ferber Fields to create "For Thee, America."[47] The press in New York, and later the national press, caught wind of Maloof's growingly popular song. By 1915, the debate about the need for a national anthem intensified, and Maloof had since composed and published more songs and had recorded with the Victor Talking Machine Company. In an effort to promote his song, Maloof penned a letter to the *New York Times*:

> In this morning's issue of the *New York Times* I happened to glance at the enclosed article relative to a new national anthem. I wish to call attention to the fact that a new national anthem has been composed by me, entitled "For Thee, America," and has been adopted by the Board of education of New York for use in the public schools, and endorsed by such men as Walter Damrosch, David Mannes and many other musical celebrities in the United States. This anthem is now being used in no less than twenty States, with the prospect that it will be adopted in other cities.[48]

The use of Maloof's song in New York and approximately twenty states during the same year the "prospective fate" Syrian Americans hung in the balance is, to say the least, ironic. The previous year, early twentieth-century music scholar, Frank R. Rix, who served as Director of Music for the City of New York, and authored "The Assembly Song Book," "The High School Assembly Song Book," and "Voice Training for Children," included Maloof's "For Thee, America" in "Patriotic Songs" section of the "The Junior Assembly Song Book" along with "Hail, Columbia," "The Star-Spangled Banner," "The Battle Cry of Freedom," "Flag of Freedom," "The Battle Hymn of the Republic," and other songs.[49] Newport, Rhode Island approved the use of "For Thee, America" and "The Star-Spangled Banner" for use in its 1917 public school graduation exercises.[50]

Although music produced by Arab immigrants to the United States rarely appeared in sources about or created by Mahjari writers, at least one case proved worthy of note. A rare Columbia records advertisement appeared in *Al-Funoon* magazine in October 1916 that encouraged Arab immigrants and Arab Americans to purchase one of the four special reissue disks that featured Nahim Simon's band or Naim Karacand's band.[51] Two disks starred Nahim Simon's band #2947 "Loan-Elhawagib No. 1 & 2," and #2948 "Ashti-Eshtibaky No. 1 & 2," produced in June, 1916, and two disks showcased Karacand's band- #2949 Azrbar Bishro No. 1 & 2," and #2950 "Bitar Bishro No. 1 & 2" recorded August, 1916.[52] The catalog numbers, which also appear in the runout section on the disks, as well as the labels, should not be confused with the matrix numbers, the records companies tracking and filing system to help them locate recording masters among its vast holdings. The point of the ad was to announce that these sessions, with a nearly designed label displaying a woman in the middle of a war-torn-burning-village with two children clinging to her legs, asked, buyers to "Support those in need" and "the proceeds would go to the Syrian Relief."[53] The artists reportedly donated any royalties to the relief effort as well. *Al-Funoon* was, of course, one of the first Arabic literary magazine's in the United States. Founded by Nasib Arida in 1913 and co-edited by Mikhail Naimy. Arida, was of course, was a founding member of the Pen League and Naimy among its more noted members. This ad demonstrates the Mahjari writers and musicians did not labor isolated from one another.

Nearly a dozen Arab immigrant and Arab American musicians recorded with Columbia and/or Victor between 1913 and 1920, some like Louis Wardiny, Naim Karacand, and Nahim Simon enjoyed unparalleled success. A.J. Macksoud continued to sell records and changed locations a few times. As Victor and Columbia added Arab American musicians to their roster of performers, Macksoud continued to sell Baidaphon and Odeon alongside Victor and Columbia.[54] Most musicians recorded two or three songs over the course of one or two days and then fell into obscurity. Columbia recorded fourteen different Arab immigrant and Arab American musicians between 1914 and 1919. Victor, on the other hand, recorded two during the same period. Similarly, Columbia recorded eight Arabic-language artists, and Victor recorded three between 1920 and 1928. One of the three Arab Americans to have sessions with Victor in the 1920s was Alexander Maloof.[55] Even as Columbia cut back on recording Arabic-language records by Mahjari musicians for Mahjari audiences and Victor demonstrated little interest in them, Alexander Maloof and A.J. Macksoud established their own record labels.

The story of Maloof Phonograph Company and A.J. Macksoud defies detailed accounts in the absence of catalogues and written sources saved by these companies or preserved on their behalf. Despite their cultural influence and reach, stories about these two businesses beyond advertisements in some Arab American newspapers, magazines, and business directories do not reveal much of the inner workings of these companies. Maloof appears to have started his record label around 1920 and maintained it through 1934.[56]

The famed Gennett Records in Richmond, Indiana, pressed most of Maloof's records and by 1921 Gennett had recording studios at its headquarters in Indiana and at 11 East 37th Street in New York City. Maloof artists and their accompanists recorded at both locations between 1921 and 1927 and at the Gennett studios on Woodside Avenue in Long Island City from 1927 to 1932.[57] Sources reveal less about the studios in which Macksoud artists recorded. The walk from Little Syria where Maloof and Macksoud set up shop and Columbia's studios at 233 Broadway was a short half mile walk that would have taken twelve minutes.[58] Gennett's East 37th Avenue recording studio was 3.5 miles apart.

Self-Determination, Arab American Music, and Mahjari Musicians

Despite their shared language, Mahjari musicians who recorded for Maloof and Macksoud had all taken rather circuitous paths to their respective labels; some musicians recorded exclusively for one label and others recorded on both Maloof and Macksoud. Exclusive Macksoud musicians included Beirut-born Andrew Mekanna who had recently arrived in the United States in 1920 via Cherbourg, France, and played with violinist Naim Karacand and oudist Toufic Moubaid and Assad Dakroub, a Muslim musician and music teacher from Tebnine who immigrated to the United States not via Ellis Island but via the Mexico–Texas border.[59] Maloof, too, signed musicians exclusive to his label including the elusive Lateefy Abdou, Saint Louis-born Anthony Shaptini, Tripoli-born Arab classical musician Midhat Serbagi, and Fedora Kurban, the "defiant" Palestinian-born daughter of an American University of Beirut professor.[60] Salim Doumani, who recorded for both Maloof and Macksoud, arrived in the United States in 1920 after time in prison for his refusal to fight for the Ottoman Army during World War I, family oral-history maintains Doumani's incredible singing voice earned him enough favor from a prison guard that he eventually fled to the United States.[61] The most prolific musicians became those like Constantine Souss and Louis Wardiny who recorded for Victor and/or Columbia in the 1910s, for Maloof and/or Macksoud in the 1920s, and recorded on independent, sometimes their own labels, in the 1940s and 1950s.

Constantine Souss and Louis Wardiny arrived in the United States from Jerusalem in 1903 and Beirut in 1904, respectively. Both made enough of a name for themselves in Syrian American fundraising concert circles to record for Victor on May 16, 1917, in the case of Wardiny and October 8 and October 10, 1917, for Souss. Interestingly, the Victor Talking Machine Company required both to complete trial recording sessions before the label agreed to full recording sessions.[62] Wardiny recorded ten songs for Victor in addition to the trial recording and Souss cut thirteen songs with Victor, plus his trial recording, although Victor rejected four of his recorded songs. Souss, with a variant spelling of his surname, recorded in Columbia in May and June of 1919 and February, 1920.[63] After a few years of performing for various Near East fundraising concerts, Souss recorded two songs # 8313 "Ya Meet Masa" and #8315 "Michjata 'l Sab" on Maloof's label on April 4, 1923. Louis Wardiny recorded over twenty-nine songs on Maloof between 1921 and 1925 and over five songs on Macksoud. He played hafli and mahrajan for most of the 1930s and 1940s and established Wardatone, his own record label, in Detroit in 1951.[64]

Alexander Maloof's and A.J. Macksoud's phonograph companies shipped records all over the United States to cities as close as Newark, New Jersey, and Boston, Massachusetts to remote towns like Janesville and La Crosse, Wisconsin, and as far away as San Francisco and Los Angeles, California. Music from songs on their record labels resounded from phonographs and gramophones in church basements, living rooms, parlors, restaurants, and other Arab American businesses in Little Syrian neighborhoods and streets wherever Syrian immigrants and Syrian Americans settled. Songs like Macksoud #1520 "Syria, the Nation," "Mount Lebanon," Maloof # 1320 "Syria, My Country," Maloof #900 "Take Me By Plane to My Country," and Maloof #2006 "In the Land of My Ancestors," recalled and celebrated home and loved one's left behind.[65] Indeed, Kay Kaufman Shelemay argues that music was sometimes "associated with the locale and situation at which they were originally heard whether at a concert, at home, or at school."[66] Some of the songs on Maloof and Macksoud were folk or classical Arabic music, some were poems set to new arrangements, other music, particularly that composed by Maloof himself, was a hybrid of Western and Eastern musical forms. Not all records contained music, some included comedic skits and routines like Macksoud # 710 "Invitation of Tom & Dorothy for Supper," Macksoud #301 "Comic Telephone Tom & Dorothy," and Macksoud # "Tom and Dorothy Visit Coney Island."[67]

The growth of Macksoud and Maloof meant the expansion of business and opportunity as Macksoud became a wholesaler with dealers in states on the East Coast and in the Midwest; Maloof appeared on air in radio program performances. Two articles in the *Talking Machine World* mention Macksoud. One maintains, "Mr. Macksoud making prompt deliveries to the dealers" and the other noted that the Euclid Music Co. "secured wholesale representation for the foreign records imported by Macksoud, of New York."[68] Taken together, it seems that although Abraham J. Macksoud served as the primary owner of the record company, his family worked as dealers at different locations and he had to establish relationships with other businesses to sell records to Arab American communities outside of New York's Little Syria.

Outside of phonograph records, Maloof's most consistent work involved him and/or his orchestra playing on the radio, the industry that nearly destroyed the phonograph record business. For example, from October 1925 and through 1926, listeners could tune-in to hear Alexander Maloof's Orchestra on WEAF New York's "Oriental Hour" at 10:00 pm. In 1927, the station moved Maloof to the 7:30 p.m. slot.[69] Maloof gave regular solo and group performances on WGBS in 1928 and in 1929 and 1930 audiences could catch Maloof on WOR where he directed the Bamberger Salon Orchestra. Maloof and Fadwa Kurban were also a part of a one-hour block of Arabic music and dialogue from 8:00 p.m. to 9:00 p.m. on WBBR in 1929.[70]

Alexander Maloof seemingly worked non-stop in the 1920s and early 1930s, and it should come as no surprise that he collaborated with many of the musicians that recorded on his labels for live performances. For example, in 1923, Maloof and Midhat Serbagi gave a joint recital at the Brooklyn Academy of Music.[71] He and Fadwa Kurban teamed up to perform at the Academy of Music in May 1929 for a Syrian Orphanage benefit and the Poughkeepsie Lebanon American Club annual fundraiser in August 1929. Novelist and Pen League writer Ameen Rihani wrote convincingly in November 1930 of the "compositions of Alexander Malouf, the voice of Midhat Sarbaji" as evidence of the Arab Americans contribution to the arts.[72] He maintained that Maloof's songs were "sung in Syrian and American homes" and Serbagi's "voice has been coupled by an authority with [Einrico] Caruso's."[73] Rihani's praises for Serbagi and Kurban did not stop there. Of Serbagi he concluded, "when I first heard him sing Arabic in an opera technique, I realized the possibilities of a supreme harmony in the art of two worlds. Here was for me the fascination of double magic."[74] Similarly, Rihani raved of Fedora Fadwa Kurban, "Even the birds in the olive groves must have wondered at the voice of this Syrian nightingale;" "At that moment I felt that I was receiving a message, through Fadwa Kurban, from the gods."[75] Alexander Maloof and Fedora Kurban performed at two separate concerts on December 7 for Bengali poet and musician Rabindranath Tagore and December 14 for physicist Albert Einstein in 1930.[76] By 1930, too, Alexander Maloof and A.J. Macksoud literally moved from working in the same neighborhood to conducting business from addresses on the same block—92 Washington Street and 88 Washington Street.

A combination of the Great Depression and radio's growth nearly wiped out the record industry as Maloof Phonograph Company recorded its last songs and A.J. Macksoud's career came to an end. The stock market crash of 1929, the result of over speculation and inflated stock values, left 25 percent of the country's population unemployed. Consumers had the wages and wealth to purchase over 100 million records in 1925, but the Depression reduced this to six million records sold per year. Maloof and Macksoud felt the devastation of the market collapse and economy left Maloof recording music for skating rinks and funeral parlors. Palestinian-born Fedora "Fadwa" Kurban, at her career's peak, performed at the Khedivial Opera House in Cairo with King Faud I in the audience.[77] In 1930, Kurban sang as a soloist at the Westminster Presbyterian Church in Utica, New York, on the program was Presbyterian minister Rev. Khalil A. Bishara, author of *The Origin of the Modern Syrian*, who had come to the defense of Syrian immigrants and the Syrian American masses back in 1914 and 1915 in the George Dow naturalization case. Bishara, himself, recorded a rare phonograph record with the song "My God's Love" in the 1920s on a vanity or personalized label produced by the Electric Recording Laboratories in New York City.[78] The Electric Recording Laboratories is notable, because it permitted anyone with $35 and the inclination to record opportunities to make professionally recorded and produced phonographs records. At least one other Syrian American minister, Rt. Rev. Agapios Golam, once considered as a possibility to lead the Antiochian Orthodox Church in North America, cut approximately eight liturgical songs in Arabic and Greek on a vanity label with the same company.[79] Mahjari writer Kahlil Gibran died in April 1931. Kurban made her final Maloof recordings in March and June of 1932.[80] Within the year, Joseph Beilouny and Sabri Andria launched the Arabian Nights Radio Program in 1933 on Brooklyn's WCNW, and later New York's WWRL.[81] Albert J. Macksoud's business disappeared from the New York City directory in 1934, and Macksoud died four years later. Radio's much less expensive format and transition from live band to record use created new obstacles and opportunities for the record industry.

The End of the Mahjari Era

In the uncertain times that were the Great Depression, Alexander Maloof returned to the professional habits he knew best—teaching, composing, and publishing music. Although Maloof first conceived of a school in the 1920s when he maintained residency at Carnegie Hall, he established the Carnegie School of Music in Englewood, New Jersey, in 1934. After building the faculty, Carnegie collaborated with the Bergen Junior College in Teaneck, New Jersey, to share resources and facilities. Moreover, between 1931 and his death in 1956, Maloof's published books of music and compositions increased from five to 12.[82] As Maloof grew older, and with A.J. Macksoud deceased, a new generation of Arab American musicians and record companies including larger labels like Al-Chark and Alamphon, and small labels like Al-Kawakeb, Karawan, Star of the East, and Mazloom emerged. Yet in his later years, Alexander Maloof, the composer, record label owner, pianist, and music teacher went into the studio one last time to record with members of his old orchestra. The result was a 78 RPM album set of eight sides on four disks released by Continental Records that included a newly recorded release of one of his first recorded songs "A Trip to Syria" and several previously recorded and never-before-recorded compositions. The advertisement in *Billboard* magazine, one of the leading periodicals of music in the United States, listed Maloof's "Music of the Orient" alongside records by popularly known acts like Andrew Sisters, the Nat "King" Cole Trio, and rhythm & blues pianist Mary Lou Williams.[83] There, Alexander Maloof's recorded music symbolically passed the baton from the first generation of Arab American musicians to those more commonly recognized, studied, and centered in the scholarship of Arab American music pioneering work of more contemporary scholars of Arab American music as a part of the diaspora.

The commercial recording careers of Alexander Maloof, Constantine Souss, Louis Wardiny, and Naim Karacand, spanned nearly three decades from the 1910s to the 1940s (and even 1950s for some) consequently these Mahjari Era musicians are often mistaken for musicians of the "middle period." The musical careers of their earlier contemporaries like Salim Doumani, Midhat Serbagi, Assad Dakroub, Wadih Bagdaddy, Lateefy Abou, Andrew Mekanna, Fedora Kurban, Nahim Simon, Anthony Shaptini, and other lesser-known musicians like Sam Attaya, Mayer Morad, or the singing priests Fr. George Aziz, Rev. K.A. Bishara, and Agapios Golam, fit more squarely into the Mahjari Era and complete the story of Arab American music. Thanks to increased accessibility of newspapers, magazines, and other sources related the first wave of Arab immigrants to the United States, we are beginning to see a more complicated, nuanced, and interconnected view of the Mahjari Era, perhaps this interconnected perspective warrants a change from the Mahjar Literary Movement to the Mahjari Arts & Letters Movement.

NOTES

1. "Alexander Malouf," *The Caravan* 15 March 1956.
2. Nijmeh Hajjar, *The Politics and Poetics of Ameen Rihani: The Humanist Ideology of an Arab-American Intellectual and Activist* (New York: I.B. Tauris Academic Publishers, 2010), 43.
3. Alexandre Najjar, *Kahlil Gibran: A Biography* (San Francisco: Saqi, 2002), 50 and 55; Suheil Bushrui and Joe Jenkins, Kahlil Gibran: Man and Poet (Oxford: One World, 1998), 69 and 71.
4. Nijmeh Hajjar, *The Politics and Petics of Ameen Rihani,* 31 and 44.
5. Richard K. Spottswood, *Ethnic Music on Record: A Discography of Ethnic Recordings Produced in the United States, 1893–1942,* Volume 5 (Urbana: University of Illinois Press, 1991): 2484, See the multivolume and encyclopedic, but incomplete

set by Spottswood, Volume 5 included Middle Eastern recordings in the United States including Arabic, Armenian, Persian, and Turkish.

6. Anne K. Rasmussen, *The Music of Arab Americans*: A Retrospective Collection (Cambridge, MA: Rounder, 1997), CD-booklet. Rasmussen's work introduced many to mahjari musicians such as Alexander Maloof, Naim Karacand, Constantine Souss, and Andrew Mekanna.

7. Randa A. Kayyali, *The Arab Americans* (Westport, CT: Greenwood Press, 2006), 123. Kayyali lumps "Macsoud, Malouf, Maarouf, Ash Shark, and Alamphone" together as existing between 1920 and 1940. I have never seen evidence of Maarouf Records despite its mention in several texts, Ash Shark or Al-Chark was not founded until after 1940 by Albert Rashid although Rashid began his business around 1935. Alamphon, too, began in the 1940s.

8. Rassmussen, *The Music of Arab Americans*, 4; Anne K. Rasmussen, "The Music of Arab Americans: Aesthetics and Performance in a New Land," in Sherifa Zuhur, ed. *Images of Enchantment: Visual and Performing Arts of the Middle East* (Cairo: American University in Cairo Press, 1998), 136–139.

9. Ali Jihad Racy, "Record Industry and Egyptian Traditional Music, 1904–1932," *Ethnomusicology* 20:1 (1976), 23–48; Racy explores the multiple impacts of recorded Arabian music on companies' selection of material, the recording process, and methods of commercial distribution in A. J. Racy, "Arabian Music and the Effects of Commercial Recording," *The World of Music, the Arab World* 20, 1 (1978): 78.

10. Rassmussen, *The Music of Arab Americans: A Retrospective*, 4; Stanley Rashid, "Cultural Traditions of Early Arab Immigrants to New York," in Kathleen Benson and Philip M. Kayal, eds. *A Community of Many Worlds: Arab Americans in New York City* (New York: Museum of the City of New York/Syracuse University Press, 2002), 79.

11. Rasmussen, The Music of Arab Americans: A Retrospective, 4.

12. Rashid, "Cultural Traditions of Early Arab Immigrants," 79.

13. Linda K. Jacobs, *Strangers No More: Syrians in the United States, 1880–1900*, kindle edition (Kalimah Press, 2019): loc 6618–6647.

14. Linda K. Jacobs, *Strangers in the West: The Syrian Colony in New York City, 1880-1900*, Kindle Edition (Kalimah Press, 2015): loc 807–818.

15. "Alexander Ragi Maloof, Petition for Naturalization," Ancestry.com. *New York, State and Federal Naturalization Records, 1794–1943* [database on-line]. Provo, UT, USA: Ancestry.com Operations, Inc., 2013.

16. *1900*; Census Place: *Brooklyn Ward 6, Kings, New York*; Page: *2*; Enumeration District: *0053*; FHL microfilm: *1241044*, Ancestry.com. *1900 United States Federal Census* [database on-line]. Provo, UT, USA: Ancestry.com Operations Inc, 2004.

17. "Abraham Macksoud," "Elias Macksoud," "Gabriel Macksoud," Brooklyn Elite City Directory (1904), 589, Ancestry.com. *U.S. City Directories, 1822-1995* [database on-line]. Provo, UT, USA: Ancestry.com Operations, Inc., 2011.

18. Racy, "Record Industry and Egyptian Traditional Music," 24, 25, and 26.

19. Spottswood, *Ethnic Music on Record*, 2483 and 2487.

20. Racy, "Record Industry and Egyptian Traditional Music," 23.

21. Racy, "Record Industry and Egyptian Traditional Music," 25.

22. Rusmussen, *The Music of Arab Americans: A Retrospective*, 4; Racy, "Record Industry and Egyptian Traditional Music," 27–31.

23. Racy, "Record Industry and Egyptian Traditional Music," 33–36.

24. One of the original Baida Records has the words, "Baida Cousins Beyrouth Syrie," on the label. See Baida Records #900, authors collection.

25. Racy, "Record Industry and Egyptian Traditional Music,"40.

26. Original copy of Alexander Maloof and George Marguard, "Only My Mother's Picture," (1901) in author's collection. Another copy of this song has a 1900 copyright date.

27. "Torrington," *The Hartford Courant*, 9 June 1903, p. 15; Alexander Maloof, "Robin's Serenade," sheet music in author's collection.

28. "Henius Music Studio Ad," *The Brooklyn Eagle*, 4 February 1905, p. 13 and 9 February 1905, p.13.

29. Dr. Nagib Abdou, *Travels in America: A Commercial Directory of Arabic Speaking People of the World* (Nagib Abdou: 1907),188 and 234, Original located at the Moise A. Khayallah Center for Lebanese Diaspora Studies, https://lebanesestudies.omeka.chass.ncsu.edu/items/show/13912#?c=0&m=0&s=0&cv=0.

30. "A.J. Macksoud '80 Greenwich' Dealer Sticker," See Baida Records #900, authors collection.

31. Ad for A.J. Macksoud," in *The Syrian American Directory Almanac* (1930). Original in of the Khalil Gibran Digital Archive. https://www.kahlilgibran.com/digital-archive.html?category[0]=1&category_children=1&own=0&tag[0]=almanac.

32. Sarah M. A. Gualtieri, *Between Arab and White: Race and Ethnicity in the Early Syrian Diaspora* (Berkley: University of California Press, 2009), 57, 58, 60–61.

33. "Syrians Barred from Franchise," *The Los Angeles Herald*, 21 October 1909, p. 8.

34. "Alexander Ragi Maloof, Declaration for Intention," "Alexander Ragi Maloof, Petition for Naturalization," The National Archives and Records Administration; Washington, D.C.; *Petitions for Naturalization from the U.S. District Court for the Southern District of New York, 1897–1944*; Series: *M1972*; Roll: *104*, Ancestry.com. *New York, Naturalization Records, 1882-1944* [database on-line]. Provo, UT, USA: Ancestry.com Operations, Inc., 2012.

35. "Abraham J. Macksoud," *New York City Directory* (1913), 970, Ancestry.com. *U.S. City Directories, 1822–1995* [database on-line]. Provo, UT, USA: Ancestry.com Operations, Inc., 2011.

36. Zaki Effendi Mourad, "Mazloumah Wayak I," AJ Macksoud 89 Washington Street label, author's collection.

37. "Damascus Lodge, F & A.M.," *The Brooklyn Daily Eagle*, 8 March 1911, 17; "Brilliant Assemblage At Masonic Reception," *The Brooklyn Daily Eagle*, 17 October 1911, 7; "Fraternal Societies: Damascus Lodge F and A.M.," *The Brooklyn Eagle*, 26 December 1911, 15; "Syrian Women on Stage Break Away from Custom," *The Brooklyn Daily Eagle*, 1 April 1912, 4.

38. Spottswood, *Ethnic Music on Record*, 2484.

39. Alexander Maloof, "A Trip to Syria," and "Al-Ja-Za-Yer," Victor #17443A & B in author's collection.

40. Spottswood, *Ethnic Music on Record*, 2486.

41. "Naim Sa'man," Discogs.com, https://www.discogs.com/artist/4714740-%D9%86%D8%B9%D9%8A%D9%85-%D8%B3%D9%85%D8%B9%D8%A7%D9%86.

42. "History of Saint Elias Maronite Church," Birmingham, Alabama, http://www.stelias.org/history.htm.

43. "Rev. George Aziz," *Scranton Republican*, 2 May 1936, 8.

44. Spottswood, *Ethnic Music on Record*, 2479.

45. Gaultieri, *Between Arab and White*, 72–73; Kalil A. Bishara, *The Origin of the Modern Syrian* (New York: Al-Hoda Press, 1914), original located at The Internet Archive. https://archive.org/details/originmodernsyria00bishrich/page/n6.

46. Gaultieri, Between Arab and White, 73.

47. "New National Anthem Pleases Musicians," *The Buffalo Evening News*, 22 May 1912, 10.

48. Alexander Maloof, "For Thee, America," *The New York Times*, 15 July 1916.

49. Frank R. Rix, *The Junior Assembly Song Book* (New York: A.S. Barnes Co., 1914), Table of Contents and 9.

50. Annual Report of the Public School Department of the City of Newport in Rhode Island (Newport: Mercury Publishing, 1916–1917), 64.

51. "Columbia Advertisement," *Al-Funoon* Magazine (October 1916), 12–13.

52. Spottswood, *Ethnic Music on Record*, 2482 and 2493–2494.

53. "Columbia Advertisement," *Al-Funoon* Magazine (October 1916), 12–13.

54. "A.J. Macksoud Ad," *Talking Machine World magazine* (October 15, 1923), 168.

55. Summary of recordings listed in Spottswood, *Ethnic Music on Record*, 2477–2500.

56. Spottswood, *Ethnic Music on Record*, 2484–2487. The author's collection includes approximately 62 Maloof 78 RPM Records, the oldest includes a date of 1920 and the most recent include the date 1927.

57. Finding Aide, "John K. Mackenzie Gennett Record Company Collection, 1887–1976," 4–6, Collection #M0428 OM0133, Indiana Historical Society Archives, Indianapolis, Indiana; "A Rare Look Inside Gennett Studios (1925)," https://the78rpmrecordspins.wordpress.com/2013/03/02/a-rare-look-inside-gennetts-new-york-studio-1925-courtesy-main-spring-blog/.

58. Ian Nagoski, Isil Acehan, Todd Fine, "The Music of 'Little Syria' and 'Ottoman New York' Walking Tour," 21 September 2019.

59. Richard M. Breaux, "Andrew MeKanna: A Life in Music and Theater Arts," 22 November 2019, Midwest Mahjar: The Recorded Sounds on the Greater Syrian Diaspora in the 78 RPM Era blog, http://syrianlebanesediasporasound.blogspot.com/2019/11/andrew-mekanna-life-in-musical-arts-and.html.

60. Richard M. Breaux, "Midhat Serbagi: A Classical Arab Music in Early 20th Century America," 18 May 18, 2019, Midwest Mahjar: The Recorded Sounds on the Greater Syrian Diaspora in the 78 RPM Era blog, http://syrianlebanesediasporasound.blogspot.com/2019/05/midhat-serbagi-musician-midhat-serbagi.html.

_____Richard M. Breaux, "Anthony Shaptini: Songs of the Midwest Mahjar in America's Heartland," 6 September 2019, Midwest Mahjar: The Recorded

Sounds on the Greater Syrian Diaspora in the 78 RPM Era blog, http://syrianlebanesediasporasound.blogspot.com/2019/09/anthony-shaptini-songs-of-midwest.html.

⎯⎯⎯⎯⎯⎯. Richard M. Breaux, "Fedora 'Fadwa' Kurban: The Defiant Daughter and the Last Years of Maloof Records," 14 September 2019, Midwest Mahjar: The Recorded Sounds on the Greater Syrian Diaspora in the 78 RPM Era blog, http://syrianlebanesediasporasound.blogspot.com/2019/09/fedora-fadwa-kurban-defiant-daughter.html.

61. Roy Simon interview with author, 1 July 2019; Richard M. Breaux, "Salim Doumani: One of Arab America's Earliest Recorded Vocalist," 3 July 2019, Midwest Mahjar: The Recorded Sounds on the Greater Syrian Diaspora in the 78 RPM Era blog, http://syrianlebanesediasporasound.blogspot.com/2019/07/salim-doumani-one-of-arab-americas.html.

62. Spottswood, *Ethnic Music on Record*, 2495–2497 and 2497–2499.

63. Spottswood, *Ethnic Music on Record*, 2495–2497 and 2497–2499.

64. "New Detroit Label Features Orientals,' *Billboard Magazine*, 14 July 1951. Anne Rasmussen defines the hafli or hafla as musical event that's "a cross between a sahra (an evening house party involving live music) and a concert." Paid entertainers perform live, like at a concert, and the audience sits at tables, have food and drink, and some people participate in folk dance. A mahrajan is "an extended outing lasting two or three days where music is played both in the afternoon and evening. Originally, mahjaranat were church picnics where musicians would play, would dance, and the old folks would tell their stories to the young." Both serve as a space where cultural practices and histories passed from one generation to the next and often possessed a fundraising component where money was used to help a church, charity, cultural group, disaster relief, or philanthropic organization. Anne K. Rasmussen, "The Music of Arab Americans," in *Images of Enchantment: Visual and Performing Arts of the Middle East*, ed. Sherifa Zuhur (Cairo: American University Press, 1998), 140 and 144.

65. These titles are taken from Maloof and Macksoud records in the author's collection.

66. Kay Kaufman Shelemay, *Let Jasmine Rain Down: Song and Rememberance Among Syrian Jews* (Chicago: University of Chicago Press, 1998), 48.

67. These titles are taken from Maloof and Macksoud records in the author's collection.

68. "Catalog of Imported Records," *The Talking Machine World*, 15 October 1923, 51.

69. "WEAF," *The Boston Globe*, 5 October 1926; "WEAF, New York," *The Ithaca Journal*, 5 February 1927.

70. "WBBR," *The Brooklyn Times Union*, 23 May 1929.

71. "Joint Recital Given by Midhat Serbagi and Alexander Maloof," *The Brooklyn Daily Eagle*, 18 May 1923.

72. Ameen Rihani, "The Syrian in American Art," *The Syrian World* (November, 1930), 10, Michael W. Suleiman Collection, 2010.51.00, Box 72, Syrian World, Arab American National Museum Archives, Dearborn, Michigan.

73. Rihani, "The Syrian in American Art," 11.

74. Rihani, "The Syrian in American Art," 11.
75. Rihani, "The Syrian in American Art,"11.
76. "Maloof Plays for Einstein and Tangore," *Syrian World* magazine (January 1931), 51, Michael W. Suleiman Collection, 2010.51.00, Box 72, Syrian World, Arab American National Museum Archives, Dearborn, Michigan; Roger S. Vreeland, "Music," The Hackensack New Jersey *Record,* 16 October 1935, 11.
77. "Madame Fedora Kurban Eagerly Works for Great Operatic Change," *The Windsor Star*, 1 August 1930, 9.
78. Richard M. Breaux, "Dr. Khalil A. Bishara: a Presbyterian Minister Who Defended the Rights of Syrians and Others," 15 January 2020, Midwest Mahjar: The Recorded Sounds on the Greater Syrian Diaspora in the 78 RPM Era blog, http://syrianlebanesediasporasound.blogspot.com/2020/01/dr-kalil-bishara-presbyterian-minister.html.
79. Antony Gabriel, "A Retrospective: One Hundred years of Antiochian Orthodoxy in North America," in George S. Corey, Peter Gillquist, Anne Glynn Mackoul, Jean Sam, and Paul Schneirla, eds. *The First One Hundred Years: A Centennial Anthology Celebrating Antiochian Orthodoxy in North America* (Englewood: Antakya Press, 1995), 257; Richard M. Breaux, "Rt. Rev. Agapios Golam: Ancient Antiochian Orthodox Music at 78 RPM," 3 November 2018, Midwest Mahjar: The Recorded Sounds on the Greater Syrian Diaspora in the 78 RPM Era blog, http://syrianlebanesediasporasound.blogspot.com/2018/11/ancient-antiochian-orthodox-music-at-78.html.
80. Spottswood, *Ethnic Music on Record*, 2483–2484.
81. Department of State and Justice, the Judiciary, and Related Appropriations: United States Information Agency: Hearings Before the Subcommittee of the Committee on Appropriations House of Representatives 86th Congress, Frist Session (1960), 348–349.
82. "A.R. Maloof, Wrote Music," *The Bergen Evening Record*, 1 March 1956, 1.
83. "Popular Record Releases," *Billboard Magazine*, 25 November 1944, 20.

Chapter 10

"Welcome, But Be Ready to Work"

Negotiating Gender Norms as Refugees in America

Manal al-Natour and Rita Stephan[1]

Refugees are neither victims nor free riders, they are individuals who found themselves, though due to no fault of their own, in a new—and sometimes hostile—cultural, economic, geographic, and political environment, as unwanted or pitiful outsiders. Syrian refugees arrived in the United States during a time of heightened Islamophobic and xenophobic feelings. Though some individuals and groups came to their assistance, others viewed them as a threat and their Syrian culture as inferior. Refugees, as agents, were faced with the choice of integration, withdrawal, or cultural exchange. Children, work, learning English, and familial relations became determinants of assuming agency. However, gender norms were at the forefront of defining the extent to which they embrace American life and values.

Using an ethnographic approach, this chapter examines the integration of Syrian refugees into local communities in Connecticut. Based on in-depth interviews with eight Syrian refugee families, this project analyzes the complex ways in which women assumed the role of agents in adapting to the new life. We specifically ask: How has the need to adapt to the new environment and step outside their comfort zone shape Syrian women's gender performances and restructure their ideas about rights within the family? Focusing on how they challenged gender norms through engaging in economic activities, our findings suggest that women demonstrated a growing awareness of the economic challenges in the United States and normalized this awareness based on their situation. Their responses varied between exerting agency as active participants in shaping their new lives, exercising ambivalent agency by mechanically embracing work and English learning for their families' sake, or as passive—and sometimes helpless— subjects of yet another form of social control.

THEORY

To portray the experiences of Syrian women refugees in Connecticut, we approach this subject from a reflexive research perspective, asking questions about the conditions of women's lives in contexts that have previously ignored them. This chapter portrays these women's stories informed by "feminist curiosity"— "*not* taking for granted [. . .] the relationships of women to families, to men, to the state, and to globalizing trends" (Enloe 2007, 10). Placing refugees within the discussion on gender rights of the "Third World difference," construct them in a reductive and homogeneous manner to describe a "stable, ahistorical something that apparently oppresses most if not all the women in these countries" (Mohanty 1991, 54). Furthermore, when discussing gender within the context of refugees, multiple layers of discrimination and victimization are often cited, such as race, religion, and class (Fiddian-Qasmiyeh 2014; Pittaway and Bartolomei 2001). Hence, we reflect how Syrian women refugees' status could have shaped their gender identity and performance.

To reflect on this question, we build on Collins' (2000) approach to framing women's agency as dialectic or dialogical. To Collins, the dialogical approach produces a transformation in the thinking within an individual sphere or a group paradigm that eventually leads to new actions when the lived experience is recognized, analyzed, and materialized into "a changed consciousness" (2000, 30). Alternatively, in a dialectical approach, agency does not require intellectual activity; rather, it comes out of experiences of daily life (Collins 2000, 274). This particular theory is directly applicable to understanding how some Syrian women refugees adopted transformational thinking in their new environment while others dealt with their daily lived experiences with either ambivalent agency or vulnerability. Collins' claim of intersectionality and interrelated domains of power can be applicable to how Syrian women responded to the conflict in Syria, in refugee camps or even in their new host countries (al-Natour 2020). It also informs our analysis of Syrian women refugees' agency as it is reinforced by the fusion of their gender identity.

BACKGROUND

Why Connecticut?

Upon entering the United States, settlement is determined based on refugees' "family ties in the United States, health, age, family composition, and language, as well as the cost of living and the availability of jobs, housing, education, and health services in potential placement sites."[2] While 30 percent of all Syrian refugees were placed in California, Michigan, and Texas, the distribution of others was more spread throughout the United States. After the Paris terrorist attacks in 2015, "31 U.S. governors issued statements opposing the resettlement of Syrian refugees in their states" and several states "initiated legal challenges to the placement of Syrians."[3] Connecticut was slowly becoming a welcoming home for refugees, especially after a Syrian family that was prevented from landing in Indiana, in 2015, was diverted to Connecticut and welcomed by its people.

Numerous humanitarian, faith-based, ethnic, and civil rights organizations rushed to sponsor Syrian refugees across the United States and advocate on their behalf.[4] In this vein, a handful of churches and synagogues in Connecticut were instrumental in bringing Syrian refugees to their communities. The personal touch that these faith-based organizations added made refugees feel welcomed and accepted. Speaking about his new life in Glastonbury, Connecticut, Zeyad Al Abas "felt kindness from the people around him," and "thanks the church that is sponsoring him. They're very supportive of him. He felt that, when he arrived here, that he was being welcomed by his own family, and he can't forget that."[5]

"Welcome, But Be Ready to Work"

Dennis Wilson, a manager with Integrated Refugee and Immigrant Services (IRIS), describes the message that refugees receive upon their resettlement in the United States as double jeopardy: Refugees constantly have to prove themselves as not being a security threat or a financial burden vis-à-vis the American people. Wilson posits: "Fewer than 1 percent of refugees who begin the screening are actually settled in the United States." Furthermore, these refugees are "required to repay the government for their airfare to get to the United States." Indeed, refugees understand this message and internalize it. During the Community Conversation on "The Muslim Ban: An Examination of the Underlying Factual, Legal, Religious, Humanitarian, Policy and Economic Considerations," on May 11, 2017 in Glastonbury, Connecticut Syrian refugee Zeyad Al Abas responds to these fears saying: "While we are here, we will not be a burden. We will get back on our feet. . . . Don't think that we are a burden on your country. Once we've built up ourselves, we will be giving back to society. If Syria were to be peaceful again, and free, we would wish to go back."[6]

After the ban on further admission of Syrians to the United States in 2018, many of these organizations advocated to reunite refugees with their families who were still stranded in transition camps. A resettlement officer we interviewed was successful in helping one respondent's family launch a media campaign that resulted in her family unification. In assessing the impact of the campaign, the officer recalls:

> Two thousand refugees were left when the administration lowered the gates of safety here in this country and those stories are human stories, each story is a family or an individual story, babies, old people, working people, mothers. When you see an actual story in a family who was affected by this political move, it opens people's hearts and minds. You can change people's hearts and minds with a human touch, and there was a lot of feedback after this program [the MBC television program] was aired on television here in Connecticut. All the television broadcasters started to come after us for more stories; television and media. (Officer Interview June 2019)

Syrians in Connecticut

As of 2018, 192,497 Syrians were living in the United States and less than 2,500 lived in Connecticut.[7] The Syrian population in the United States is bifurcated comprising descendants of immigrants that left Syria as early as the 1800s during the Ottoman Empire (Suleiman 1999), immigrants, who came after the 1960s with the rise in political and economic hardships in the region, and the latest arrival of the refugee population. According to the American Community Survey 2018, 70 percent of Syrians in Connecticut are foreign-born naturalized U.S. citizens and around 65 percent are foreign-born and not U.S citizens.

While Syrians born in the United States constitute the majority of those who identify with this ethnic and national origin, the immigrant population is at minimum divided equally between those who entered the United States before 2010 and those who did so after 2010, most likely as refugees or asylees. According to the American Community Survey 2018, around 60 percent of the Syrian refugees entered Connecticut in 2010 or later and around 49.4 percent entered the United States before 2010.

Syrian Refugees

Overall, 21,247 Syrian refugees sought residence in the United States since 2000, of which only 62 arrived in 2018. According to the Migration Office of Admissions and the Department of Homeland Security, 1,682 refugees settled in the United States in 2015, 12,587 in 2016, and 6,557 in 2017.[8]

The Connecticut General Assembly's Office of Legislative Research reports that 61 Syrian refugees settled in Connecticut in 2015, 367 in 2016, 91 in 2017, and zero in 2018.[9] These handful Syrian refugees constitute less than four percent of the 9,317 refugees who moved to the state in 2016.[10]

Of the Syrian refugees admitted to the United States since the beginning of the conflict, 72 percent (or 13,014) were women and children under age 14. Close to half (47 percent) of Syrian refugees were under age 14, and 12 percent were between the ages of 14 and 20.[11] About 98 percent of the Syrian refugees were Muslim and less than 1 percent were Christians.

METHODOLOGY

Using a snowball sampling method, we conducted in-depth interviews with eight Syrian refugee families living in various small communities in Connecticut. The majority of these were working and middle-class families. Most of them were Sunni Muslim who did not have a college education or the financial means to have paid their way to the United States.

With the exemption of one woman, Nicole, all respondents were married with children. These women were accompanied by their spouses and children. To examine Syrian women's agency and how their adaptation to their economic challenges shapes their gender performances, we have interviewed men and women. All men were civilians who escaped with their families to a transition country before coming to the United States, often Jordan, Egypt, or Turkey. Western pseudonym were used to protect the identity of refugees interviewed.

FINDINGS

Syrian refugee women demonstrated an awareness of the economic challenges in the United States and normalized it based on their situation. Their responses varied between exerting agency as active participants in shaping their new lives, embracing work for their families' sake, or as passive and sometimes helpless subject of yet another form of social control. We use a three-prong approach to organize the enactment of gender identification and agency. Although the three gendered roles may seem somewhat rigidly demarcated, women moved between them, particularly given the changing particularity of their lived experiences. Evidence below shows that one cannot assume clear demarcation between the groups. Nonetheless, three general scenarios of gender performance are discernible: assuming agency, exercising ambivalent agency, and embracing feminine vulnerability.

In this chapter, we define refugees as "individuals who are unable or unwilling to return to their country of origin or nationality because of persecution or a well-founded fear of persecution. Refugees are eligible for protection in large part based on account of race, religion, nationality, membership in a particular social group, or political opinion."[12]

Claiming Agency: The Iron Woman

Womanhood and motherhood were sources of empowerment for women who claimed agency as they embarked on their new lives in the small communities in Connecticut and navigated the emotional turmoil of resettlement. It is noteworthy that these women did not necessarily have better resources than the other women we interviewed. Rather, they proclaimed a proactive agency in their gender performance. Not once did these women fall into the vulnerable feminine position. They acted almost mechanically and systematically to do what's needed to adjust, succeed, and advance in their new lives. With various degrees and expressions of agency, Adeebah and Elsa are two refugee women who orchestrated their families' new life in the United States actualized strategic gender interests by employing the dialogic approach. These women affected change within the arena of their relations to power.

Adeebah is from Homs in Syria, married with four children. Having never worked while in Syria: "I was a housewife who is dedicated to her house, children, and husband," in a blink of eye, she became "the mother and the father at the same time." When the Syria regime detained her husband and male relatives, she was not prepared to take the leadership role she did. Left without a choice but to stand up for her husband, she appealed to the regime for his release. It is then that she found her agency: "I felt that I was the Iron woman."

Fleeing to Jordan, she had to find a way to help her husband pay for rent and make a living. Learning how to work toward finding a voice in her displacement and a job that would place her on equal footing with the man, she actualized strategic gender interests by tutoring an American girl, who later helped her sell in the United States the wool hats she knitted. It was then that she claimed: "I discovered myself and my capabilities." Only nine months after her arrival in the United States, she obtained her driver's license despite her poor English skills. To her, this was the first step to gain financial freedom and contribute to the household along with her husband who became a driver with Amazon. Being proactively curious to enhance her life, she defied her husband and sought to open a catering business. Right after learning how to drive, she pursued a business license: "I asked how to obtain a cooking certificate. My husband doubted me and replied, 'Are you crazy?' I told him it was none of his business." Apparently, Adeebah's relationship with her husband is not what one would expect from vulnerable victims. She also defies the stereotypes of being a submissive wife. However, Adeebah seems to exchange mutual appreciation and respect with her husband whom she recognizes as hard working and supportive of her.

Adeebah has challenged social and gender norms. Her interaction with the other sex was not hindered by any cultural or religious restrictions. In fact, she was able to obtain the cooking certificate with the help of an American man. With this license, she began selling Syrian food at a hospital in Hartford. Attracting business was hindered by her appearance, "it was not easy for me to do so since I am a veiled woman." But Adeebah would share with her clients her story and her art. In order to advance reform in her life and her female peers, Adeebah used her economic situation in sales to assert her claim to her national origin and her agency as a refugee. Such an action is read as a mechanism to defy the universal labeling of Third World women as submissive, victim, and lacking of agency.

Adeebah remained committed to furnishing the groundwork for representing an image of Third World women that defies homogeneity and reduces her and her peers to a single collective other. She sustained her advocacy to achieve equal rights for women even in her displacement in the United States. She was immediately touched by the American value of realizing one's potential. She claims, "Here people appreciate those who have skills and hobbies." Encouraged by her American friends, she began making greeting cards and selling them from her home. Then she would display her art at her food stand. "I tell people who come to eat and buy my paintings, please buy my paintings only if you like them not because you want to help me." And she has been successful in selling some of her paintings for as much as $150. She even caters to consumer demands by making her paintings as affordable e-cards.

Her paintings reflected her expression of freedom as she depicted birds and feathers that can roam freely. She reflects: "I used to paint anything nice I see, but now I paint birds more than anything. Birds have freedom to go wherever they wish. Birds have wings can go wherever they want without a passport."

Figure 10.1 Adeebah's Paintings. Adeebah. *Birds as Freedom*. 2020. Medium size. Personal Photos.

Adeebah's journey was not easy but her agency fueled her desire to persevere. She defied political oppression she and her family were subjected to in Syria as well as the social and cultural judgment of her as a third world woman in the West. She reflects on having to do what's needed to advance:

> I am a mother of five children, I need to work and help my husband financially even more than before, and I need to master the English language in order to be able to communicate with American people and integrate in the society, and I need to follow up with my children's needs and schools especially that there is a difference between the two cultures. And since I have two teenagers, more work was added to my plate as a woman . . . . The difference between the two cultures added to my struggles, but most of the times I do not sleep more than three to four hours a day because after I put my children to bed, I work on my paintings.

Despite feeling weak sometimes, she decided to take up the challenge for the sake of herself and her children. Adeebah fits into what Suad Joseph coins in "intimate selfing" as having a present and asserted individuality and agency. She embodies what Joseph claims as relational selfing that is neither individualist nor corporatist but "embedded in relational matrices that shape their sense of self but do not deny them their distinctive initiative and agency" (1999, 11). In addition to caring for her children, she finds fulfillment in the pride that her children express toward her, especially as they tell her that their dream is to become as determinant as she is.

While Adeebah enjoys the support of her husband who is also active, Elsa's husband is too wrapped up in his own challenges. In addition to struggling with learning English, he is unemployed. His inability to learn English has impacted his opportunity to obtain a good job. According to Nancy, the social worker volunteer with the resettlement agency, Elsa's husband struggled: "He worked in a dryclean for a while then he moved to New Britain and worked for two years in an Arab store . . . . Working in an Arab store did not help learning the language since most of communication is in Arabic. He did not work on learning the English before as his wife did" (Interview 2019). Indeed, a number of refugee men feel intimidated and vulnerable in their attempt to learn English, especially when their wives and children surpass them in their learning ability. A part of their fragile masculinity gets shattered as providers and caregivers and they retreat to inaction and depression.

Elsa did not have the chance but to step up and lift up her family with her. Being "self-motivated, go-getter, she figured out a way to study English at pretty high level and she is doing very well in her classes. She is at the top of her class" says the social worker who helps Elsa's family. To earn a living, she teaches Arabic at the local mosque and has ambitions to further her education: "I am planning to join college and study after finishing the highest level of English, maybe radiology. I have a community college degree in Syria. I am ambitious since I was a little girl." In order to pursue her dreams, she plans not to have any more children in the near future and stresses the need for both men and women to work and provide for the family. She emphasizes, "In this country the man and the woman need to work to pay for essential life expenses." Elsa's individuality is focused on her own personal achievements, but not without recognition of the ultimate benefits to her family at large.

In her attempt to best represent the image of the Third World woman, Elsa implemented strategic interests in her society and extended her agency to the community as well. She was one of the main coordinators of "A Taste of Ramadan" event, which was held to familiarize her community with the positive attributes of her culture and religion. She invited the larger community to share food during the holy month and to convey a larger message of love, peace, and appreciation.

Adeebah and Elsa are examples of women who overcame hardships and challenges and never gave up or waited for other social agents to design a settlement plan for them. They have challenged social and gender norms strategically, even promoting a real feminist image among Syrian refugee women and in their Connecticut community. They were proactive in pursuing and designing the new life for their families. The literature on migration and refugee studies have not paid attention to such women. The behavior of women in this category contradicts conventional theorizing on vulnerable femininity and feminine vulnerability. However, as mentioned earlier, these behaviors cannot be rigidly viewed as a dichotomy but are much more complex.

Ambivalent Agency

Four women did not fit the perfect dichotomy of proactive agent versus vulnerable feminine. Their consciousness was neither proactively claiming their agency nor totally submitting to vulnerable femininity and helplessness. Yes, their selfing was embedded in their patriarchal, cultural, and situational settings, employing dialectical practices according to Collins (2000). Such practices emerge from daily experience. In their resettlement efforts, these women did not behave or identify themselves in a binary way, as either dependents or agents—they were rather ambivalent. Ambivalent agency has been studied in relations to arts and law (Andersson and Edgren 2018; Gover 2015) and can be defined as assuming agency without the consciousness to proactively and strategically do what is needed or be motivated by the right causes.

Grace fits in this category. She and her family were among the first Syrian refugee families to arrive in New Britain. Having never worked in her 50 years of life in Syria, she was behind in many aspects. However, Grace's love for her family pushed her to reach out to the larger community. Her quest for social connection and her husband's encouragement motivated her to participate in cooking for the Taste of Ramadan event and doing a presentation about a Syrian dish in the church despite not speaking English well. She also participated in "Jiran" program with the cooperation with IRIS in welcoming American community members to her home and teaching them her Syrian dialect as they enjoyed her Syrian dishes. In a nutshell, Grace became involved in the larger community outreach by educating, planning, and supporting community activities freely and openly. Although her stance emerged suddenly and was not based on intellectual tradition or feminist thought that privileged equality or women's rights, she never felt vulnerable, withdrawn, or victimized.

Submitting to the status quo, Anna felt that by improving her English she can achieve a peace of mind: "The more I master English, the more I feel settled down here." In fact, she has accepted her new reality and tried to make the best out of it, without feeling excited or sad: "Our situation is very fine, we feel settled down." She did feel vulnerable upon her arrival and after she learned that her son was diagnosed with autism. However, she eventually accepted her situation and did what was needed. She has learned English and tried to integrate in the community and to befriend her neighbors. Furthermore, she sought freedom of mobility as a way to help her family: "Obtaining the driver's license was very important for me in order to give my children rides to their schools and to go to my ESL classes, and shopping, and to give my husband a hand." Her stance emerged as a response to the urgent social and familial situation that resulted from her displacement. She was pushed to act upon her situation and perform the role of feminine rescuer despite lacking the necessary resources and knowledge.

Fay is another woman who employed dialectical practices that emerged from daily experience. She arrived in the United States with no English skills and only seventh grade education. She immediately started attending ESL classes and worked in a restaurant. Her motivation to learn English stems from her desire to communicate with her son's doctors as her son was diagnosed with autism. Fay's dedication to her family and her children has also motivated her to encourage her husband to launch an entrepreneurial initiative. She is currently helping him export used cars to the Middle East in collaboration with his brother-in-law who is residing in the Gulf. While Fay did not proactively assume agency or seek her own individuality, her rationality with her family defines the parameters of her willingness to do what is needed to improve her family's life.

Finally, Rose is a fifty-year-old single mother of two children. As a cancer patient, Rose learned to be resilient. Left without a choice but to be self-sufficient, she refused to depend on welfare for her survival. Not having a male protector, she felt free to do what other women would not do like taking public transportation and integrating in the American society. Like Grace, Anna, and Fay, Rose is an ambivalent agent who employed dialectical strategies in her response to her displacement and refugee status. She is making the best out of her situation, given her lack of access to traditional resources (read male protector), but possibly empowered by the vulnerability of social and health situations. These women's agency emerges as existential, not in the individualized sense but rather in their relational role, regardless whether or not they fulfill the duties assigned to their roles; however, they still offered new inroads into the examination of feminism and third world women's gender performance.

Embracing Feminine Vulnerability

Women in this category expressed the greatest sense of normalcy. For them, nothing changed from their limited life in Syria, the camp, or here in the United States. By putting their fate in the hands of their family members or resettlement agency, these women did not feel as strained, nor did they seem as exposed to feelings of humiliation, suffering, and displacement (Stephan 2020). Despite the security and normalcy that these women felt from submitting to society's expectations of them as vulnerable feminine, they ultimately forfeited their agency.

Eva and Nicole are excellent examples of these women. Eva did not work in Syria and when she moved to the United States, she did not exert any efforts to learn English. Despite acknowledging that life in the United States is expensive, and requires both spouses to work, she did not feel that she can commit herself to a job. Instead, she complains that life back in Syria was better and that the United States is complicated and overwhelming: "Here everything is different from our country. Everything costs money." Having lived in her multigenerational family home and walked everywhere within her two-mile radius community, her family now has to pay for rent and purchase a car in the United States. She compares, "Car back home is not necessary. It is like a luxury, but here it is necessary for shopping, doctor's appointments, taking kids to school. It's one of the house's primary pillars."

It is noteworthy that public transportation is complicated for refugees for two reasons: First, their tight community in Syria did not require them to use the male-dominated space of public transportation, which is believed to increase women's vulnerability to sexual harassment. Second, the public transportation system in the United States is inefficient and complicated. Unlike European cities, most American cities are not well-connected. Furthermore, a number of refugees found the façade of American streets confusing with nothing but cookie-cutter houses, green lawns, and trees.

Therefore, venturing out to the street can take a lot of courage, especially for women who rarely left the house in their home communities. Nicole, a 37-year-old single woman who lives with her brother and mother and relies on both of them for survival, explains her refusal to take public transportation to go to the ESL classes: "I do not like to take public transportation. It is something that I am not used to and I cannot force myself to adjust. My brother has a car, but he cannot commit to the ESL classes schedule because of his work."

Eva tried working as a janitor at a school when she first arrived in Connecticut. Having come from a middle-class family, she was ashamed to have such a low status job. She did not ascribe to the American mentality of "there is no shame in work." Eva lasted only a short time in her job and finally decided that such a job does not suit her class and the prestige she is used to having in Syria. Class is an interesting aspect of refugees' lives as some would assume that the mere status of being a refugee summons a person to the lowest, entry-level, low-skill jobs, regardless of their previous socioeconomic background. Hence, the status of being a refugee dominates and erases any social status the person assumed before becoming a refugee.

In assessing Eva's individualism, relationality, and selfhood from Joseph's perspective on "intimate selfing," her individuality is almost absent. Instead Eva's relationality as a mother defines her selfhood. She gives up having a job and drops out of English classes in order to raise her children. Indeed, she prefers to adhere to cultural norms of putting motherhood ahead of any other purpose in life (Stephan 2014). Looking at Nicole's case from the lens of intimate selfing, she emerges as someone who totally relinquishes her agency. She chooses to rely on her brother to survive and does not even try to learn English language, find a job, or integrate in the local community.

As a mother, Eva's dilemma emerges from her urge to raise her children. As a mother of four children, she declares: "I cannot handle both working and taking care of my children, it is either or." Eva's helplessness goes even further. She chooses to rely entirely on her husband who, in addition to working full time at a restaurant, is in charge of scheduling doctor's visits for his children, attending teacher–parent conferences, helping them with their homework, shopping for groceries and clothes, and paying utilities.

While Eva's husband and Nicole's brother are perceived to be engaging in performing positive masculinity, by being good providers, these settings create opportunities for unequal gender power and relations, unequal distribution of roles, and rigid social norms that perpetuate domestic violence.[13] Likewise, the retreat of Eva and Nicole from pursuing knowledge and self-fulfillment through work can have several explanations. They either do not have a consciousness of themselves in such a manner or they feel so overwhelmed by the avalanche of the competing new demands that they have never experienced before. Either way, their gender identities are embedded in patriarchal norms and structure that prevent them from exercising agency.

LIMITATIONS

The sample in this study is narrow in scope, featuring the small group of women to whom we gained access, and all attempts at generalizability must acknowledge this limitations. The data falls short of representing the voices of evacuees with diverse age, class, and sexual identification. For instance, the experiences of homosexual men and women, the elderly, children, individuals with disabilities, or single or married heterosexual men were not captured in this study, although they too endured the affliction of being refugees.

Another limitation to the study lies in gaining access to respondents. A number of potential respondents were hesitant to grant us interviews, because they feared that providing their data could jeopardize their security. Ironically, spouses of these women were the source of much of this paranoia. It has been our experience in conducting these interviews that respondents were often concerned about their anonymity, given the political atmosphere surrounding their departure from Syria. Therefore, we assured respondents that we would respect their anonymity by guarding any information we collected and by assigning Western pseudonyms to respondents and their relatives.

CONCLUSION

Studying gender within the context of refugees in a Western culture is challenging, especially since most of the refugee studies assume as a priori that women refugees lack agency. This study has examined the integration of Syrian refugees into local communities in Connecticut. Through the lens of intersectionality, this chapter has illustrated how the need to adapt to the new environment in their displacement in the United States shaped Syrian women's gender performances and restructured their ideas about rights within the family. Focusing on how they challenged gender norms through engaging in economic activities, our findings suggest that women demonstrated awareness of the economic challenges in the United States and normalized it based on their situation. While none of these women were submissive or had contentious relationships with the male members of their kins, they all remained embedded in their patriarchal structures and relations. The two main strategies Syrian women refugees have employed are: dialogical practices, which link intellectual work and activism, and dialectical practices, which link experience and ideas.

Just as women's voices are often silent in the mainstream migration studies, they were also absent from the reports that reached Western audiences about Syrian refugees. In the same fashion that Youngs (2006, 3) differentiates between change "for women" and change "by women"—"the former too often denying women's agency, and the latter asserting it"—this study reports on the acculturation of women as being driven by women. However, instead of presenting their agency in a dualistic manner, the stories in this study show that, whether proactive or ambivalent agents, or even vulnerable feminine, some women's overarching motivation for adjusting to their new lives was embedded in the gender norms they felt within their family structure. These modes of adaptation and acculturation stand as remarkable to the Third World feminist movement, in general, and the Syrian feminist movement, in particular. Third world women's activists and Syrian women's journey toward social justice is still ongoing, regardless of the interlocking spheres of oppression that they seek to dismantle.

NOTES

1. The views expressed in this chapter are those of the authors and do not represent the views of, and should not be attributed to, the U.S. Department of State.

2. Jie Zong and Jeanne Batalova, "Syrian Refugees in the United States," Migration Policy Institute, last modified January 12, 2017, https://www.migrationpolicy.org/article/syrian-refugees-united-states.

3. Zong and Batalova, "Syrian Refugees in the United States."

4. "500+ national and local organizations sign letter to the Senate in support of Syrian refugees and opposing HR4038," Refugee Council USA, last modified January 19, 2016, https://rcusa.org/resources/letter-signed-by-500-national-and-local-organizations-to-the-senate-in-support-of-syrian-refugees-and-opposing-hr4038/.

5. Steven Smith, "Syrian Refugees Speak About New Life in Connecticut," Hartford Courant, last modified May 25, 2017, https://www.courant.com/community/glastonbury/hc-gr-glastonbury-syrian-refugees-0525-20170525-story.html.

6. Smith, "Syrian Refugees Speak."

7. American Community Survey 2018 and 2015.

8. Andrew Bolger, "Refugee Processing and Settlement," Office of Legislative Research, Connecticut General Assembly, last modified May 30, 2018, https://www.cga.ct.gov/2018/rpt/pdf/2018-R-0134.pdf.

9. Christopher Reinhart, "Refugee Processing and Settlement," Office of Legislative Research, Connecticut General Assembly, accessed May 13, 2020, https://www.cga.ct.gov/2015/rpt/2015-R-0293.htm.

10. "Table 22. Persons Naturalized by State or Territory of Residence: Fiscal Years 2016 to 2018," U.S. Department of Homeland Security, last modified January 6, 2020, https://www.dhs.gov/immigration-statistics/yearbook/2018/table22.

11. MPI tabulations of data from the U.S. Department of State Refugee Processing Center.

12. Zong and Batalova, "Syrian Refugees in the United States."
13. "Positive Masculinities in a Refugee Context: A Case Study from Uganda," CARE, accessed May 30, 2020, https://insights.careinternational.org.uk/images/in-practice/EMB/Positive-Masculinities-Refugee-Context_Uganda_2019.pdf.

REFERENCES

Andersson, Ulrika and Monika Edgren. 2018. "Vulnerability, Agency and the Ambivalence of Place in Narratives of Rape in Three High-Profile Swedish Cases." *NORA - Nordic Journal of Feminist and Gender Research* 26, no. 3: 197–209. https://doi.org/10.1080/08038740.2018.1472140.

Collins, Patricia. 2000. *Black Feminist Thought: Knowledge, Consciousness, and the Politics of Empowerment*. 2nd ed. New York: Routledge.

Enloe, Cynthia. 2007. *Globalization and Militarism: Feminists Make the Link*. Lanham: Rowman & Littlefield.

Fiddian-Qasmiyeh, Elena. 2014. *The Ideal Refugees: Gender, Islam, and the Sahrawi Politics of Survival*. New York: Syracuse University Press.

Gover, K. E. 2015. "Ambivalent Agency: A Response to Trogdon and Livingston on Artwork Completion." *The Journal of Aesthetics and Art Criticism*, 73, no. 4: 457–60. Accessed June 7, 2020. www.jstor.org/stable/44510194.

Joseph, Suad, ed. 1999. *Intimate Selving in Arab Families: Gender, Self, and Identity*. Syracuse: Syracuse University Press.

Mohanty, Chandra Talpade. 1991. "Under Western Eyes: Feminist Scholarship and Colonial Discourses." In *Third World Women and the Politics of Feminism*, edited by Chandra Talpade Mohanty, Ann Russo and Lourdes Torres, 51–80. Bloomington: Indiana University Press.

al-Natour, Manal. 2020. "Strategies of Nonviolent Resistance: Syrian Women Subverting Dominant Paradigms" In *Women Rising: In the Arab Spring and Beyond*, edited by Rita Stephan and Mounira Charrad, 330-8. New York University Press.

Pittaway, E. and L. Bartolomei. 2001. "Refugees, Race, and Gender: The Multiple Discrimination against Refugee Women." *Refuge: Canada's Journal on Refugees* 19, no. 6: 21–32. https://doi.org/10.25071/1920-7336.21236.

Stephan, Rita. 2020. "Citizenship and Gender in a Time of Crisis: Lebanese-American Women in the 2006 War." In *Arab American Women* edited by Michael Suleiman, Suad Joseph and Louise Cainkar, 670-705. New York: Syracuse University Press.

———. 2014. "War and Gender Performance: The Evacuation of Lebanese-American Women in the 2006 War." *International Feminist Journal of Politics* 16, no. 2: 297–316. https://doi.org/10.1080/14616742.2013.849969.

Suleiman, Michael. 1999. *Arabs in America: Building a New Future*. Philadelphia: Temple University Press.

Youngs, G. 2006. "Feminist International Relations in the Age of War on Terror: Ideologies, Religions and Conflict." *International Feminist Journal of Politics* 8, no. 1: 3–18. https://doi.org/10.1080/14616740500415409.

Chapter 11

The Influence of Nativity (or Lack Thereof) on Arab-American Muslim Attitudes and Behaviors

Youssef Chouhoud

INTRODUCTION

The story of immigrants in the United States typically centers on the process of cultural assimilation. Ethnic minorities arriving on America's shores as foreigners will, the belief goes, eventually and collectively blend into the national landscape. The once precarious, now indelible status of Irish- and Italian-Americans is often pointed to as evidence of this phenomenon. While "No Irish Need Apply"[1] signs and affirmative action for individuals with Italian heritage (Scelsa 2011) now seem wholly anachronistic, the process that relegated these phenomena to a bygone era is thought to be ever-operable. Similarly subsumed within the vaunted American "melting pot" are religious minorities. There are indications that many members of these communities also follow an assimilative path, along the way diluting (if not altogether discarding) their distinctive beliefs and practices. Such is the case with American Jews, 62 percent of whom reported in 2013 that Jewish identity was mainly a matter of "Ancestry/Culture" rather than religion (Pew Research Center 2013).

As both an ethnic and religious minority, Arab-American Muslims (AAMs) are in a unique position to test the guardrails of cultural assimilation. While a majority of AAMs are foreign-born, there is a substantial (and growing) proportion that is native-born U. S. citizens. The attitudinal and behavioral differences between these first-generation immigrants and their successors are key indicators of the degree to which this minority population is following a so-called "straight line" assimilationist pathway or one that is more staggered/segmented (Portes and Zhou 1993). On the one hand, as Yvonne Haddad

(2007, 252) notes in her study of hijab adoption post-9/11: "The integration and assimilation of second and third generation Muslims into US society was expected to proceed according to a predictable trajectory noted among previous immigrant groups. The children of the immigrants would shed their parents' religious and cultural markings and become more Americanized." On the other hand, the general public's abiding suspicion of AAMs (particularly, though not exclusively, since the September 11th attacks) could affect this community's ability or even willingness to adopt certain markers of mainstream culture.

To help gauge the degree and mode of acculturation among this population, this chapter empirically examines the effect of nativity on AAM attitudes and behaviors. The study draws on pooled data from three waves of Pew's nationally representative surveys of American Muslims (2007, 2011, and 2017) and five waves of the American Muslim Poll (2016–2020) fielded by the Institute for Social Policy and Understanding. Analyses of these data demonstrate that (1) U.S.-born AAMs are no less religious than their immigrant counterparts, (2) nativity partially moderates social and political attitudes, and (3) AAMs experience and process discrimination in ways that highlight both the added conspicuousness of this minority group and the paradoxes of "cultural fluency" (Lajevardi et al. 2020). Where these findings ultimately place AAMs on the spectrum from isolation to assimilation is hard to say, especially given how nascent this community is relative to other recognized/potential "White ethnics" and the inexactness of terms such as "assimilation." Nonetheless, the results presented in this chapter provide a rare and wide-ranging empirical reference to help adjudicate claims of AAMs status in American society.

The next section briefly introduces the subject population before subsequently describing the data sources and the unique lens they offer into this largely overlooked minority group. The analysis then begins by highlighting demographic differences between foreign-born and U.S.-born AAMs, including key metrics of socio-economic status. With this foundation set, the study moves to the core examination of how nativity influences religiosity, social and political attitudes and behaviors, and experiences with discrimination. A concluding section puts these findings in a broader context and suggests fruitful avenues for research.

ARAB-AMERICAN MUSLIMS AND THE ASSIMILATION PARADOX

A Brief History of Arab-American Immigration and Identity Formation

Although America's relations with the Arab world stretch back to the country's founding,[2] large-scale immigration from the Middle East and North

Africa (MENA) to the United States did not take place until the late nineteenth century. From about 1870 through the 1910s, scores of predominantly Levantine Christian subjects of the failing Ottoman Empire came to America seeking economic opportunity and mobility (Foad 2013). The next influx took place over two decades beginning in the 1940s, but official quotas largely limited immigration during this period to individuals seeking asylum from war-torn countries and oppressive regimes—most of whom were Muslim, well-educated, and often members of influential families.[3] In 1965, however, the passage of the Immigration and Nationality Act (INA) removed many nativist restrictions to immigration and paved the way for the bulk of Arab migration to America. As a result, the MENA immigrant population would increase four-fold between 1980 and 2010 (Batalova and Cumoletti 2018). Yet, even though the vast majority of Arab immigrants (particularly Muslim ones) entered the United States around the turn of the twentieth century, those initial immigrants from the Levant left a lasting impact on Arab-American identity.

For decades, the official Census taxonomy has categorized individuals of Middle Eastern descent as racially White. This designation was not haphazard but rather advocated for in courts and through public campaigns by immigrants early in the twentieth century—a time when "Whiteness" was a prerequisite for citizenship in America. In an early landmark decision, *Shishim v. United States* (1909), a Syrian Christian argued against his "Chinese-Mongolian" racial classification, stating: "If I am a Mongolian, then so was Jesus, because we came from the same land." The judge found this argument persuasive and the plaintiff became the first Arab naturalized as an American. Arab Muslims, however, were routinely denied citizenship (and "White" status) until 1944 (*Ex Parte* Mohriez). Eventually, in 1977, the Office of Management and Budget (OMB) designated "persons originating in Europe, the Middle East and North Africa" as officially White, a classification which maintains to this day.

In recent years, however, a number of Arab-American civic organizations, activists, and celebrities have lobbied for the OMB to recognize Middle Easterners as a distinct ethnic group. Although this movement began in the 1980s, the 2000s and 2010s witnessed a more concerted and widespread effort on the part of advocates. In large part, this increased advocacy tracks the increased discrimination many Arab-Americans faced post-9/11 and the limited recourse to address these incidents in the absence of reliable population data needed for accurate reporting of these crimes. Notably, in the lead up to the 2010 Census, there was an organized effort on the part of multiple civil society organizations imploring persons of MENA descent to "Check it right; you ain't White!" (Kayyali 2013)—a call that was renewed once the decision came down that the OMB would jettison a proposed "Middle Eastern and North African" on the 2020 Census form.

The Complications of Assimilation

In the context of America's long-preserved racial hierarchy (whether *de jure* or *de facto*) and more recent targeted racialization and discrimination, AAMs find themselves stuck in something of an identity conundrum. Fundamentally, success for ethnic and racial minorities is to a large degree predicated on assimilation to White mainstream culture. This association is occasionally made explicit in official forums. For instance, in the landmark 1922 case *Takuji Yamashita v. Hinkle*, the attorney general for the state of Washington argued in a brief titled "The Japanese are Not Assimilable" that like "the Negro, . . . the Indian, and the Chinaman," the Japanese were unassimilable due to their immutable "marked physical characteristics." Yet, more often, socio-economic metrics are used to proxy an implicit adoption of the dominant culture. Viewed through this alternative lens, Asian-Americans are not only assimilable but are "achieving trajectories considered most proximate to the assimilation of European groups in the past" (Alba and Nee 2005, cited in Lee and Kye 2016, 254).

In terms of either the explicit or implicit renderings of assimilation, AAMs are in a seemingly advantageous (if not entirely unproblematic) position. Their aforementioned placement on the racial taxonomy forecloses questions into whether they have the requisite "assimilable" traits, yet it is worth once again emphasizing that religious affiliation played no small role in this assigned status. As Beydoun (2013) chronicles in his survey of Arab-American racial identity formation, early immigrants from the Levant leveraged Christianity as a "passage into Whiteness," allowing judges to consider Syrian Christians as racially distinct from Arabs (whom they still conflated with Muslims). In empirical terms, Ajrouch and Jamal (2007) find that Christians in the Detroit Arab American Study were significantly more likely to think of themselves as White compared to Muslim respondents.

Socio-economically, AAMs similarly appear to have the inside track on the path to assimilation. While there is sparse extant data on AAMs specifically, the first nationally representative survey of American Muslims was notably titled "Middle-Class and Mostly Mainstream" (Pew Research Center 2007). Along these same lines, a brief put out by the U.S. Department of Commerce following the 2010 decennial census reported that Arab-American household income was approximately 8.5 percent higher than the national average (Asi and Beaulieu 2013). Here, too, however, a cautionary note is in order as a closer examination of this census tally by country of origin reveals that the Arab-American households with the highest median income are also the ones that hail from areas with a significant Christian minority (i.e., Lebanon, Egypt, Syria, and Palestine), and thus it is unclear what proportion of this broader community's income is attributable to AAMs.

These narratives of assimilation, however, contrast with the othering and discrimination that AAMs have endured since even before the attacks of September 11, 2001. With Said's (1979) masterwork as a foundation, scholars have tracked how orientalist tropes filter depictions of Middle Easterners, and Muslims more broadly, both in popular media (Alsultany 2012; Shaheen 2014) and news broadcasts (Lajevardi 2020). These (mis) representations facilitate not just the public's perception of Arabs as the "other" but also make salient to Arab-Americans their distinctiveness from the broader society. Discrimination toward persons thought to be Middle Eastern or Muslim, particularly since the 2016 election, further reinforces this dynamic. Moreover, this heightened discrimination, depending on the source, could lead to alienation and disengagement with the broader society (Oskooii 2015).

These competing accounts thus frame the following analysis. To be sure, given both geo-politics and the domestic socio-political environment since the turn of the century, it is hard to imagine that AAMs are on a pathway toward the same "ethnic White" status that Italians and the Irish now occupy. Yet, this assumption should not lead to the conclusion that AAMs wish to isolate themselves or otherwise settle into a permanent underclass. Put differently, the concept of assimilation could be too analytically limiting. To the extent that we observe differences between immigrant and native AAMs, they may be best considered through a broader lens of social and political adaptation that sets aside the normative connotations associated with a particular cultural pathway. The conclusion takes on these debates and discourses in more detail, but for now, let us turn to the analysis.

Data and Demographics

Undoubtedly, part of the reason that systematic research on AAMs has been lacking is the dearth of viable data sources. The Arab American Institute (AAI) estimates that those with MENA heritage ties constitute approximately 1 percent of the U. S. population. Myriad challenges face researchers seeking to survey such low-incidence populations (Berry, Chouhoud, and Junn 2018). It is no wonder, then, that (to my knowledge) the only publicly available survey data dedicated to this population comes from the 2003 Detroit Arab American Study. While the dataset from this project is an invaluable resource, its temporal and spatial bounds limit its utility. Additional proprietary data coming out of AAI and/or Zogby International buttress much of the descriptive knowledge we have on Arab-Americans, but does little to help us make inferences about this community.

While dedicated data on Arab-Americans remains sparse, surveys of American Muslims more generally have markedly increased since the mid-2000s. Yet,

Table 11.1 Demographic Differences

Variable	Source	N (Foreign Born)	Mean (SE) Foreign Born (1)	N (US Born)	Mean (SE) US Born (2)	T-Test Difference (1) – (2)
Less than $30K	ISPU	340	0.35 (0.04)	242	0.26 (0.05)	0.09
$100K or more	ISPU	340	0.14 (0.02)	242	0.17 (0.03)	-0.03
College Graduate	ISPU	340	0.40 (0.04)	242	0.39 (0.05)	0.01
18 to 29	ISPU	340	0.37 (0.04)	242	0.57 (0.05)	-0.21***
55 or over	ISPU	340	0.13 (0.02)	242	0.03 (0.01)	0.10***
Married	ISPU	340	0.61 (0.04)	242	0.39 (0.05)	0.22***
Women	ISPU	339	0.36 (0.04)	242	0.49 (0.05)	-0.14**
Democrat/Lean D	ISPU	340	0.65 (0.04)	242	0.74 (0.05)	-0.09*
Republican/Lean R	ISPU	340	0.20 (0.03)	242	0.18 (0.04)	0.02
Somewhat/Very Liberal	ISPU	340	0.23 (0.03)	242	0.31 (0.04)	-0.08
Less than $30K	Pew	597	0.41 (0.03)	172	0.27 (0.06)	0.14**
$100K or more	Pew	597	0.09 (0.02)	172	0.05 (0.02)	0.04
College Graduate	Pew	597	0.28 (0.03)	172	0.26 (0.05)	0.03
18 to 29	Pew	597	0.32 (0.03)	172	0.72 (0.05)	-0.39***
55 or over	Pew	597	0.12 (0.02)	172	0.02 (0.01)	0.10***
Married	Pew	597	0.70 (0.03)	172	0.34 (0.06)	0.36***
Women	Pew	597	0.44 (0.03)	172	0.57 (0.06)	-0.13**
Democrat/Lean D	Pew	597	0.64 (0.03)	172	0.77 (0.06)	-0.13**
Republican/Lean R	Pew	597	0.07 (0.02)	172	0.12 (0.05)	-0.06
Somewhat/Very Liberal	Pew	597	0.23 (0.03)	172	0.25 (0.05)	-0.02

Source: Institute for Social Policy and Understanding, American Muslim Poll (2016-2020); Pew Research Center (2007; 2011; 2017).
* $p<0.10$, ** $p<0.05$, *** $p<0.01$.

since the percentage of Muslims in America with MENA heritage ranges from 14 percent (Pew Research Center 2017) to 24 percent (Mogahed and Chouhoud 2017),[4] no one survey can provide any statistically valid insight into how intra-Arab opinion varies. To overcome this limitation, I pool the three waves of Pew's groundbreaking surveys of U.S. Muslims (2007, 2011, and 2017) along with five waves of the annual American Muslim Poll (2016–2020) commissioned by the Institute for Social Policy and Understanding (ISPU). This method yielded a sample size of 769 respondents from the Pew surveys and 585 from the ISPU polls. Pooling data from these two sources provides greater confidence when analyzing the metrics they share while also widening the breadth of analysis by incorporating those measures that only appear on one source. The full wording for all the non-demographic items discussed below (as well as any coding adjustments) can be found in the Appendix.

Table 11.1 provides a demographic comparison between foreign-born and U.S.-born respondents in the ISPU and Pew samples, respectively. While some estimates vary, the two survey sources evidence significant differences for nearly all the same traits and, just as important, all these differences point in the same direction. On the key socio-economic indicators of income and education, there appears to be little difference among AAMs on the basis of nativity. Age represents the largest statistical divide between U.S.-born and immigrant respondents, with clear majorities of the former falling into the 18–29 range while only a small fraction are over 55-years old. In terms of political leanings, it is important to note the higher proportion of U.S.-born Arabs self-identifying as Democrats may have more to do with immigrant aversion toward affiliating with political parties in general rather than any ideological divergence, as evident by the statistical parity when it comes to describing oneself as "Somewhat/Very Liberal." Taken together, these demographic disparities (not least on the basis of sex) indicate that any observed attitudinal or behavioral correlations with nativity could be an artifact of compositional differences. Therefore, in addition to Survey Year fixed effects, the analyses in the next section control for the suite of demographic variables in table 11.1.

NATIVITY AND THE ARAB-AMERICAN MUSLIM EXPERIENCE

Religiosity

The first set of analyses considers Arab-American Muslim religiosity. This factor features prominently in general assessments of assimilation, but takes on added analytical weight when considered in the context of this particular population. Its increased significance is rooted in the (sometimes implicit,

Figure 11.1

RELIGIOSITY
- ISPU: Attends religious services weekly
- ISPU: Religion very important to R's life
- Pew: Attends religious services weekly
- Pew: Religion very important to R's life
- Prays 5 daily salat
- Always wears hijab
- Active in the mosque

SOC/POL ATTITUDES & BEHAVIORS
- Registered to Vote
- Homosexuality should be accepted by society
- Use of military force in Afghanistan was wrong decision
- Thinks of self as 'American First'
- Thinks of self as 'Muslim First'
- Thinks of self as both American and Muslim, Equally
- Most friends are Muslim
- Hardly any friends are Muslim

DISCRIMINATION
- People acted as if they are suspicious of you
- Been called offensive names
- Been singled out by airport security
- Experiences discrimination more than rarely
- Better quality of life for Muslim in the US
- Holds Some Anti-Muslim Bias

Legend: Not Significant / Significant

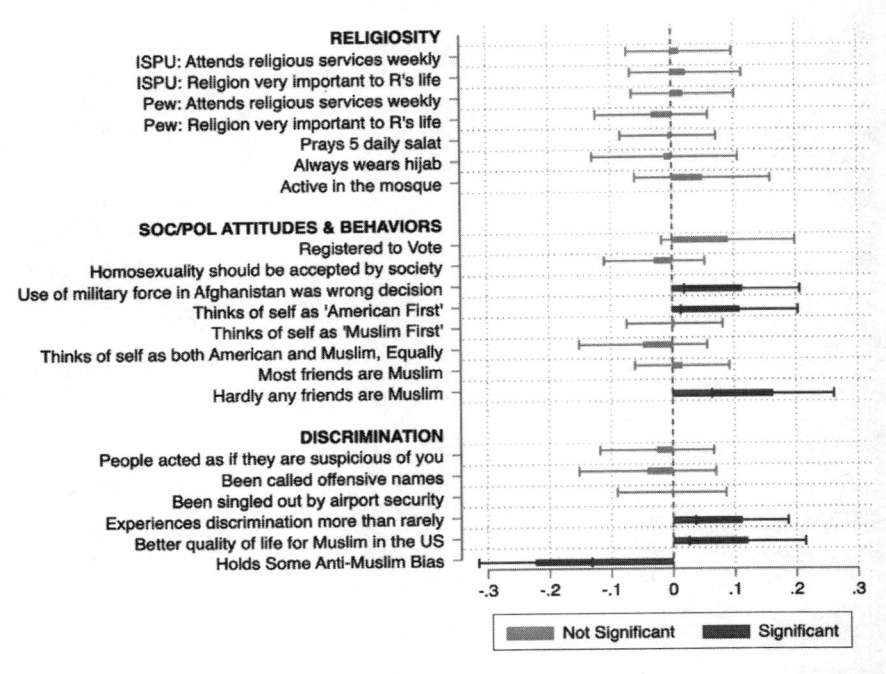

Figure 11.1 Multivariate Analyses: Predicted Probability of Being U.S. Born (90% CI).

often explicit) presumption that religiosity and societal disaffection tend to go hand-in-hand when it comes to Muslims in the West. An Oxford Analytica (2009, 1) brief distributed as incidents of domestic terrorism in America were beginning to multiply, typifies this association: "A sizeable portion of the immigrant Muslim-American population is becoming more religious and alienated from mainstream US society. This is true particularly among second-generation Muslims. This trend is similar to the growing religiosity among Muslims in many countries in Western Europe."

A landmark NYPD counter-terrorism study similarly casts suspicion on rising religious sentiment among American Muslims. In the radicalization process, the report outlines, for example, the second of four stages is described as "Self-Identification," in which an individual undergoes "religious seeking" by means of "trusted social networks made up of friends and family, religious leaders, literature and the Internet" (Silber and Bhatt 2007, 32). Moreover, while acknowledging that American Muslims have adapted (and have been allowed to adapt) far more than their European counterparts, the report nonetheless cautions that "[d]espite the economic opportunities in the United States, the powerful gravitational pull of individuals' religious roots and identity sometimes supersedes the assimilating nature of American society" (Silber and Bhatt 2007, 8).

In light of these dire warnings, it is particularly noteworthy that, as figure 11.1 demonstrates, there is no discernible difference between foreign-born and U.S.-born AAMs on any of the five unique measures of religiosity. This parity manifests with both subjective attitudes, such as the importance of religion in one's life, and objective behaviors, such as always wearing a *hijab*. Similarly, whether asking about private actions, like praying the five *salat*, or public ones, like attending weekly religious services or being active in the mosque, there is simply no drop-off in religiosity based on nativity. This finding is certainly at odds with the assimilative paths that other minority groups have taken in the past and, by extension, the one that American Muslims in particular were expected to be on. The preservation of religiosity past the first generation is all the more notable given that, in many instances, second-generation American Muslims often exhibit a commitment to religion that actually *exceeds* that of their immigrant parents (Chouhoud 2011).

Social and Political Attitudes and Behaviors

Does the stickiness of religiosity among AAMs translate to feelings of alienation and efforts to isolate? To examine whether this association—observed among European Muslims and presumed to be operable among American Muslims—holds, figure 11.1 also scrutinizes several relevant social and political attitudes and behaviors. These include preferences and actions that are tracked among the general public, as well as measures particular to Muslims in the United States.

Each of the general indicators tells a potentially rich story about the ways in which AAMs interact with society. First, there is no difference between immigrants and those born in the United States in terms of voter registration. Admittedly, this is a less-than-ideal item to have as the sole measure of political participation, given its susceptibility to social desirability bias, however, it is the only relevant question asked multiple times across either the set of Pew or ISPU survey years. A number of dynamics could be at play here. It may be that, since this question is only asked of those who can legally vote, naturalized immigrants wish to take advantage of the rights afforded to them, especially since many came from countries where voting was not particularly meaningful. Alternatively, perhaps the native-born in the sample either do not perceive voting to be the only or the best way to affect change. Given that Chouhoud, Dana, and Barreto (2019) found that Arabs were the most politically active in their study of American Muslim political participation (which included more comprehensive items), it is unlikely that this result reflects a generalized political apathy among U.S.-born AAMs.

There is also no difference on the basis of nativity when it comes to believing that society should accept homosexuality. This parity, however, masks a marked shift in sentiment over time. A secondary analysis of this item revealed that the predicted probability of supporting the societal acceptance of homosexuality more than doubled over the span of a decade, on average, for both foreign-born and U.S.-born AAMs. This trend mirrors the one found among American Muslims generally as well as the broader public (Pew Research Center 2017, 27). This dramatic attitudinal swing also highlights that foreign-born AAMs can be just as adaptable to changing norms as their U.S.-born counterparts. Both natives and immigrants, after all, are clustered in the same macro environment and subject to the same societal stimuli. Given this context, we should not think that nativity is the only means by which individuals process society's ebbs and flows.

One preference that does exhibit a clear disparity on the basis of nativity is opposition to the use of military force in Afghanistan. A normatively neutral interpretation of this finding would be that native-born AAMs are simply more attuned to geo-politics, although that reading would presume that their immigrant counterparts are not consuming news from the MENA region, where geo-politics are perennially top-of-mind. A more promising reading, and perhaps one that is more likely, is that U.S.-born AAMs are more willing to voice their disapproval of American policies. Of course, the converse may also be true. That is, foreign-born AAMs could be self-censoring for fear of the consequences. Given that there is no compelling *a priori* justification to expect that immigrant respondents would be less critical of America's incursions into Muslim-majority countries, it is certainly possible that some measure of social desirability bias is driving this sub-group's responses to this question.

Turning to the Muslim-specific questions, they collectively evidence a socialization that does not run neatly along the more constrained pathway of straight-line assimilation. Native-born respondents are more likely to think of themselves as American first, but are just as likely as their foreign-born counterparts to think of themselves as Muslim first. Moreover, no group is more likely than the other to volunteer that they see themselves as equally American and Muslim. To be sure, what "Muslim first" means to respondents is not entirely clear and so this blunt ordering of identity may not be all that informative in itself. Indeed, as Naber (2005) argues, the prioritization of a Muslim identity may in part arise out of a desire to combat various racial and gender hierarchies in one's ethnic community. In this way, pronouncing a "Muslim first" identity may actually indicate an organic integration of religious conviction and American norms of multi-culturalism that eschew a deference to one particular cultural lens. Along these same lines, both native and immigrant AAMs are just as likely to report that most of their friends are Muslim, but those born in the United States are more likely to have a network where hardly any of their friends are Muslim. Taken together, this particular mix of parity and disparity suggests a process, discussed more in the conclusion, by which cultural adaptation coincides with (rather than supersedes) existing attitudes and behaviors.

Discrimination

A final set of indicators in figure 11.1 track experiences with discrimination. On each of the first three items in this grouping, which ask about particular circumstances, foreign-born AAMs are just as likely to report being discriminated against on the basis of their religion as those born in the United States. These findings diverge somewhat from recent research on American Muslims. More specifically, using this same Pew data, Lajevardi et al. (2020) find that native-born American Muslims are more likely to report having experienced suspicious looks and being called offensive names although being singled out at the airport was not related to immigrant status. Chouhoud (2018) finds an even starker pattern using ISPU data and speculates that native-born Muslims "are more attuned to the varied forms of discrimination that they may encounter on a day-to-day basis in America and thus can more easily code discriminatory behavior when they experience it." For AAMs, however, it seems that the discriminatory behavior they experience is overt enough that immigrants need not "read between the lines."

That is not to say, however, that nativity does not factor into the way that AAMs perceive discrimination. Indeed, in terms of overall frequency, U.S.-born respondents report experiencing religious discrimination either occasionally or regularly at a significantly higher rate. This could be where the ability to discern more subtle discriminatory interactions comes forth. That is, the higher rate of reported discrimination among U.S.-born AAMs could be a function of recognizing less explicit slights, such as micro-aggressions, or a sense that they are entitled to a certain level of treatment that their foreign-born counterparts may not be as cognizant of. Paradoxically, this heightened sensitivity to discrimination may actually be an indicator of "cultural fluency" that comes with integration (Lajevardi et al. 2020).

Moreover, the processing of discrimination appears to vary by immigrant status. The fact that U.S.-born respondents are significantly more likely to believe that America offers Muslims a better quality of life than most Muslim-majority countries speaks to the subjective toll that minority status exerts on immigrant Arab-Americans. It is worth emphasizing that this attitudinal divide is not a function of material well-being as education and income are held constant in the analysis. Rather, the gap indicates that native-born AAMs are better equipped with the social and cultural resources that allow them to filter their experience as a minority in the United States in a more productive manner—neither denying the experience nor letting it weigh them down. By that same token, as the final item in figure 11.1 demonstrates, AAMs born in the United States are much more likely to wholly reject anti-Muslim tropes rather than partially internalize them. In line with the prevalence of religiosity among this sub-population, the tendency to reject Islamophobic stereotypes is yet another indication that U.S.-born AAMs are simply not inclined to abrogate their ethnic and religious background in favor of a more mainstream identity.

CONCLUSION

What emerges from the analyses in this chapter is a wide-ranging, empirically grounded depiction of how the sons and daughters of Arab immigrants to the United Stated have adapted to their minority status. The data demonstrates that the attitudes and behaviors of native-born AAMs both diverge from their foreign-born counterparts in notable, and occasionally predictable, ways, but also demonstrate parity when the expectations of assimilation theory would predict otherwise. Ultimately, whether and to what degree this community is assimilating is, in part, a function of the academic or pundit leveraging the term. Indeed, the slippage between assimilation, integration, acculturation, and socialization can constrain the utility of any of these terms. To the extent that any of these phenomena do apply to the Arab-American Muslim experience, they would likely require additional modifiers. One viable contender in this regard is "selective acculturation" as articulated by Portes and Rumbaut, meaning "the acquisition of English fluency and American cultural ways *along with* preservation of certain key elements of the immigrant culture" (2014, 350, emphasis in original).

This chapter is certainly far from the final word on Arab-American social and political adaptation. At minimum, the stark divide in age between native and immigrant AAMs, coupled with the similarly wide gulf in marriage rates, urges researchers to revisit the above findings once most Arabs born in the United States have gone through their prime earning years and started families of their own. Another fruitful avenue of research would be to dive deeper into the broad correlations discussed above. Empirically modeling the mechanisms that drive these surface-level observations would further refine our understanding of the ways in which AAMs navigate and negotiate minority status in America. What is clear at this point, however, is that AAMs are neither wholly alienated from the broader society nor do they seek to uncritically meld into the dominant culture. As with many discourses surrounding Muslims over the past two decades, this one, too, could use added nuance.

NOTES

1. While there remains a general consensus on the prevalence of anti-Irish discrimination in the latter half of the nineteenth century on through World War I, the incidence of "No Irish Need Apply" signs (or its variants) has recently been a topic of dispute (Lind 2015).

2. Morocco was the first country to officially recognize United States independence in December 1777.

3. These included Palestinians displaced by the founding of Israel, Egyptians whose property had been nationalized by President Gamal Abdel Nasser, Iraqis fleeing their country after the 1958 revolution, elite Syrians excluded from government participation, and Eastern European Muslims escaping Communist rule (Haddad 1997).

4. The seemingly large gap in these estimates is most likely a result of Pew extrapolating MENA heritage based on respondents' country of origin (or that of their parents), whereas ISPU directly asks respondents for their race/ethnicity.

REFERENCES

Ajrouch, Kristine J., and Amaney Jamal. 2007. "Assimilating to a White Identity: The Case of Arab Americans." *The International Migration Review* 41 (4): 860–79.

Alba, Richard, and Victor Nee. 2005. *Remaking the American Mainstream: Assimilation and Contemporary Immigration*. Cambridge: Harvard University Press.

Alsultany, Evelyn. 2012. *Arabs and Muslims in the Media: Race and Representation After 9/11*. New York: NYU Press.

Asi, Maryam, and Daniel Beaulieu. 2013. "Arab Households in the United States: 2006–2010." American Community Survey Briefs. Washington, D.C.: U.S. CENSUS BUREAU. https://www2.census.gov/library/publications/2013/acs/acsbr10-20.pdf.

Batalova, Jeanne, and Mattea Cumoletti. 2018. "Middle Eastern and North African Immigrants in the United States." Migrationpolicy.Org. January 8, 2018. https://www.migrationpolicy.org/article/middle-eastern-and-north-african-immigrants-united-states.

Berry, Justin, Youssef Chouhoud, and Jane Junn. 2018. "Reaching Beyond Low-Hanging Fruit: Surveying Low Incidence Populations." In *Oxford Handbook of Polling and Polling Methods*, 181–206. Oxford; New York: Oxford University Press.

Beydoun, Khaled. 2013. "Between Muslim and White: The Legal Construction of Arab American." *New York Annual Survey of American Law* 69 (1): 29–76.

Chouhoud, Youssef. 2011. "(Muslim) American Exceptionalism: Contextualizing Religiosity among Young Muslims in America." Master's Thesis, Bethlehem, PA: Lehigh University.

———. 2018. "Born in the USA: How Nativity Affects the American Muslim Experience." *Institute for Social Policy and Understanding* (blog). November 27, 2018. https://www.ispu.org/born-in-the-usa-how-nativity-affects-the-american-muslim-experience/.

Chouhoud, Youssef, Karam Dana, and Matt Barreto. 2019. "American Muslim Political Participation: Between Diversity and Cohesion." *Politics and Religion* 12 (4): 736–65.

Foad, Hisham. 2013. "Waves of Immigration from the Middle East to the United States." In *Proceedings of American Economic Association Annual Meeting,* San Diego.

Haddad, Yvonne. 1997. "A Century of Islam in America." *Hamdard Islamicus* 21 (4): 3–5.

———. 2007. "The Post-9/11 Hijab as Icon." 68 (3): 253–67.

Kayyali, Randa. 2013. "US Census Classifications and Arab Americans: Contestations and Definitions of Identity Markers." *Journal of Ethnic and Migration Studies* 39 (8): 1299–1318. https://doi.org/10.1080/1369183X.2013.778150.

Lajevardi, Nazita. 2020. *Outsiders at Home: The Politics of American Islamophobia.* Cambridge, United Kingdom: Cambridge University Press.

Lajevardi, Nazita, Kassra A. R. Oskooii, Hannah L. Walker, and Aubrey L. Westfall. 2020. "The Paradox Between Integration and Perceived Discrimination Among American Muslims." *Political Psychology* 41 (3): 587–606. https://doi.org/10.1111/pops.12640.

Lee, Jennifer C., and Samuel Kye. 2016. "Racialized Assimilation of Asian Americans." *Annual Review of Sociology* 42 (1): 253–73.

Mogahed, Dalia, and Youssef Chouhoud. 2017. "American Muslim Poll 2017: Muslims at the Crossroads." Washington, DC: Institute for Social Policy and Understanding.

Naber, Nadine. 2005. "Muslim First, Arab Second: A Strategic Politics of Race and Gender." *The Muslim World* 95 (4): 479–95. https://doi.org/10.1111/j.1478-1913.2005.00107.x.

Oskooii, Kassra AR. 2015. "How Discrimination Impacts Sociopolitical Behavior: A Multidimensional Perspective." *Political Psychology* 37 (5): 613–40.

Oxford Analytica. 2009. "UNITED STATES: Young Muslims' Piety, Alienation Rise." Oxford Analytica Daily Brief Service.

Pew Research Center. 2007. "Muslim Americans: Middle Class and Mostly Mainstream." Washington, DC: Pew Research Center.

———. 2013. "A Portrait of Jewish Americans." Washington, DC: Pew Research Center.

———. 2017. "U.S. Muslims Concerned About Their Place in Society, but Continue to Believe in the American Dream." Washington, DC: Pew Research Center.

Portes, Alejandro, and Rubén G. Rumbaut. 2014. *Immigrant America: A Portrait.* Fourth Edition, Revised, Updated, and Expanded edition. Berkeley and Los Angeles, California: University of California Press.

Portes, Alejandro, and Min Zhou. 1993. "The New Second Generation: Segmented Assimilation and Its Variants." *The ANNALS of the American Academy of Political and Social Science* 530 (1): 74–96.

Said, Edward W. 1979. *Orientalism.* New York, NY: Vintage.

Shaheen, Jack. 2014. *Reel Bad Arabs: How Hollywood Vilifies a People.* Northampton, MA: Olive Branch Press.

Silber, Mitchell D., and Arvin Bhatt. 2007. "Radicalization in the West: The Homegrown Threat." New York, NY: NYPD Intelligence Division.

Appendix 1
Question Wording

RELIGIOSITY

Variable	Survey Source	Survey Year(s)	Question Wording	Response Options
Attends religious services weekly	ISPU & Pew	Pew: ALL ISPU: ALL	Aside from weddings and funerals, how often do you attend religious services?	More than once a week; once a week, once or twice a month; a few times a year; seldom; or never [rendered dichotomous for at least "once a week"]
Religion very important to R's life	ISPU & Pew	Pew: ALL ISPU: ALL	How important is religion in your life?	Very important; somewhat important; not too important; or not at all important [rendered dichotomous for "very important"]
Prays 5 daily salat	Pew	ALL	Concerning daily salah (sal-AH) or prayer, do you, in general, pray all five salah (sal-AH) daily, make some of the five salah (sal-AH) daily, occasionally make salah (sal-AH), only make Eid (EED) Prayers, or do you never pray?	[rendered dichotomous for "Pray all five salah"]

Variable	Survey Source	Survey Year(s)	Question Wording	Response Options
Always wears hijab	Pew	ALL	When you are out in public, how often do you wear the headcover or hijab (hee-jab)? Do you wear it all the time, most of the time, only some of the time, or never?	[rendered dichotomous for "All the time"]
Active in the mosque	Pew	2007, 2011	And outside of salah (sal-AH) and Jum'ah (joom-AH) prayer, do you take part in any other social or religious activities at the mosque or Islamic Center?	Yes; no

SOCIAL AND POLITICAL ATTITUDES

Variable	Survey Source	Survey Year(s)	Question Wording	Response Options
Registered to vote	ISPU	ALL	Are you registered to vote at your present address or not?	Yes; no
Homosexuality should be accepted by society	Pew	ALL	Here are a few pairs of statements. For each pair, tell me whether the FIRST statement or the SECOND statement comes closer to your own views — even if neither is exactly right.	1 Homosexuality should be accepted by society [OR] 2 Homosexuality should be discouraged by society
Use of military force in Afghanistan was wrong decision	Pew	2007, 2011	Do you think the U.S. made the right decision or the wrong decision in using military force in Afghanistan?	Right decision; Wrong decision

Appendix 1

Variable	Survey Source	Survey Year(s)	Question Wording	Response Options
Thinks of self as "American First," "Muslim First," "American and Muslim, Equally"	Pew	2007, 2011	Do you think of yourself first as an American or first as a Muslim?	1 American 2 Muslim 3 Both equally (VOL.)
Most Friends / Hardly Any Friends are Muslim	Pew	ALL	How many of your close friends are Muslims?	1 All of them 2 Most of them 3 Some of them [OR] 4 Hardly any of them 5 (VOL. – DO NOT READ) None of them [rendered dichotomous for at least "most of them" or "hardly any of them," respectively]

DISCRIMINATION

Variable	Survey Source	Survey Year(s)	Question Wording	Response Options
People acted as if they are suspicious of you	Pew	ALL	have people acted as if they are suspicious of you	Yes; no
Been called offensive names	Pew	ALL	have you been called offensive names	Yes; no
Been singled out by airport security	Pew	ALL	have you been singled out by airport security	Yes; no
Experiences discrimination more than rarely	ISPU	ALL	How often, if at all, have you personally experienced discrimination in the past year because of your religion?	Never; rarely; occasionally; regularly

Variable	Survey Source	Survey Year(s)	Question Wording	Response Options
Better quality of life for Muslims in the U.S.	Pew	2007, 2011	What's your impression, do you think that the quality of life for Muslims in the U.S. is [RANDOMIZE: better, worse], or about the same as the quality of life in most Muslim countries?	[rendered dichotomous for "better"]
Holds some anti-Muslim bias	ISPU	2018, 2019, 2020	*	* [rendered dichotomous for greater than 0 on the Islamophobia Index.

* ISPU's Islamophobia Index scales five questions gauging anti-Muslim prejudice. The resulting measure ranges from 0 to 100. More details can be found at https://www.ispu.org/wp-content/uploads/2018/04/AMP-2018-Key-Findings.pdf

Index

activism, 19, 21, 183
Afghanistan, 99, 104, 196, 202
African, 5, 6, 67, 86, 115–19, 142, 153, 189; Africans, 15, 117, 142
agency, 8, 12, 40, 41, 171, 172, 175–84
Alabama, 158
Alawite, 34
Aleppo, 37, 154
Algeria, 115, 142, 153; Algerian(s), 115, 116, 118
Al Nabk, 34
Al Qutayfah, 34
Al Tall, 34
Al-Wehda, 92–95
Amazon, 49, 176
ambivalent agency, 171, 172, 175, 179
American Jews, 187
American(s), 3, 4, 8, 11–15, 19, 21–26, 30, 32, 35, 45, 50, 60, 64, 69, 79, 81, 88, 132, 151–65, 171, 173, 174, 176–78, 180–82, 187–98
Amity Street, 155
anti-immigration, 100, 103
Antillean, 68, 71
Arab(s), 1–9, 11, 13–15, 17–21, 23–25, 29–35, 37, 39, 40, 42–44, 46, 49–55, 57–60, 64, 67–85, 88–93, 99–102, 104, 110, 115–18, 120, 125, 129–31, 134–37, 139–46, 151–65, 178, 187–91, 193, 195, 198; Arab American Muslim(s), 187, 188, 190–98; Arab American(s), 4, 8, 151–54, 156–65, 187–91, 193, 197, 198; Arab Canadian, 130, 131, 135, 138, 139, 141, 143; Arab Christian(s), 24, 155; Arab communities, 1, 2, 4–8, 15, 68, 73; Arab culture, 135, 136, 141, 144; Arab diaspora(s), 1, 3–7, 13, 30, 31, 33–35, 37, 44, 99, 100, 102, 152; Arabic, 3, 8, 15, 17, 49, 54, 68–72, 74, 76–79, 90–92, 105, 109, 136–38, 141, 143, 151–53, 155–64, 178; Arabic speaking, 68–72, 74, 77, 79, 157; Arab identity, 1–3, 6, 71, 130, 135, 138, 141–43; Arab immigrant(s), 8, 31, 33, 34, 72–76, 79, 80, 115, 116, 125, 151–53, 156, 158–60, 165, 189, 197; Arab immigration, 30, 33, 35, 80, 118, 152, 154; Arab Iraqis, 4; Arab Israeli, 14; Arab Latin American, 13, 23; Arab League, 2–4, 60; Arab media, 3, 130, 135, 136, 145; Arab migration, 5, 51, 54, 55, 71, 79, 189; Arab Muslim, 60, 80, 145, 189; Arab-Singaporeans, 83; Arab youth, 7, 129, 130, 134, 135, 137, 138, 141–43, 145, 146

205

Index

Argentina, 5, 7, 13, 15, 29–46, 50, 79, 80
Argentine-Arab, 29–31, 39, 40, 42–44
Argentine-Syrian, 35
Argentinian/Argentine society, 35–37, 39, 44
Argentinian(s), 7, 32, 35–37, 39–41, 45
Asia, 84, 89, 92, 93, 129, 142, 152; Asian(s), 8, 15, 53, 70, 71, 84, 157, 190; Asian Turkey, 70, 71
assimilation, 5, 18, 25, 80, 81, 101, 107, 119, 122, 132, 144, 146, 158, 187, 188, 190–91, 193, 196, 198; assimilation theory, 101, 197
association(s), 3, 18, 20–25, 33, 34, 38, 40, 43, 54, 60, 68, 75–77, 79, 80, 84, 92, 93, 116, 117, 119, 125, 190, 194, 195
Assyrian, 2, 4
Asturias, 67
Asylum, 9, 99–104, 106–8, 110, 111, 189
Atlantic coast, 14, 17, 21
authority-disorder, 35–37, 39

Baathist, 2
Baghdad, 94
Baidaphon, 155, 156, 160
Barranquilla, 15
Beirut, 54, 55, 58, 64, 67, 69, 152, 154–56, 161
Beit Jala, 14, 15
Beit Sahour, 14, 15
Berlin, 99–101, 104–11
Bethlehem, 12–16, 19, 24
Birmingham, 158
Bolivia, 18
Boston, 162
Brasilia, 50, 60, 64
Brazil, 7, 13, 15, 30, 42, 49–64; Brazilian, 49, 50, 52–61, 63, 64; Brazilian Muslims, 60
British: British Muslims, 60
Brooklyn, 151, 155–57, 163, 164
Btaaboura, 64

Buffalo, 158
Bukele, 11–14, 16, 50
business owners, 11, 16, 19, 21–23

Cairo, 152, 155, 164
California, 157, 162, 173
Canada, 4, 7, 129, 130, 132–46; Canadian, 4, 7, 41, 129–33, 135, 137–44, 146; Canadian-Arab, 130, 135, 137, 138, 140, 141, 143; Canary Islands, 67
Caracas, 15
Carnegie Hall, 164
Catalonia, 67
Catholic, 11–13, 19, 34, 40, 73–75; Catholic Maronite, 74
caucus, 50, 60–64
Central America(n), 13, 15, 17, 20–22, 25, 26
Centro Habana, 73
Cherbourg, France, 161
Chicago, 154, 155
children, 8, 9, 15, 16, 30, 70, 75, 88, 90, 99–110, 133, 144, 151, 154, 159, 160, 171, 175, 176, 178–80, 182, 183, 188
Chile, 8, 13–15, 17–21, 23–26
Chilean(s), 4, 17–21, 23, 25
Chilestino/Palestinian-Chilean, 4, 11, 17, 20, 25
Chinese, 15, 16, 21, 67, 68, 73, 83, 87–89, 91, 93; Chinese-Mongolian, 189
Christian(s), 5, 12, 13, 15–19, 24–26, 34, 53, 59, 69, 73–75, 80, 155, 175, 189, 190; Christian Catholic, 11–13, 19, 34, 40, 73–75; Christian Evangelical, 13, 25; Christian Orthodox, 12, 17, 34, 40, 74, 75, 80, 164; Christian Palestinians, 16, 17; Christian Protestant, 75; Christian Zionist Evangelical, 25
Cleveland, 158
Colombia, 13, 15, 16, 50
colony, 57, 76, 77, 152

Index

Columbia, 155, 156, 158–62
commerce, 16, 22, 33, 34, 50, 55, 57, 61, 190
committee, 29, 40, 41, 43, 46, 77–79, 85, 92, 124, 126
community, 4–8, 12–23, 25, 29–35, 39, 40, 43, 44, 51, 53, 54, 56–61, 67, 68, 71, 74, 75, 77, 79–81, 83, 85–88, 90–95, 102, 103, 116, 118–20, 123–25, 130, 132, 136, 138, 142, 144, 155, 157, 173, 174, 179–82, 188, 191, 196, 198
composition, 74, 122, 124, 125, 151, 156, 163–65, 172, 193
Connecticut, 8, 156, 171–76, 179, 182, 183
Córdoba, 33, 41
corruption, 14, 23, 57, 59
Costa Rica, 70
Council of the Muslim Faith (CFCM), 120, 124, 125
Creil, 118
Cuba(n), 5, 7, 21, 24, 43, 67, 68, 70–81; Cuban Arab, 7, 80
culture(s), 8, 26, 32, 67, 75, 76, 84, 86, 89–94, 101, 102, 109, 132, 135–38, 141–45, 171, 178, 179, 183, 187–90, 198
Cuyo, 34

Damascus, 34, 37, 40, 41, 54, 154, 155, 157
Detroit, 162, 190, 191
Diario Sirio Libanés, 35, 37–39
diaspora(s), 1, 3–9, 11, 13–15, 17, 19, 20, 23–26, 30, 31, 33–35, 37, 44, 51, 54, 83–86, 88, 89, 91–95, 99–102, 105, 107, 108, 110, 111, 115, 123, 125, 131, 132, 143, 146, 152, 153, 165; diaspora space, 101, 102, 107, 108, 110, 111; diasporic communities, 1, 7, 8, 99, 101, 106, 107, 109, 111; diasporic individuals, 102

discrimination, 1, 16, 17, 21, 33, 53, 102, 106, 117, 122, 125, 130, 133, 172, 188–91, 197, 198
displaced children, 105, 110
Dominican Republic, 13
dramatization, 35–37, 39
Druze, 43, 69
Dutch, 84

East African, 86
Eastern Europe, 94
Eastern Yemen, 84
East Mediterranean territories, 69
Ecuador, 13, 50
Egypt, 67, 142, 152, 153, 155, 156, 175, 190, 199; Egyptian, 69, 155, 156, 158, 198; Egyptian Armenian, 156
El Salvador, 8, 11–16, 20–23, 25, 50
emigration, 6, 16, 68, 69
England, 4, 69, 70
English, 45, 86, 134, 135, 137, 151, 153, 158, 159, 171, 176, 178–82, 198
Escalon, 11
ethnic, 2–6, 8, 9, 52, 57–59, 64, 67, 68, 71, 75–78, 80, 81, 84, 86, 89, 90, 99, 100, 104, 108, 110, 115–17, 120, 122, 124, 129, 130, 134, 135, 138, 141, 142, 145, 146, 165, 173, 174, 187, 189–91, 196, 198; ethnic groups, 67, 75, 76, 80, 89; ethnic identity, 3–6, 75, 130, 135, 146; ethnic origin, 57, 84; ethnocultural community, 130, 138; ethnocultural identity, 132, 135; ethnocultural minorities, 131, 132
Eurasian, 88
Europe, 2, 8, 21, 32, 33, 36, 41–43, 81, 94, 100, 101, 104, 105, 118, 121, 126, 130, 189, 194; European Muslims, 195, 199; European(s), 88, 100, 101, 103, 104, 111, 119, 121, 181, 190, 194, 195, 199; European Turkey, 70

family reunification, 29, 39, 40, 43, 44, 116
famine, 69, 84
foreign-born, 174, 184, 188, 192, 193, 195–98
fragmentation, 35–37, 39, 125
framing, 35–37, 39, 90, 172
France, 8, 21, 38, 73, 76, 115–18, 120–26, 145, 161
French, 31–33, 53–55, 58, 67, 72, 115–26, 134, 135, 145
French Muslims, 119–23, 126

Galicia, 67
gender, 6, 8, 101, 102, 106, 109, 110, 125, 171, 172, 175, 176, 179, 181–84, 196
geopolitical, 60, 125
Georgia, 157
German(s), 17, 99–111, 155; German-born children, 101, 107, 108, 110;
Germany, 5, 9, 21, 99–106, 108–10
Glastonbury, 173
Greater Syria, 51, 153, 154
Greek, 74, 75, 80, 102, 164; Greek Catholic, 75; Greek Orthodox, 74, 75, 80
Greenwich Street, 154, 156

Hadhrami, 83–95; Hadhrami diaspora, 83–86, 89, 91, 92, 94, 95; Hadhrami identity, 83, 84, 86, 91, 93–95; Hadhrami Singaporean, 87, 90, 93, 95; Hadhramout, Yemen, 8, 84; Hadramaut/Hadhramaut, 84, 86, 91–94
Haiti, 43, 70
halal, 60, 122, 124, 125
Havana, 70, 72, 74–77
Hebrew, 78
Homeland(s), 1, 4, 5, 7, 8, 15, 24–26, 50, 54, 55, 84, 85, 91, 94, 95, 116–23, 130–32, 143, 145, 174
Homs, 33, 34, 176
Honduras, 8, 13–15, 20–23, 25, 50

host society, 8, 99–101, 107–11, 132
humanitarian crisis, 2, 7, 29, 30, 39
humanitarian visa, 29, 39–41

identity, 1–8, 11, 12, 17, 20, 21, 23–25, 33, 40, 51, 53, 68, 71, 75, 80, 83–95, 104, 115–20, 122, 125, 130–36, 138–46, 172, 187–90, 194, 196, 197
immigrant(s), 5, 7, 8, 15, 21, 30–34, 36, 44, 67, 68, 70–76, 79, 80, 99–103, 106–11, 115–19, 121, 125, 131–33, 135, 138, 143–46, 151–54, 156–60, 162, 164, 165, 173, 174, 187–98
immigration, 2, 6, 14–17, 20, 21, 30–37, 43, 45, 68, 70–74, 77, 78, 80, 85, 94, 95, 99–104, 106–10
independence, 51, 52, 54, 58, 70, 76, 78, 85–91, 115
Indonesia, 84, 85, 91
intermarriage, 21, 84, 86, 89
Iran, 2, 38; Iranian(s), 103; Iranian Revolution, 118
Iraq, 2, 99, 104, 142, 152
Iraqi(s), 2–4, 103
Islam(ic), 2, 8, 12, 24, 26, 33, 40, 58, 75, 80, 83, 84, 86, 87, 89–92, 103, 106, 107, 116, 118–25, 159
Islamism(ization), 103, 118, 122
Islamophobia(ic), 26, 100, 125, 171, 197, 204
Israel, 2, 12, 13, 16, 19–21, 38, 59, 60, 94
Israeli/Israelite, 12, 14, 24, 33, 38
Italian(s), 31, 32, 34, 52, 64, 67, 102, 156, 187, 191

Jerusalem, 12, 16, 60, 69, 154, 161
Jews(ish), 5, 20, 26, 77–79, 94, 187
Jordan, 67, 142, 152, 157, 175, 176; Jordanian(s), 137

Kurban, 161, 163–65
Kurds(ish), 2
Kuwait, 3

Index

La Nación, 35–39
Latin(a) America(n), 4, 7, 9, 11, 13–17, 19–21, 23–26, 64, 68, 69, 73, 76, 79–81
Lebanese, 2, 4, 7, 13, 15, 24, 31, 33, 34, 40, 41, 49–62, 64, 67, 69–77, 79–81, 102, 155, 158; Lebanese American(s), 158; Lebanese Canadian, 4; Lebanese community, 53, 60, 61; Lebanese descent, 7, 49–51, 55, 57, 59–61, 64; Lebanese migrants, 49–59, 64; Lebanese-Syrian, 15
Lebanon, 15, 24, 33, 34, 40, 41, 43, 51–55, 60, 61, 64, 67, 69, 72, 75–77, 80, 102, 142, 152–54, 157, 158, 162, 163, 190
Levantine, 13, 54, 57
Libya, 142, 153
Little Syria, 152, 154–56, 161, 162

Macksoud, 152, 154–57, 160–65
Madrasah, 84, 87, 88, 93, 97
Magazine, 54, 93, 151, 159–60, 165
Maghrebi(s), 8, 115–26
Mahjari, 151–65
Malay, 8, 83–84, 86–93, 95; Malay-Indonesian, 86; Malay Singaporean, 8
Mali, 106
Maloof, 151, 152, 154–65
Maronite, 33, 71, 74, 75, 80, 158
Marseille, 73
Mashriq, 152, 153, 155, 156
Massachusetts, 162
Mecca, 124
media, 2, 3, 7, 9–11, 14, 20, 23, 25, 29–48, 100, 103, 105, 110, 117, 119, 122, 130–32, 134, 136, 137, 141, 143–45, 174, 191; media bias, 35, 44
Melkite, 75
MENA, 2, 3, 6, 146, 189, 191, 193, 196
Mendoza, 41
Mexico, 12, 13, 15, 26, 70, 71, 79, 80, 161

Michigan, 26, 173
Middle East, 1–11, 23, 24, 26, 35, 50, 53, 59, 60, 68–70, 72, 74–76, 79–81, 93, 95, 118, 129, 130, 135, 136, 142, 152, 154, 180, 188, 189; Middle Eastern(er), 2, 4, 35, 53, 79, 142, 154, 155, 189, 191
migration, 1, 5, 7–10, 13, 15–17, 20, 21, 23–25, 32, 33, 39, 40, 42, 44, 46, 51, 52, 61, 62, 67–69, 71, 79, 84, 99, 100, 105, 106, 111, 115, 117, 130, 133, 176, 179, 184, 189
minority, 7, 23, 25, 26, 75, 87, 90, 94, 104, 115, 116, 118, 122, 129, 134, 187, 188, 190, 195, 197, 198
mobilization, 8, 116–20
Mongolian, 189
Montreal, 129, 134, 146
Moroccan(s), 102, 115, 117, 124, 126
Morocco, 10, 115, 142, 143, 153, 199
Mount Lebanon, 67, 69, 162
multi-axial, 101, 102, 105, 110
multiculturalism, 90, 95, 129, 132, 141
multiracialism, 83, 89, 90
Munich, 100
music, 5, 8, 17, 76, 93, 107, 136, 137, 143, 151–65
Muslim(s), 5, 8, 12, 17, 24, 26, 34, 59, 60, 75, 80, 83, 85–91, 100, 103, 104, 107, 115–31, 145, 155, 161, 173, 175, 187–98; Shia/Shiite, 26, 34, 80; Sunni, 26, 175

Nablus, 69
national anthem, 152, 159
national identity, 2, 3, 10, 25, 92, 97, 130, 132, 135, 144
nation-state, 2, 4, 51, 101, 103, 131
nativity, 187–98
New Jersey, 20, 162, 164
New York, 8, 27, 41–43, 46, 152, 154–59, 161–65
newspaper, 18, 19, 21, 35, 37, 46, 54, 55, 58, 71, 77, 88, 97, 103, 151, 153, 160, 165

Nicaragua, 21, 22, 24
North Africa, 1, 4, 5, 116, 118, 188;
   North African(s), 5, 6, 117, 142, 153, 189
Nuevo Cuscatlán, 11

Odeon, 155, 156, 160
"official politics", 50–52
Ontario, 129
Orchestra, 163, 165, 176
Osorno, 17
Ottawa, 129, 134, 146
Ottoman Empire, 2, 3, 7, 9, 15, 16, 26, 31–33, 53, 54, 69, 174, 189

Palestine, 9, 10, 12, 15, 16, 18–20, 23, 25–28, 33, 34, 59, 67, 69, 75, 77–79, 142, 135, 152, 154, 157, 190; Palestinian Chileans, 17–19, 23; Palestinian descent, 20, 22, 23; Palestinian Honduran, 22, 23; Palestinian identity, 12, 20, 23–25; Palestinian nationalist movement, 13; Palestinian(s), 2, 4, 8–28, 31, 33, 67, 69, 71–77, 79–81, 102, 137, 161, 164, 199; Palestinian Salvadoran, 11, 13, 22
Palmyra, 38
Pampas, 34, 46
Pan-Arab, 3, 17, 24, 77–79
Pan-Canadian, 135
Paraguay, 13
Paris, 15, 45, 124, 126, 158, 173, 193
Patronato, 14, 17
pattern, 1, 6–9, 58, 62, 68, 75, 120, 123, 125, 141, 196
Pennsylvania, 158
personalization, 35–37, 39
Peru, 15
Philadelphia, 27, 154
PLO, 12, 19, 21, 22, 24, 25
policy, 7, 17, 25, 28–32, 36, 39–45, 50, 57, 59–61, 70, 78, 89–91, 94, 97, 99, 101, 130, 132, 133, 173, 184, 188, 192, 193

political attitudes, 13, 188, 195, 202
political participation, 9, 50–52, 55, 56, 61, 134, 195
poll, 116, 188, 192, 193
post-independence, 86–88, 91
press coverage, 35, 38
primo-migrants, 115–18
Protestant Christians, 75

Qatar, 3, 10, 153
Quebec, 129

Rachiin, 72, 75
refugee(s), 2, 7–10, 23, 24, 29, 30, 33, 36, 37, 39–46, 93, 94, 99–101, 103–5, 110–11, 171–79, 181–84
religion, 2, 5, 8, 28, 33, 83, 88, 89, 91–94, 111, 116, 117, 119–23, 126, 172, 175, 179, 184, 187, 193, 195, 197, 201
religiosity, 116, 120–22, 125, 188, 193, 194, 195, 197, 201
relocation, 30, 40–45, 68
Republic of Singapore, 83
right-wing, 11, 19, 21, 23, 43, 60, 61, 130, 146
Russian, 31

Salvadoran, 11–13, 22
Santiago, 14, 17, 18, 27, 28, 74, 76
São Paulo, 15, 49–64
Saudi Arabia, 10, 38, 142, 152
second-generation, 81, 118, 120, 133, 144, 194–95
secular(ism), 24, 34, 88, 97, 118–26
security, 30, 36, 37, 39–41, 44, 100, 123, 173–74, 181, 183, 184
Senegal, 104, 106
Singapore, 83–95
social elite, 73, 77
social mobility, 7, 50, 55, 57, 144
Sonsonate, 14
South America(n), 17, 27, 30, 42, 45, 61, 70
Southeast Asia, 84, 89, 93, 95; Southeast Asian, 84

Index

Southern Cone, 30
Southern Europe/an, 32
South Indian, 86
Spain, 38; Spaniard(s), 32, 34, 67, 73; Spanish, 16, 19, 31, 45, 63, 67, 69, 70, 73, 81
Syria, 2, 7, 15, 24, 30, 33–39, 42–44, 51–53, 55, 64, 67, 69, 72, 75–77, 99, 104, 105, 109, 151–57, 161, 162, 165, 172, 173, 176, 178, 179, 181–84, 190; Syrian American, 156–59, 161–62, 164; Syrian Christian, 189, 190; Syrian conflict, 29, 30, 35–40; Syrian immigrants, 31, 44, 75, 156–58, 164; Syrian Lebanese, 24, 33, 34, 40, 51, 52, 56–59, 65, 69, 73, 74, 76, 77, 80; Syrian Program, 29–31, 35, 39–44; Syrian refugees, 7–9, 29, 36, 39, 40, 43, 45, 171, 173–75, 181, 183, 184; Syrians, 16, 30, 36, 41–44, 53, 54, 67, 76, 77, 81, 103, 154, 157–59, 173, 174, 190, 199; Syrian women, 171–75, 183–84

Tamil, 88
Tebnine, 161
Tel Aviv, 12, 37, 60
Television, 5, 9, 23, 35, 99–111, 136, 143, 144, 174
Texas, 26, 65, 161, 173
The Middle East/North Africa, 2, 4, 5
The United States. *See* United States
Tiscornia Camp, 72, 73
Toronto, 129
Torrington (in Connecticut), 156
trade, 33, 34, 55, 61, 70, 73, 74, 76, 77, 80, 84, 85, 117, 122
transnational, 2, 3, 8–10, 65, 84, 86, 104, 118, 119, 126, 130–34, 137, 141, 143, 144, 146
transnationalism, 118, 130–33, 143, 144, 146

Tripoli, 62, 69, 161
Tunisia, 10, 115, 153; Tunisian(s), 102, 115
Turk(s), 15, 33, 52, 53, 55, 69, 71, 102; Turk-Arabs, 52; Turk-Asians, 53; Turkey, 1, 16, 46, 70, 71, 175; Turkish, 17, 24, 36, 42, 53, 69, 104, 106, 108, 109, 119, 124, 126, 154; Turkish-German, 108; Turkish Muslim(s), 124, 126; Turkish-Ottoman empire, 69

United States, 4, 5, 8, 13, 17, 21, 23, 25, 32, 38, 70, 71, 78, 79, 81, 101, 145, 151–62, 165, 171–77, 180, 183, 184, 187, 189, 193–99
Uruguay, 30, 45
U.S., 22, 25, 50, 51, 58, 59, 65, 152, 156–58, 173, 174, 184, 187, 188, 191, 193–97
U.S.-born, 158, 188, 193–97

veil, 20, 121–23, 125, 177
Venezuela, 15, 43
Veracruz, 15
vulnerable, 9, 176, 179–80, 184

waqaf, 86, 87
Washington, 152, 154, 157, 163, 190
Western, 3, 12, 35, 38, 55, 56, 92, 109, 126, 130, 131, 135, 137, 141–44, 152, 153, 162, 183–93
Western Europe, 101
West Germany, 102
West Scranton, 158

Yemen, 67, 84, 93, 94; Yemeni, 92

Zaleh, 154
Zgarta, 72
Zionist, 24, 25, 79

About the Contributors

Mariam F. Alkazemi is an assistant professor at the Robertson School of Media and Culture at Virginia Commonwealth University (VCU). She has served as a Carnegie fellow at University of North Carolina Chapel Hill and a research fellow at the London School of Economics. She has authored over twenty-five peer-reviewed publications on a range of topics from honor-based violence to political cartoons in the Arab world. Her first co-authored book on Kuwaiti media law was published in May 2018. Dr. Alkazemi served as an officer of the Religion and Media Interest Group, which is affiliated with the Association for Education in Journalism and Mass Communication (AEJMC) for five years. In 2020, she was the recipient of the 2020 Gerner Award by the International Studies Association. She holds degrees from the University of Florida, Michigan State University, and George Washington University.

Claudia E. Youakim is the deputy director of knowledge management and research at the Center for Inclusive Business and Leadership in the Olayan School of Business at the American University of Beirut. Her work focuses on socio-cultural and political structures and how they impact policies and practices in the Middle East and North African region and in the United States. She earned her doctorate in sociology with a concentration on the intersection of race, ethnicity, and women and gender studies from the University of Florida. Her dissertation sheds light on Arab American millennial identity development and social networks. She completed her MA from DePaul University and BA Loyola University, Chicago. Dr. Youakim has served as an assistant professor of sociology at Finlandia University.

Imène Ajala is assistant professor in international relations at the University of Wollongong in Dubai. She completed her PhD in international relations at the Graduate Institute of International and Development Studies in Geneva and previously taught at Webster University. Dr. Ajala's research interests are comparative politics, foreign policy analysis, diaspora studies and multiculturalism with a particular focus on Muslims in Europe. Her work has appeared in the *Journal of Muslim Minority Affairs*, *Contemporary Islam*, the *Journal of Islamic Law and Culture*, *French Politics*, *Politique Etrangère* and *Behavioral Sciences of Terrorism and Political Aggression* among others. In 2018, her first book titled *European Muslims and their Foreign Policy Interests, Identities and Loyalties* was published by Gerlach Press.

Manal al-Natour is associate professor and director of Arabic Studies in the World Languages, Literatures, and Linguistics Department, West Virginia University. She earned a PhD in comparative literature and cultural studies at the University of Arkansas. Her research and teaching interests include modern Arabic literature and language, postcolonial studies, contemporary women's writings, feminism, and the Arab Spring. Her most recent publications have appeared in *Women Rising: In and Beyond the Arab Spring* (New York University Press, 2020); *The Routledge Handbook of Arabic Translation*; *Literature and Psychology: Writing, Trauma, and the Self*; and *Arab Spring and Arab Women: Challenges and Opportunities*, in addition to several peer-reviewed essays in *Alif: Journal of Comparative Poetics*, *Journal of International* Women's Studies, *Comics through Time*, and *Women's ENews*.

Aisha Sahar Waheed Alkharusi is a career diplomat with the Ministry of Foreign Affairs of the Sultanate of Oman since 2007. She served a five-year tour of duty in Singapore (2011–2016) as deputy consul general. She obtained her bachelor's degree at George Washington University (2007) majoring in international affairs (International Economics and Middle Eastern Studies) minoring in cultural anthropology, and a master's of science in international relations from Nanyang Technological University, Singapore (2014). Her master's thesis entitled "The Sunni-Shia Divide and the Modern Middle East" was the recipient of the Tay Seow Huah Book Prize (NTU 2014). She is currently a first secretary at the Political Affairs Office at the Minister's Department.

Diogo Bercito is a journalist and scholar. He worked with Brazil's leading newspaper *Folha de São Paulo* (300,000 daily copies) as a correspondent both in Jerusalem and Madrid from 2013 to 2018. In 2018, he was part of the team of Brazilian reporters who received the prestigious Rey de España award, bestowed by the Spanish king to the best journalistic works of the year in the Hispanic world. Currently, a graduate student at Georgetown University, Bercito worked as a research assistant with Professor Yvonne

Haddad on a project about Arab migration to Latin America. He was awarded the Laurie Fitch Endowed Scholarship Fund as a recognition of his academic merit. He also received a grant to study the archives of the Khayrallah Center for Lebanese Diaspora Studies at North Carolina State University (NCSU).

Richard M. Breaux is an associate professor of ethnic and racial studies at the University of Wisconsin–La Crosse. His research interests include African American cultural history, Arab American Cultural History, the Harlem Renaissance, and the history of African American and Arab American music. He has published in the *Journal of African American History*, the *History of Education Quarterly*, the *Journal of Pan-African Studies*, and the *Great Plains Quarterly*. He is also the creator of "Midwest Mahjar," a blog about Arab American music and musicians on 78 RPM records.

Youssef Chouhoud is an assistant professor of political science at Christopher Newport University, where he directs the minor in Human Rights and Conflict Resolution. His research in the United States and Middle East models support for core democratic norms, with a focus on political tolerance. He is the author of two studies on religious doubt in the American Muslim community, commissioned by the Yaqeen Institute for Islamic Research, and is co-author (with Dalia Mogahed) of the 2017 and 2018 American Muslim Polls from the Institute for Social Policy and Understanding. Prior to joining CNU, Dr. Chouhoud was a Provost's Fellow at the University of Southern California where he earned his PhD.

Manal Deeb is a visual artist who studied studio arts and psychology. Manal describes her artwork, displayed on the book cover, as "Sacred Moments," a visual representation of identity. Her passion for reading, especially poetry, created an unbounded stability and instability at the same time. "I recognized that even though I'm away from Palestine, I still live in it and it still lives within me," she wrote. Her struggle to redefine home led her to create art. In the following section, Manal shares her experience as an artist and as a woman who is part of the Palestinian diaspora. Manal's art has been exhibited around the world and has been featured in magazines, journals, newspapers, art education research publications, television and radio shows.

Jodor Jalit is professor of postcolonial security studies at Instituto de Artes y Ciencias de la Diversidad Cultural at Universidad Nacional de Tres de Febrero. He earned an MA in national defense from Universidad Nacional de la Defensa, and holds two BA degrees, one in political science from Armstrong Atlantic State University and another in international studies from Universidad Torcuato Di Tella. In addition to Spanish-language fluency, he possesses full command of English and acquired elementary skills on Arabic through stays in Lebanon and Jordan. His interests are security and civil–military relations in the Muslim-Arab World, and his expertise was featured by Argentinean and international media. Most recently, he has established the website El Intérprete Digital (The Digital Interpreter) to publish Arab opinions on current issues translated into Spanish to strengthen Latin American and Muslim-Arab relations.

Bessma Momani is professor of political science at the University of Waterloo. She is also a senior fellow at the Centre for International Governance and Innovation (CIGI), the Arab Gulf States Institute in Washington, DC, and formerly at the Brookings Institution in Washington, D.C. She is a 2015 Fellow of the Pierre Elliott Trudeau Foundation and a Fulbright Scholar. She has authored and co-edited over eleven books and over eighty scholarly, peer-reviewed journal articles and book chapters that have examined international affairs, the Middle East, the global economy, diversity, and pluralism. She is a recipient of multiple research grants from Canada's Social Sciences and Humanities Research Council (SSHRC), Immigration, Refugees and Citizenship Canada, and Department of National Defense.

Michael Ahn Paarlberg is an assistant professor in the Political Science Department at VCU. He specializes in immigration, labor, and Latin American politics. Dr. Paarlberg is also an associate fellow at the Institute for Policy Studies in Washington, D.C. He has published in *Comparative Politics* and the *Journal of Ethnicity and Migration Studies*, as well as *The Guardian*, *Washington Post*, *The New Republic*, and *El Faro*, and is currently writing a book on diaspora politics in Mexico, El Salvador, and the Dominican Republic. Prior to coming to Virginia Commonwealth University, Dr. Paarlberg was a postdoctoral fellow at the University of Pennsylvania's Center for the Study of Ethnicity, Race, and Immigration.

Rigoberto Menéndez Paredes is the director of the Arabic Museum of Havana in Havana, Cuba. He holds a doctorate in history and has published three books and several articles about the Arab diaspora in Cuba and Latin America. In Cuba, Dr. Menéndez-Paredes gives lectures about the Arab community in Cuba and other issues. The Boloña Publishing House published his book, *Arabic Components in the Cuban Culture* in 1999 and *The Arabs in Cuba* in 2007. The Madrid-based publisher, Huerga y Fierro Publishing House, published his book, *Arabs from Stories and Novels,* in 2011. Dr. Menéndez-Paredes was awarded the Prize of the National culture of Cuba in 2006.

Naomi Sakr is professor of media policy at the Communication and Media Research Institute (CAMRI), University of Westminster in the United Kingdom. Her books include *Satellite Realms: Transnational Television and the Middle East*, winner of the 2003 British Society for Middle Eastern Studies book prize, *Arab Television Today* (2007) and *Transformations in Egyptian Journalism* (2013). She has edited/co-edited volumes of research on women and media, media and politics, and Arab media moguls. She co-edited *Children's TV and Digital Media in the Arab World* with Jeanette Steemers (2017) and is co-author (also with J. Steemers) of *Screen Media for Arab and European Children: Policy and Production Encounters in the Multiplatform Era* (2019).

Christine Singer is an immersive audience researcher at StoryFutures/Royal Holloway, University of London and a research affiliate at King's College London. Her research centers on the intersections of screen media, childhood, race, and gender. She holds a PhD from SOAS University of London, with her thesis, *Transnational Narratives: Youth and Screen Media in Contemporary South Africa* (2017), exploring childhood and coming of age in relation to film, television, and digital media in post-apartheid South Africa.

Nawroos Shibli is a PhD candidate in global governance at the Balsillie School of International Affairs (BSIA) at the University of Waterloo where her research focuses on institutional responses to Islamophobia in Europe. She also holds a master of arts degree in global governance from BSIA. Nawroos was previously a senior research fellow at the Canadian Arab Institute and serves as an editorial assistant for *Stability: International Journal of Security and Development*.

Jeanette Steemers is professor of culture, media, and creative industries at King's College London. She has published widely on European media industries and policy, including numerous articles and a book on preschool television. She is co-author of *Screen Media for Arab and European Children* (2019, with Naomi Sakr) and co-editor with Sakr of *Children's TV and Digital Media in the Arab World* (IB Tauris, 2017).

Rita Stephan is a research fellow at The Moise A. Khayrallah Center for Lebanese Diaspora Studies at North Carolina State University and the director of the Middle East Partnership Initiative at the U.S. Department of State. She is the co-editor of *Women Rising: In and Beyond the Arab Spring* (New York University Press, 2020) and *In Line with the Divine: The Struggle for Gender Equality in Lebanon* (Abelian Academic 2015) and the author of several publications on Lebanese women's movement, social movements, social networks, and Arab-Americans.

ABOUT THE COVER ART

Manal Deeb is a visual artist who focuses on preserving Palestinian identity in her original paintings and digital art. She was born in Ramallah, Palestine, and traces her ancestry back to the town of Dir Tariff, occupied 1948 land around Lud and Ramleh. She moved to the United States for college, studying studio arts and later attained a degree in interdisciplinary studies in psychology of art from George Mason University.

Her first art series was exhibited in the United Nations' headquarters in New York, titled "From There." She wrote, "the painful memories of living as a teen under occupation and the imposed curfews, all fueled my perseverance and imagination for the creation of a new life standard." She feels privileged to be able to channel her painful experiences into creative artistic expressions that put forward a reminder of her ancestry and identity. She is a globally recognized artist who has been featured in several exhibits, that includes having her work displayed at the first Palestinian Museum in the United States. Manal's work has been recognized in the *Washington Post*, Workhouse Arts Center, Taubman Museum of Art, to name a few, and she has been named Palestinian artist of the month and Arab woman of the year.

Manal Deeb describes her artwork, displayed on the book cover, as "Sacred Moments," a visual representation of identity. Her passion for reading, especially poetry, created an unbounded stability and instability at the same time. "I recognized that even though I'm away from Palestine, I still live in it and it still lives within me," she wrote. Her struggle to redefine home led her to create art. In the following section, she shares her experience as an artist and as a woman who is part of the Palestinian diaspora.

The art is a symbolic and continuous conversation of my life and journey as a Palestinian living in exile. The artwork reveals an alternative to an ideal medium to fight stereotypes that have misconstrued my experience and that of Arab Americans more broadly. The bright colors in the art piece provide a message of hope, where in reality, identity is superficially politicized and obscure terms are imposed.

Several curators refer to my artwork as "metaphoric" art expressions because it combines symbols of psychological layers that we all carry of our own experiences, cultures and traditions. Despite the painful content of my work, as it reminds people in exile of their multifaceted selves and origins, it contains hope and provides empowerment. For instance, many young American-born Arab women have expressed that they positively connect to the modern female portraits in my art. My art was another form of expression that made them feel as though they belong and can positively contribute to their culture, although in different ways than their ancestors. Along with the personal histories that their parents or grandparents share from their homeland; they've expressed that my art has helped them visualize and shift their cultural identity from that of their ancestors to their own. Additionally, even when their families are living in the calamity of exile and separation, they can continue to thrive to succeed and belong in new ways. It allows them to embrace and celebrate their heritage and the parts that will live on through them as a part of the diasporic community.

Art is a global language that crosses all boundaries and has the ability to be universally recognized. Arabic calligraphy is a recurring motif in my work because I believe it can conceal emotions but it also communicates meaning. For me, art is a language I wear, as if it is my skin. Most of my art is based on peeling layers of images, paints, wood, tree bark, cloth and other materials, mimicking the process of revealing the memories that help me understand the sorrow of living in exile. Accordingly, one of my exhibitions is titled "Defaced Yet Appealing" in which the artwork illustrates the strength and power of Palestinian women with facing socio-political and gendered obstacles. It also represents that scars or disfigurement may be present at the surface but not to one's core "self". In sum, it is a combination of the preservation of self-pride and emotional power that has led Palestinian women to great achievements, respect and recognition.

Digital art has provided me with a beautiful immediate outlet for my creativity. Someone once told me that my digital art "shakes the walls and stiff shackles," explaining that it transcends the feeling of exile and home, helping others to feel connected. To me, this is because digital art provides infinite opportunities for self-expression in a modern form. It provides a spatial framework that cultivates the "unhealable rift" between "the self and its true home" as called by Edward Said.

I dig deep into my subconscious, attempting to make sense of troubling emotions and memories that have lingered with me since I left my home in Ramallah, Palestine. My art offers and rewards me with tranquility and provides us, as Arab Americans, with a sense of resilience to unapologetically embrace our identities. My identity as a Palestinian often wavers between living in a daily conflict of *being* and *not being* that Arabs in exile tend to share due to the scarcity of choice with regards to returning home. As a promise to live a loving life even with the many conflicts that come with being a Palestinian in the diaspora, I say "your home is where your art is" to those who say, "home is where your heart is."